IN THE PRESENCE OF EACH OTHER:
A PEDAGOGY OF STORYTELLING

JOHANNA KUYVENHOVEN

In the Presence of Each Other

A Pedagogy of Storytelling

UNIVERSITY OF TORONTO PRESS
Toronto Buffalo London

© University of Toronto Press Incorporated 2009
Toronto Buffalo London
www.utppublishing.com
Printed in Canada

ISBN 978-0-8020-9915-0

Printed on acid-free paper

Library and Archives Canada Cataloguing in Publication

Kuyvenhoven, Jo, 1953–
In the presence of each other: a pedagogy of storytelling/Jo Kuyvenhoven.

Includes bibliographical references and index.
ISBN 978-0-8020-9915-0

1. Storytelling – Study and teaching (Elementary).   2. Oral communication –
Study and teaching (Elementary).   3. Language arts (Elementary).   I. Title.

LB1042.K89 2009   372.67'7   C2008-907215-4

University of Toronto Press acknowledges the financial assistance to its
publishing program of the Canada Council for the Arts and the Ontario
Arts Council.

University of Toronto Press acknowledges the financial support for its
publishing activities of the Government of Canada through the Book
Publishing Industry Development Program (BPIDP).

Contents

Acknowledgments

When Linda Stender invited me into her classroom to learn about storytelling, she opened her heart, her wisdom, her teaching work to all of us. Without Linda, this book would not exist, and I am grateful for the learning and friendship we shared. The students in her classroom were my other teachers. They gave joy in company and delight in working together to learn, and shared their bright insights and sharp perplexities. I am humbled by their gifts of knowledge to all of us who want to learn about storytelling in school, and hope I have honoured their generosity. Many, many thanks to the school community of other teachers, staff, administrators, and parents who made me welcome in their learning place.

The initial impulse and foundational knowledge of this work were nourished by my storytelling friends in Sierra Leone. Yagbe Tarawale, Mamorie Marah, James Karanke Marah, and others taught me about the roles of stories and storytellers in a community of experts within a traditional oral culture. Four years of their tutelage in Badala taught me much about the extraordinary power of spoken language.

In Canada I went on to learn with some of our nation's very finest tellers. I thank my friends and fellows of the Vancouver Society of Storytelling. With gladness, I acknowledge the help of Anne Anderson, Nan Gregory, Kevin MacKenzie, and Kate Stevens. I cherish the long conversations with Kira Van Deusen, a folklorist, teller, writer, and musician, who kept reminding me to root my writing in talking and listening. The Storytellers of Canada (SC/CC), my community of story-wise folks, have more responsibility than they know for directing my thinking. I think of Jan Andrews, Jennifer Cayley, Linda Howes, Glenna Janzen, Celia Lotteridge, Carol McGirr, Melanie Ray, Kay Stone, Carol Leigh Wehking, and Dan Yashinsky. The gifts of all these and other teller-listeners in the troupe yielded me sustenance and substance for my studies. Pennishish, also known as Louis Bird, Cree elder and storyteller, was one of my counselling guides during my course of learning. I also owe much to Karen Lander, my most constant of listeners – there is no story without one.

My studies and research were informed and guided by some of Canada's most excellent scholars. Let me hasten to add that the directions and understandings I came to are my own doing. But every time I remember the journey that led to these pages, I feel my debt. It began with Sean Kane, who insisted on the *Wisdom of the Mythtellers* as foundational to thinking about the world and living in it. Allison Tom, ethnographer and educator, led me through my studies. I thank Jo-ann Archibald, storyteller and scholar of the University of British Columbia's First Nations House of Learning, and Maureen Kendrick, who brought her rich breadth of understanding about the life of stories in play. I am grateful for the formative questions and conversations and guidance of Julie Cruikshank, Kieran Egan, and Joseph Sobol generously given. Finally, I thank the Social Sciences and Humanities Research Council of Canada (SSHRC), who gave me the funding I needed to take up full-time studies. SSHRC's support was a significant gesture of confidence in my ability to pursue the question.

The beautifully expressive cover was designed by Jessica Hiemstra van der Horst, who also helped me develop the images and diagram for the concept described in chapters 6 and 7. My thanks to Helena Van Eek, Barbara Carvill, and Terry Teskey for their reading responses and editing work. I am grateful for the support of Calvin College, who affirmed my work by assisting in the publication of this book.

Finally, writing while teaching full time necessitated gifts of grace. I had them in abundance. I enjoyed the never-waning encouragement of my large family. Always, I valued the support of my smaller family circle: my three children Rachel, Jessica, and Joshua, with their partners Fredrick, Gregory, and Teema. They tolerated my distractedness, and listened, laughed, made stories, and advised me well. They were my devoted teachers, and I thank them.

Because I am a storyteller, I sometimes felt the solitariness of writing. When that happened I turned my ear inward to memory. There I heard the host of friends, tellers and listeners, readers and writers, singers and players, I met along my long way. To all of you, *Thank you.* You granted me the storyteller's fabulous privilege: to tell a story that will belong to each of us afterwards.

IN THE PRESENCE OF EACH OTHER:
A PEDAGOGY OF STORYTELLING

Introduction

The story of this book began on a warm September morning. Along with hundreds of children, I made my way through a neighbourhood to arrive on time for the first day of school. I went to the back of the large school building and entered Ms Linda Stender's Grade 4/5 portable classroom, taking my seat in the room among twenty-six children. Like them, I'd come to learn. However, unlike my lively new companions, my subject of study wasn't listed on the classroom schedule.

I wanted to learn about storytelling in school. What happened during a storytelling? What were the stories? When did they get told? Why do teachers and children tell stories? How often did they do it? How and why did they listen? What happened afterwards? I expected the answers to be these questions to be complicated. But I had no idea how varied the shapes of storytelling were, nor how deeply enmeshed such activities were in the fabric of a school day. Myriad bits of story were woven throughout conversations. The teacher used sharp little story tools in the midst of math and social studies lessons. Children talked about books, news, movies, and they remembered things that happened. During times of play, fights, and group discussions, storytelling happened. And once in a while, on the classroom floor, storytelling was a tumble of listeners, sprawled limp and dreaming inside the spun web of a storyworld. Thus began my learning about the many ways of storytelling and the diversity of stories.

Before going on, it's important to realize that when I write about storytelling I mean *telling*. It's an act in which a person speaks a story from memory to a listener or group of listeners. For some of my readers, this will demand a change of thinking while reading this book. Usually, when teachers want to tell children a story they go to the library, not their memories. In the culture of print, illustrations, keyboards, DVDs, and movies, we mostly reach for a book or an electronically fed device when we want a story. The word 'storytelling' has lost its original meaning. When educators, readers, and the popular media write or say 'storyteller,' they mean a successful writer, film-maker, or journalist. Teachers call writing 'storying,' and scholars write about reading aloud as storytelling. I revert to the original meaning: always, in this book, storytelling is an action in which the teller shares a story from memory. In common parlance, the storyteller 'tells by heart' to gathered listeners.

As I emphasize throughout this book, telling and listening to a story is not the same thing as reading or writing it. Even if a storyteller uses the same words as are found on paper, the story is transformed when lifted into talk and experienced in each other's presence. In the classroom, the place of storytelling, stories out loud include sounds, colors, and the touch of each other. The story gathers meanings and possibilities that are different from its written version. Sometimes this is a fresh aspect or emphasis. Other times the spoken and read versions become so dissimilar that they aren't 'the same story' at all. They are as different as two children from the same parents. This difference matters. As we'll see in Linda Stender's classroom, storytelling offers experiences, kinds of understandings, skills that can be learned only inside a storytelling event. Storytelling involves a particular language and set of relationships; it's a body of knowledge and abilities that are activated only within its happening. Its learning and teaching are loosed when people share stories with each other, from memory for memory.

In this book, I share what I have learned about storytelling in school. I found that all storytelling events were part of a single, unified pedagogy. Whenever tellers and listeners shared a story, learning happened. The participants gained abilities, acquired knowledges, and developed understandings that were available inside the circle of a storytelling. I've written my explanation of this in the shape of a story. If readers follow me, chapter by chapter, they'll take a journey beginning with a setting of persons, a problem, and a place. They'll come with me into a lively classroom, crowded with talk, action, and drama. Then we'll come to an ending. But, like a good story, I hope the ending becomes another beginning.

Let me briefly outline the chapters that follow. In the first chapter I introduce myself. This helps readers to know about the eyes, ears, and person through which they experience and learn about the classroom.

In chapter 2, I introduce the storytelling teacher, Linda Stender. In chapters 3 and 4, I introduce another important participant: the school, the place of storytelling. This is the setting.

In chapters 5 and 6, I explain how I organized my description of storytelling in Linda's classroom. The hundreds of different storytellings formed a complex but unified way of teaching and learning together. I'll show that storytelling was used in three main ways: participants would *talk* with stories, *think* with them, and sometimes *be inside* them. These three participations form a single pedagogy. Children developed specific kinds of abilities, understandings, and knowledges inside each of the storytelling participation, ones that could only happen during storytelling. Together, the activities and engagements created a pedagogy of storytelling. Chapter 7 presents a conceptual model of this theory, a picture to make the idea visible.

In the three following chapters, I discuss each of the three kinds of storytelling participations in detail. In chapter 8 we learn about what happens when children and their teacher talk with stories. There was a lot of this kind of storytelling. From the first moments of the schoolday to the final bell's cut-off, children and their teacher talked about news, movies, sports, accidents, and playground events. These anecdotes, memories, rumours, and 'rundowns' filled the room with story-talk. This participation helped students develop vocabulary and language abilities. Talking with stories also developed social awareness and facility. It nourished the relationships necessary to bring a class of diverse strangers into a kind of accord. It made learning together possible.

Chapter 9 is about being inside the storyworld conjured by storytelling. These were times of deep play and pleasure. Children embarked with noisy anticipation that fell into hushed intensity. They took up a deep imaginative engagement with the story. Weeks or even months later, they remembered it with fresh delight. During this participation with a story, they learned how to imagine. They learned about being human in its states of triumph, despair, hilarity, and horror. Such storytelling events offered critical means to explore complex questions that were philosophical, ethical, psychological, political, religious, and ontological.

In chapter 10 I discuss thinking with storytelling. The chapter looks at those times Linda used storytelling to help children learn about something. For instance, she used storytelling to contextualize information, give relevance to historical events, make social issues pertinent, or create sturdy frames for abstract knowledge. One of the astonishing parts of this chapter is the extraordinary effect of deep imaginative engagement on reading and writing abilities.

In chapter 11 I summarize storytelling events and participations throughout the schoolday as a pedagogy. It is a way of teaching specific kinds of abilities and understandings, and a body of knowledge taught and learned through three kinds of participation with a story. It is a teaching practice. I discuss what this suggests for education. By this point, I have created a way for teachers to formalize and plan oral language instruction led by storytelling. I offer a strong rationale and compelling evidence for the significant contribution of storytelling to children's learning in school, for lives inside and beyond those walls. For this reason, in chapter 12 I offer some help and suggestions for readers who would like to develop their storytelling abilities.

This book is the outcome of a research project: I have written a classroom ethnography into a description. It is a qualitative social-scientific study of what happens when a story is told in school. Such a study is not widely encouraged by funding today. Most of our current thinking and learning about language arts in school is directed by scientifically based reading research. I have deliberately taken a different route in writing about what I discovered and experienced in Linda Stender's classroom: unabashedly, I have fully entered into the study and been personal about my experience. I hope that with this book I can introduce a new consideration into our teaching of language. In a time of so much anxiety about learning to read and write, the wellspring of those activities is drying up. Led by demands for measurement and narrow ideas about language arts, many educators emphasize decoding of letters and genre forms, and the patterns and strategies of communication, rather than its driving impulse. These mechanistic approaches risk forcing story-talk, story-thinking, and imagination out of the classroom. Surely we know that language facilities, with text or talk, comprise more than a skill set. Comprehension is more than reiterating or organizing information. Yet instruction *driven* by standards captured on bubble sheets risks the reduction of children's learning work to such outcomes. An uneven emphasis threatens the very foundation of learning: human imagination and relationships. The sanctity of persons, the unplumbed fullness of being human, the marvellous varieties of intelligence are poorly acknowledged by tests that have, in many schools, replaced the reasons for which we talk, listen, read, write, and learn together about our lives.

School is a place where still-new persons gather together to learn about where they are, what to do, and how to do it. Importantly, they are learning *why* they should do anything at all. The answers to such questions are developed in minds invigorated by curiousity and written slowly on the growing hearts and minds of children. With every new story, answers grow, change, or crumple. This was the learning that happened in a portable classroom, in a circle gathered around a storyteller and in each other's presence.

1 Growing into Storytelling

Childhood

My early years were spent in a home full of stories and storytellers. Many of the stories were in books. Our house was full of them: covers invited me from beside my bed, from living room shelves and kitchen counters. There were Dutch children's books as well as heaps of 'Canadian' ones. I read fluently in both of them before I finished grade 1. To keep me and my sisters and brothers happily reading, my dad also took us every Saturday to the library.

My grandmother was an uncommonly lively storyteller. Sitting on her lazy-lady chair, the sun streaming through her fine white hair, she told the tales of our family's life during 'the war.' The immigration from Holland became a series of vivid accounts. There were the terrifying stories of the Second World War and the occupation, then the journey out of devastation and, through immigration, into a new home. There were the stories of packing and farewells, and stories of the boat, the trans-Canada train belching soot, and the unimaginable expanse of the new country. There were the stories of a family of eleven squeezing into their new home: a two-room chicken coop on a sugar beet farm. We heard funny stories about language learning, first new cars that were too old, the trouble with jobs and crazy courtships. My grandmother, whom I called Oma, transformed our family life into stories that extended my memory of who I was and what I might become.

My family was big. When everyone got together there was lots of talk. The room filled with gossip and anecdotes, remembering and postulating. I listened for stories on the borders of the grown-up conversations. While they talked, I hunkered down somewhere just out of sight to get those stories that were juicier and more interesting. The same thing happened in the church community life that dominated much of my childhood.

My father was a storyteller. He told us stories during long trips in our Volkswagon station wagon, at the dinner table, and before bed. Six children grew up under his gentle rain of stories. He made some of them up; others were about the daring, terrible things he did in his youth. Very often my father, who was a theologian, told Bible stories and stories of moral courage; these were stories of brilliantly coloured images and passion. At the end of nearly every day of my early years, he told me and my siblings a story to close the day and open the night's time for dreaming. To this day, my spiritual life is nourished and formed by a long root tapping into stories.

So much storytelling happened outside the hearing of grown-ups. Over the long easy days we made our storyworld playgrounds. We argued about who we were while we made and mapped out a world for us to play in. Sometimes it was a place made out of book stories. Sometimes it was from stories we shared, like fairy tales or the Second World War or Jesus stories. More usually, we patched together what we needed. Zorro and Calamity Jane joined in one story. In another the Mouseketeers Annette and Darlene were with the Lost Boys of *Peter Pan* or Jesus anointing us. We also made up our own story people and places. I was Joe-the-Pirate in the tumbleweed forts we built in Lethbridge alleyways. Playing inside stories didn't restrict us to our mortal shapes either. We were horses, wolves, and troll families. At school we leavened baseball, soccer, and chasing games as well as taunting with the heroes and history we had learned about a few minutes earlier in the classroom.

I had just one or two teachers I would call 'storytellers.' I think of Mrs Van Belle in Grade 6, who would come into the classroom and promptly drop all her books on the front desk. She stood for a moment, gathering up our anticipation. Then she'd say, 'Okay, let's see. Where were we … Oh! Yeah! Well, when Jacques Cartier passed Anticosti Island on his way to the mouth of the Saguenay River …' All of us jumped in to join the canoe flotilla to explore New Canada. History class was one long fabulous adventure story. Interestingly, this remains the only slice of all the history I learned in school that still comes easily to mind.

Storytelling transformed our apparent circumstances of homes and playgrounds. The walls of the ordinary world gave way like the back of a wardrobe or the brick wall in a Muggle train station. The common places, like the classroom, backyard, or kitchen table, disappeared. Even the places we made with a blanket thrown over tables and chairs in the kitchen or stacked tumbleweeds in a prairie-town alleyway were utterly changed. The intense and significant realities of storyworlds displaced the mundane places, people, and events of our commonplace lives.

I had an uncommonly rich diet of stories, tellers, and listeners in my childhood. All those early years shaped me into the storyteller and listener I am today. All that talking, playing, thinking, and plunging inside storyworlds by myself and with others helped me develop language abilities and a tremendous set of references and illustrations by which to understand experiences afterwards. The stories and tellers helped me think about myself as part of the wider world and acquire flexibility or openness to the unknown. They gave me friends, heroes, and enemies. As I listened, made stories, and wandered about inside them, I grew the imaginative abilities I needed to manage my days and nights ever afterwards.

Time passed. As I entered my teen years, I no longer could be found inside cardboard boxes or prancing about, screaming and whinnying, in an alley. As my high school and college years absorbed me, storytelling events diminished. In fact, they seemed to disappear. More and more, relatives talked just a little too much. Teachers explained without colour or drama. And the stories? They were now all firmly captive between book covers. They still offered experiences similar to told stories, but did not spill into my living world as easily. I entered and lived alone in the storyworlds, sliding in and along print with imagined people in places opened up by books. At the end of a book I left, quietly looking for another story. Between the covers of books I found the retreat I needed during those years.

I went on. I finished university. I got a teaching certificate. I married and helped three children into the world.

With my children I had the chance to do it all over again, in renewed ways. My two daughters, my son, and I shared storytelling time. Telling by heart and from memory, enriched by life's storms and pleasures, I gave my children stories. I became their storyteller. My children went into their play, their sleep, their work bolstered by my folk tales, read stories, and made-up stories. We grew our own family lore. Tooth fairies and secret meadows, foolish farmers and dark wood trolls transformed our ordinary world of sometime-hardships into a bright and extraordinary one. Storytelling made our shelter; it pulled a warm blanket around us. At the same time, storytelling together was our brave foray into the world. We met its dark sides and challenges with courage we didn't usually have.

Without knowing when it actually began, I started telling and being asked to tell at special events. I told stories at family reunions, on playgrounds, at libraries and other gatherings. I realized that storytelling was a cornerstone in my Grade 2 and 3 classrooms. I relied on it to make islands of delight when drudgery threatened: it was our lovely reprieve from the real work of teaching. It was 'going off track' or 'having a break.' Storytelling gave us the release we sometimes badly needed. Occasionally I used it to draw my students into attentiveness. Although my curricular materials and manuals didn't really suggest or encourage it, storytelling seemed like a good thing to do.

All of these, my childhood, motherhood, and teaching work, gathered into a stream of experiences that kept me listening, telling, and looking for storytelling. However, as I look back, there were three experiences that irrevocably led me to take up the study I write about in this book. The following events sharpened my interest, provoking questions and a keen desire to learn more about storytelling. The first experience happened over the course of more than three years during which I lived in a small Sierra Leonean village. The second was my encountering the Toronto School of Storytelling. The third was a teaching experience in high school. These led me, ultimately, to join the children in Linda Stender's portable classroom that lovely September morning.

First Encounter: Storytelling in Badala

In a small West African village in Sierra Leone, I learned about language. For several years my young family and I worked to learn the Kuranko language and better understand our neighbours in order to design a literacy project. Living and working with people who had little use or need for paper, books, or other print-carrying technologies, I was forced to listen, to watch, to participate in ways that drew my attention to presence as communication. In a culture centred on subsistence farming activities, I learned about the inadequacy of print to capture many relationships of teaching and learning, while I also worked to establish apt uses for writing. Modelled on Paolo Freire's work, the project challenged me to learn about people and language in real ways.[1] In this I learned about language as activity, among people, not from books.

My neighbours never read books, sent notes, used grocery lists, read instructions, wrote contracts, or recorded transactions. They didn't need to: all their business and social interactions were conducted in face-to-face discussions. Thus, not only did I have to learn to speak the words of a new language, Kuranko, but I had to learn new ways of interacting, remembering, and thinking about my world and people around me. The way of life was thoroughly human, and socially and intellectually sophisticated. My neighbours had abilities to remember, used complex references to argue a point, and shared wide-ranging sets of understandings that eluded me. I was a stumbling child in this language. Although the Kuranko people had given us the mandate to help bring writing and reading abilities into their rich culture of integrity, I struggled with the tension of living between a culture that depended of print and one that used presence for communication. I worried about the inexplored ramifications of my work.

In this mostly oral culture, storytellers had a high profile. Several people in the village carried that vital, cherished role. Yagbe Tarawale, my neighbour and friend, and Mamorie Marah, the chief's eldest son, were two storytellers.[2] Someone like Mamorie was charged with remembering all the stories significant to the life of the village. For most of the time storytellers were ordinary residents, working with all of us, riding the rhythm of days and seasons. Then an occasion would arise: a quarrel needed solving, children needed advice, or the moon was shining and we were all sitting together. Then storytelling began.

I remember many evenings spent sitting quietly on the veranda with others while a story was told. During the telling, participants sometimes vigorously commented, exclaimed, amended, or contested the teller. Often listeners and tellers discussed the story's applications and significance afterwards. Storytelling addressed questions of legal procedures, contractual questions, record keeping, and peace making and entailed a formalized idea of cultural entertainment. Sometimes a story was told just for fun. One evening a troupe of stilt-walkers came into the village and we had storytelling entertainment for the whole night.

In Badala I learned about oral culture and about the role of the story-teller in community. This challenged my earlier understandings. My previous ideas about stories were developed through years of schooling, reading, and living in a print-dependent culture. In the village, sitting on the veranda or setting out clothes to dry with Yagbe, I realized how much being-there-together with a story out loud mattered. The storyteller took up a vital role, filled a place to make all of us, a community, whole. I realized that print can't replace talk. All my notes and transcriptions, descriptions and pictures did not capture what happened when we talked and told stories together.

Later, when I was at Trent University, in Canada, I sought out and read works to help me learn more about the difference between communication that is writing and talking, and that which is talking and listening together. I read Eric Havelock's *The Muse Learns to Write* (1986), Walter Ong's *Orality and Literacy* (1982), and Harold Innis's *The Bias of Communication* (1951), among many other works on the same topic. But ever afterwards, it was the storytellers and people of Badala who made theory and scholarly work about language, print, and talking together understandable and real for me.

Second Encounter: Storytellers of Canada

Soon after we left Sierra Leone and returned to Canada, I was introduced to the Toronto School of Storytelling. I met Alice Kane and many other storytellers of Canada. Miss Kane was the first professional Storyteller I had heard. I was thrilled to find myself carried by a voice into stories held together in good company. I missed the company of people around a storytelling and embraced this partial replacement. Storytellers such as Dan Yashinsky, Celia Lottridge, Linda Howes, Carol McGirr, Kira Van Deusen, Kate Stevens, Nan Gregory, Jan Andrews, and many others introduced me to storytelling as a public event in Canada.[3]

Of course, this wasn't like storytelling in Badala. Most of this kind of storytelling happened on stages and looked more like the stilt-walkers or visiting tellers that came for an evening. These were special-event storytellings. The Toronto School and Storytellers of Canada taught me a great deal about storytelling as an event that happened in Canada. I began to recognize the craft that weaves together memory, talk, gesture and critical relationships with listeners into a storytelling. The people named above, with many, many other fine tellers, form the backbone of an eclectic but uncommonly strong storytelling community. I felt my shared love of stories and telling to be a privilege as we met at festivals and workshops and, shared stories, food, and books. I took up membership with the Toronto School of Storytelling and subscribed to the *Canadian Journal of Storytelling: The Appleseed Quarterly.*

As my curiosity grew stronger, I took up studies at Trent University. I met and worked with more Canadian storytellers. Most notable and influential were Pennishish (Louis Bird), a Cree elder from Winisk and a master storyteller with whom I spent time at his home in Peawanuk on the Winisk River; and Esther Jacko, Anishinabe teller from White Birch Island. These two tellers taught me much about the fraught relationship between storytellers who carry stories across languages and out of their homes onto a 'storytelling stage.' As in Badala, I learned again that storytelling activity is about being with people, sharing time, learning each other's names and stories. I learned how deeply rooted a story is in place, people, and time.

I began to wonder about the role of festivals in the development of storytelling culture. At festivals I attended across Canada, storytellers from other cultures – Haiti, Winisk, Ghana, Cuba, Ireland, and so on – were much feted. Like everyone, I experienced the diverse cultural roots of stories and tellers as fresh and invigorating. Storytelling made it possible for us to go somewhere else and be part of another tradition of stories. A program was hardly complete without an 'authentic oral traditional teller.' Powerfully affecting ideas about stories and tellers being original or 'really-cultural' were articulated and taught without our realizing it. I began to feel uneasy and confused about such important questions among storytellers as ownership, appropriation, and authenticity. I began to question the growing disparity between storytelling as a performance and storytelling as a community activity.

Storytellers like Yagbe and Pennishish make cultural borders somewhat permeable, and their storytelling creates an apparently common ground for our meeting. Indeed, this is the most common argument for the uses of 'multicultural literature,' heavily made up of folklore. By 1995 I realized that 'multicultural' stories gave us a story pulled out of its home language, away from the tellers and listeners and location that nourished it into fullness. What we heard at festivals were vital artefacts. The so-called traditional storytellers enriched listeners and expanded their images and worlds. At the same time, however, this made the stories thinner and weaker for the storytellers.

As I look back at that time of my growing into storytelling, I realize the time of festivals, storytelling, tellers, listeners, and workshops increased my familiarity with stories and my abilities to tell and listen. However, it also gave rise to a troubling, common idea that storytelling is a performance art. While I enjoyed storytelling mainly at festivals and other formal gatherings, I felt a kind of uncomfortable dissonance: storytelling does have an aspect expressed in a performance, yet its particular difference from theatre is in its steady relationship with a place, persons, stories, language, and time spent off the stage.

Third Encounter: Storytelling in School, Again

While I attended festivals, I was very busy teaching. For six years I taught Grades 2 and 3. In language arts classes, storytelling connected stories to print and motivated my students' reading and writing work. It enriched studies across all subject areas. It helped me to explain things that were too hard to explain any other way. It focused students' attention on a topic, connected them to each other, and engaged them more thoroughly with topics. Storytelling brought good talk, laughter, and pleasure into the room. And it just felt good.

After six years I left elementary school and took up a part-time secondary school position. I taught 'English.' For the first time in all my teaching years I did not take time to tell a story. My classes were empty of folk tales, book retellings, or extended jokes. I had lost all my usual reasons for storytelling when I went up several grade levels. With third graders the established relationship between literacy and storytelling gave me good reasons. Now I faced students who could read and write quite well, and storytelling seemed 'childish' in high school. More perplexingly, I felt a new and strong reluctance to tell stories. I felt personally vulnerable in front of student-listeners who were more critical of and seemingly indifferent to their teacher than younger students. I wasn't alone in my reluctance: my students seemed unenthusiastic about taking up opportunities to 'tell a story.'

One day storytelling came into my classroom, accidentally. I had come back from the Toronto Storytelling Festival, at which I was a featured teller. Just before class one of the students said to me, 'Hey, I saw you in the paper. I heard you were storytelling.'

'Yes,' I said.

He asked, 'You get money for that?'

I answered him, feeling a little uncomfortable about this question, 'Yes.'

He promptly demanded, 'How much?' When I told him, he was deeply impressed.

'Just for telling some kids some stories?'

'Well, no,' I said, 'they were nearly all grown-ups.'

Surprised, he burst out, 'No shit! So, how come you never tell us any stories?'

Why, indeed! I felt a sudden pang of confusion and shame so strong I let his language violation go. Could I tell him that I was simply scared?

Instead I said, 'Well, the rule in storytelling is that if I tell you one, you have to tell me one.'

So began a new habit in my teaching work in a Grade 11/12 class of so-called general students. We began a small storytelling tradition. Every class began with a small story, a joke, or someone's remembering. Increasingly we looked forward to the first hush of anticipation that initiated our class period. Those first ten minutes at the beginning of class profoundly changed who we were together. I confess I was very glad we weren't observed or heard during the time I opened the classroom to personal stories, bad jokes, and odd bits of urban legend. I firmly shut our classroom door to guard our privacy. Some of the stories were risky to tell, and many might be considered in bad taste. But I never once regretted the new spaciousness that grew in that room with a closed door. Before we could learn together, we had to be a group of persons, each of us made of edges, soft spots, histories, colours, and interests. Later, during class time, I opened the door for air and to declare our openness. But our classroom learning community depended on our being with each other, recognizing who each of us was, together. That happened when we told each other a story.

While almost nothing else changed about the things we did, the depth and pleasure of interaction did. It gradually became possible to learn and work together in ways that had eluded us before these rather small, ordinary, funny stories were told. I learned to listen better to my tellers and our shared circumstance: a schoolroom full of lives. I became a better teacher while we all became better learners. My understanding of storytelling, stories, and learning was challenged and reshaped by that class of tough tellers.

In this experience, again, I learned a lot about storytelling. It was a far more complicated relationship than I had appreciated. It entailed my taking risks and being personal or vulnerable. I discovered how important an honest relationship is in the circle of storytelling. It also became plain how important it is to know one's listeners. This happened during storytelling and nowhere else in our curriculum.

During these years my curiosity grew sharp. I wanted to know what was happening during a storytelling that made teaching so much better. My memberships in several storytelling guilds and participation at workshops and seminars were motivated by this interest. I met with other storytellers who taught in schools and read works by storytellers about using storytelling to teach. It was exciting to realize that there were many others who found storytelling made teaching possible and created pleasure in sometimes difficult circumstances.

Paradoxically, even as I experienced affirmation and satisfaction about using storytelling in school, I became increasingly uncomfortable about its use. I was confused. It was difficult and uncomfortable to fit storytelling into expressed frames of teaching curriculum provided by the ministry or education board. Storytelling was 'enrichment' in the books I was reading, but in my experience it was a key to successful teaching practice.

I discovered a strange and deep rift in the way teachers talk about storytelling as a classroom tool. Teachers who use storytelling declared it to be critical and fundamental to their teaching. But a vast majority of teachers report they do not and 'never' would include storytelling in their teaching practice. While teacher-tellers like me described storytelling as a kind of panacea, the key that unlocked the classroom to learning, the great majority of teachers I have met in schools and conventions do not and would not willingly put down a book and simply tell a story from memory and heart. In the meantime, at conferences and meetings with storytellers, we grinned, we nodded, we shared meaningful looks. We had reasons and ideas for our work. But none of my storytelling companions really expressed why we did it. We just *knew*. The inexpressible spur for putting down books to share a story in school eluded naming. We simply shared an experience that didn't need words.

Storytelling Pressed between Pages

I was determined to learn more. In 1999, with a change in my life's circumstances, I took an opportunity to follow my curiosity. I set out in an old loaded-up Cavalier, with my daughter and a dog, into the wilderness called university and a quest to know about what really happens during storytelling. On my journey I had the fairytale-traveller's luck of a magic boon: the Social Sciences and Humanities Research Council of Canada (SSHRC) granted me the funds I needed to manage that long journey.

At university I read a lot, I went to many lectures, and I had to learn a new language that was harder than any language I'd previously learned: academicese. The talk at university was not at all like storytelling. I had to change my way of listening, and there were many times I wanted to quit that alien country.

Yet in all this I learned. Along the way I met such story-scholar-helpers as Julie Cruikshank, Kieran Egan, Maureen Kendrick, and

Jo-Ann Archibald. My study supervisor, Allison Tom, encouraged me to pause, watch, and listen in the *place* of learning. I learned about the nature and language that is a story. In anthropology and in cultural theorists' works I learned much about the function of a story and storyteller function in social life. Among First Nations scholars I learned much more about the problematic aspects of crossings between cultures and languages; some of the ramifications I mentioned earlier came into view. I learned that a story belongs to people and people belong to stories. I learned about ethnography, narrative-inquiry, and feminist research practices that include people, place, and circumstances to understand a story's meaning. I began to appreciate how much storytelling is an activity of identity-making, healing, and counselling. Eventually I left the campus behind, but I treasured the gifts of understanding given by the many thoughtful people I had met on my way.

Finally I prepared to take up the question 'What happens during a storytelling in school?' I planned an ethnographic approach to this study. Such a methodology promised to expand my experience to include the children's and teacher's, the circumstances and landscape of storytelling. This would make it possible to plunge deeply into the complexity of classroom storytelling and include its whole world. By including interviews, a teacher's reflective journals, and children's writing, I could enlarge, confirm, amend, and correct my learning.

After successfully submitting and passing the project proposal and ethics review, I looked for a classroom whose life I could be part of. I searched for a storytelling teacher who was interested in the project and willing to invite me into the classroom.

Linda Stender was that teacher.

2 Linda Stender: The Storytelling Teacher

When I met Linda Stender at a Vancouver storytellers event in April 2002, she was telling Farjeon's story entitled 'Elsie Piddock Skips in Her Sleep.' In the story, Elsie skips rope so tirelessly that she outjumps the fairies. They give her a gift that proves invaluable many decades later. At the fabulous age of 109, spry Elsie Piddock actually saves her community by a feat of skip-roping for hours and days. Linda, in telling this story, opened the room wide to our laughter and imagining. She also sowed courage and hope with a story that urges listeners to keep skipping under the tyranny of age or bullies.

While I listened I did not know I had just met the woman who would guide and facilitate our learning about storytelling in school. Afterwards, as we all milled about, Linda Stender asked me about my search for a storytelling teacher. She'd heard from another teller that I was looking for a classroom teacher who used storytelling. Linda was interested in my reasons and plans. Why was I looking for a teacher? What would I do in such a classroom? As we talked further, I discovered that Linda met all the criteria I had for a teacher and classroom in which to learn about storytelling in school.

For several reasons, I was looking for a teacher who had a Grade 3–5 classroom. There are many fine works already available about storytelling in the early school years, where it fits into a curriculum for teaching phonemic awareness and establishing relationships between talk and text. In the early years, storytelling with books in hand or nearby is commonly used to develop language skills. It is also used to motivate children to read and write and develop vocabulary. But as the grade levels go up, storytelling goes down. By Grade 3 or 4 the role of storytelling in school becomes less obvious. Learning is facilitated and increasingly guided by text, not talk. In my study, I hoped to examine what happens when storytelling is not motivated by the teacher's urgent need to teach beginning reading and writing. However, neither did I look for a higher-level classroom where children work with several different teachers or rotate classrooms. It was important that I have as much opportunity as possible to learn about the listeners, place, and tellers. Knowing that storytelling is personal and communal, I expected I would need ample time and varied experiences to get to know the listeners and tellers as persons in the room. My studies also directed me to look for storytelling across diverse circumstances and done for a variety of reasons. What, besides language arts, sparked a storytelling? A Grade 3–5 classroom would be an ideal location for all these reasons.

I also wanted a teacher who deliberately used storytelling in his or her teaching. I hoped to find a classroom where it had been normalized, that is, storytelling was part of the usual set of teaching and learning practices. I wanted an experienced teacher, someone who could be confident and comfortable with my observing presence in the classroom. Finally, it was very important that the teacher be interested in the study and willing to talk and think together with me about storytelling and education.

Linda was experienced and had used storytelling in her teaching for a long time. She was fully engaged with questions, ideas, and stories related to being a storytelling teacher. As she later wrote me:

> My practice was shaped by quite serious exploration [of storytelling], over a long period of time. The residency with Laura Simms[1] was the catalyst which led to my enrolling in many more courses and workshops on storytelling techniques, the power of story and the value of honouring and preserving the oral tradition of story. My interest led to coursework in folklore as well as to teaching a course in folklore in the Faculty of Education at UBC. My M.Ed paper was an attempt to describe and give credence to the idea of a Storytelling or, as I called it then, a Narrative Classroom.

As Linda and I continued our discussion that April day in Vancouver, it became plain that the famed story-luck had struck. I'd found a teacher who offered even more than I dared hope for. Linda offered a situation where I could observe classroom storytelling as an ordinary, deliberate practice. She taught in a Grade 4/5 classroom. She had almost twenty years of classroom experience, most of which included her use of storytelling to teach. She was the storytelling teacher for whom I'd searched.

Before readers imagine that I had found a teacher who told stories all day, let me clarify. Storytelling was simply one activity among the many, many instructional strategies and events that filled the days in Linda's classroom. She used videos, charts, overheads, textbooks, handout pages, discussion, art response, visitors, teaching objects, charts, the blackboards, and her own teacher-talk to teach. She directed children across subjects of study and activities that included current events, math, spelling, language study, computer lab work, physical education, French, science experiments, biology, and environmental and social studies.

She was attentive to children's learning styles. To that end she created situations in which children worked alone, in pairs, in assigned groups, or in chosen groupings. They took up role play, gave presentations, and conducted surveys. Children read, drew, diagrammed, talked, and wrote under her direction. In short, Linda used every means at her disposal to make her classroom a place where children learned.

However, all through the day, storytelling guided her practice. As she described herself in our first interview:

> I'm someone who tells stories. Someone who believes in that form for learning. Storytelling informs my practice. But, knowing about the power of story, or how enjoyable it is it, doesn't make my practice necessarily conscious. It's like the alphabet, you know? /A/ says 'ahh!' and that informs your teaching of reading and spelling. Knowing the alphabet is a knowledge base. That's storytelling for me. It's underneath everything, guiding it.

Storytelling is an inescapably human activity. It happens anywhere people are together, and classrooms are certainly rich gathering places of people. Stories bubble up through the whole school day. Children remember events, talk about goals scored, accidents, and video games they play. Teachers tell stories by-the-way and solicit children's experiences in the many discussions that happen during the day. Linda listened for those stories and nourished them. They weren't interruptions or tangents; they were noticed and cherished. As she said to me, she taught with her 'head cocked for a story.' She was alert to storytelling sparks and fanned them to life. She also made spaces for more extended storytelling times in her room about once a week.

On every day I observed the class, she used storytelling in some way, more than once, in her teaching. Storytelling was her tool of choice. As she wrote in her journal about a day spent with her students:

Sunday, October 20.
None of us, least of all me, know at the start of the day what little gem will inspire enough interest to spark a story. But something usually does, and it usually happens during class meeting. Thursday, for example, Pender came in with a 'Fantastic Fact' about the miracle of the salmon returning to their birth place to spawn after four years away on their own in the wide Pacific Ocean. His parents had helped him with the facts, but it was so wonderful how the few statistics that they'd recorded on a bit of paper blossomed into their wonderful adventure, of the bruised and wounded blood-red salmon battling their way upstream to lay their eggs and die. The kids fleshed the story out. 'The male salmon's mouth forms a hook.' 'Its teeth become fangs,' and then that led to fishing stories and falling-in-the-river stories, and before you knew it, it was 10:00 and Pender was beaming and everyone had plans to go to the Adam's River Site on the Internet and to the library to follow the story even further ...
    In the best of all worlds we could have allowed that story to lead us, even for several weeks, through science study of the salmon's life cycle, through some social studies stories like Dunc Shields tells of the coastal fishing industry, some Paul Yee stories of the abuse of the Chinese cannery laborers and some Coast Salish legends that reveal how the salmon is honoured in their culture, and on and on and on.[2]

Although she used the full range of materials, strategies, activities, and teaching relationships to help children learn, as she said, 'in the best of all worlds we could have allowed [a] story to lead us' through learning. She was convinced that storytelling was efficient and enjoyable and offered the best possible means to engage children's participation in learning. As she said in our September interview:

I think in storytelling you can do a lot of quick lessons. It's a very efficient kind of teaching tool. Stories are fast and they're complete to themselves. And something else too. I think it was recognizing that storytelling was different from anything else. There was a silence that happened. And as I grew older, that silence grew more and more important to me. I found I couldn't get attention any other way. (laughs)

Linda intentionally created opportunities for children's storytelling by offering circumstances for sharing experiences, retelling or summarizing movies and books. She used stories to teach about graphing, to recount historical events, and to explain such things as migration or the origin of a holiday. Sometimes, during language arts period, Linda told a story instead of reading it. Only in the last instance did her greater ability perhaps differentiate her from other teachers.

To be sure, Linda did all this carefully. She had read many of the available books about teaching with storytelling, regularly attended festivals and workshops where conversations about storytelling in school abound, and was an active contributer to the growing body of teacher-storytellers' popular and published knowledge. Like me, she had first hand experience of the benefits the literature outlines.[3] Similar to the experiences I related earlier, Linda knew the nourishing capacity of storytelling within teaching; her experiences confirmed it. She found that storytelling crossed cultures, ages, abilities, and interests. It created understandable explanations of abstract ideas. It gave necessarily swift and apt illustrations to underscore or elaborate a point. Storytelling developed oral fluency, vocabulary, and a love of language. It stimulated classroom talk and listening abilities. Stories offered models for writing and helped children structure thought. Storytelling was highly motivational. It made children want to read books. It eased the long, hard work of decoding the story in print. Storytelling was flexible to the needs of all subject areas. It made math problems tangible, history personal, and artwork coherent. Storytelling developed social skills. It nourished self-esteem when children told their own stories to listeners. Finally, storytelling helped children explore values and ethics in issues or events discussed.

Yet something about the experience and positive effects of storytelling in her classroom was not captured by this compelling list of reasons. Although the list is long, it does not get at the quality of saturation that marked Linda's sense of its presence in the room. In our conversations before and during the first months of my study in the classroom, Linda spoke of her struggle to better understand what storytelling meant to her teaching. She wanted to know more about how and why storytelling so fully nourished her practice. She wanted a rationale to explain, even exonerate, her dependence on storytelling in teaching. She also felt a subtle conflict between her teaching practice and professional mandates. How could it be that storytelling fully informed her practice while the curricular outlines and manuals on her desk made no mention of it? How could she feel so sure that it was the right method when teacher training colleges don't teach, encourage, or even discuss it?[4] And what about that magic, breathless experience in the midst of a storytelling event? Why did that have no mention? Why did such a highly valued event, greatly anticipated and remembered with such relish by the students, have no well-established place in school?

Linda's unease and sense of conflict are shared by a few other storytellers, whose expressed rationale and real reasons for telling stories aren't always the same thing. If storytelling is just a good 'tool,' why did it feel more like the objective than the means? As early as 1942, Ruth Sawyer objected rather forcefully to the imposition of traditional educational rationale on storytelling:

> What I am decrying is the telling of stories to impart information or to train in any specified direction. The sooner this unhampering be accomplished the more positive and direct will be the approach to our goal, which I take to be creative.
>
> [It] has been with a kind of horror that I watched eager and intelligent young minds being thumb-screwed under the belief that storytelling could not stand alone as an art, that its reason for existence depended on some extraneous motive. (1962: 32)

Storytellers know their classroom experiences have a value and rationale not captured by the curriculum binders on their desks. Well-known storyteller and writer Margaret Read MacDonald expresses the tension forcefully:

> Many books have been written for the teacher suggesting story as a device for teaching structure, plot, characterization, and a plethora of other concepts. Story is suggested as a springboard for writing exercises ...
>
> If you *must* dissect the tale to meet your curriculum's guidelines, please commit the brutality only *after* everyone has had a good time, playing with their birthright – the untrammeled folktale. (1993: 44)

Storytellers like Linda Stender, Ruth Sawyer, and Margaret Read MacDonald experienced classroom storytelling as its own reason for being. While it significantly nourished teaching and learning, the most important aspect of the experience was unnamed, perhaps unnameable. Linda wanted that unacknowledged quality of storytelling experience admitted to our reasons for storytelling. She felt the presence of a unified structure, sturdily supporting her practice, but it eluded her articulation.

In our first interview, I asked her why she wanted to work with me. She expressed thoughts and questions similar to the ones that led me to her classroom.

LINDA: I'm using you as a way of showing that … that (she struggles for words) Well you know that … when you try to convince people that you need to do it this way? You know, using storytelling to teach? Well, I think, I believe there's tons of ways to teach. Some people might not base their classroom on story in the same way that I might, but there's still amazing things happening there …

I'm someone who tells stories and someone who believes in that form for learning. I help kids make meaning that way. And I try to get them to tell their own stories, like anecdotes, things that happened. I help them create listeners around them.

I want them to be able to choose, to become conscious of story. You need to help me with this. I haven't got there yet, where I can help the kids understand what they're doing. I don't think that they know that, or I haven't thought of ways.

ME: Is it necessary that you, the teacher, are conscious of that? I mean, that you understand why they need to use stories or storytelling? You, the teacher?

LINDA: Yes, because it helps me to see that there's growth. That's where the hard part comes in. I say I don't believe in measurement, but I have to know. I want to know that they are spending a year with me and at the end they're going to be more expressive …

As a storyteller, I'm sort of just taking a chance now. I don't have structure. I don't have a conscious structure to do this. I don't really get what storytelling's doing in my teaching, how it works, even though I know it works. So maybe that's some place that you can come in and show or discover ways of … or you can identify structure that is there.

ME: Find the structure you aren't aware of?

LINDA: Yeah. Because if you are going to tell about it, [if] you want other people to learn about the value of storytelling, you'll have to find that.

Linda began by saying that there were 'tons of ways to teach' and that 'amazing things happened' without storytelling. But she was a teacher who 'believes in its form' for teaching. Storytelling was the way in which she could help children learn to listen to each other, develop their identity, and find meaning. She wanted other teachers to realize the 'value of storytelling.' Her positive and successful teaching experiences with storytelling made her want to help others find that extraordinary key. But convincing others depends on finding out what is happening during a storytelling. She hoped we could find something that felt like a 'structure' that supported her teaching with storytelling.

I had the same sense of an underlying and supportive structure and shared her sense that storytelling created vital educational and nourishing experiences. But discerning that structure was a daunting project, and, truthfully, I was afraid I could not meet such high hopes. I really did not know what I would learn in the classroom, though I was sure our collaboration promised a rich description of a storyteller at work. I expected my study with a well-developed example of a teacher who used storytelling to achieve certain effects as a valuable outcome of our project. But I could anticipate little else.

I could only let myself be flooded with the excitement of being on the threshold of learning and discovery. That September morning, I simply looked forward to listening, looking, and being in Linda's classroom. With the permission of the board, her principal, and parents, I walked into the portable and took a seat among the other students. Linda would do her work of teaching; I would do my work of listening, watching, and experiencing the classroom.

3 The Neighbourhood

Linda's school was part of a neighbourhood set a few blocks away from thick streams of traffic forced through a city pressed between rivers and mountains. Just beyond sight of the school, a heavily used highway carried more than half a million vehicles on their daily trek from home to work and back. Although the school was tucked away from the heavy traffic and nearby industry, their thrumming presence was always there. We could hear traffic on the playground or through our open classroom windows. Teachers, parents, and other residents regulated their trips to and from work by tuning in to the radio station for traffic reports. A nearby river carried another kind of traffic for several large industrial enterprises. A bustling line of ships, log booms, and barges plied opaque waters that emptied into the Pacific Ocean. During my time at school, references to the river, boats, fishing, traffic accidents, working relatives, and so on reminded me often of its role in the lives of the students in our classroom.

In spite of being surrounded by these busy thoroughfares, the school was set in a surprisingly quiet little neighbourhood. Most children walked to school between the trees, across two little worn-out parks and along the narrow streets that separated modest homes. The neighborhood included a few shops and a community centre. The nearby grocery store had a postal outlet and offered a good range of staple groceries, prepared takeout foods, greeting cards, and hardware. The store was a favoured local hangout, frequently mentioned by the children. These and other aspects of the neighbourhood seeped into talk, play, and work in the classroom. References to the neighbourhood landscape, people, and issues were part of classroom talk. They were part of a shared knowledge critical to hearing stories and telling them.

Although a few families had lived in the neighbourhood for a generation or more, the population was characterized by mobility and change. A good many neighbourhood residents had impermanent work and stayed with families near the school. Many residents thought of themselves as temporarily settled, waiting for an opportunity to move into better housing or circumstances. A large percentage of the school children came from immigrant families. Nearly 35 per cent of the children in Linda's school were identified as English Second Language (ESL) students.

The Ministry of Education statistics tell us a lot about Linda's classroom. Of all the school districts in the province, hers was the fastest growing district with the largest class sizes. Yet it had nearly the lowest student-to-teacher ratios, because of the urgent needs of the large number of speakers who did not use English as a first language. Linda's school had more than double the district average of ESL students and more than four times the provincial average.

These statistics about the school and its neighbourhood were fully evident in Linda's classroom. When I took my seat in the classroom, there were twenty-six children. One left within a few days. Over the course of five months two more children moved away, and one joined us. Just 10 of the 27 children spoke English as a first language. However, only two children were born outside Canada. This suggested that children of immigrants were raised in the language of the parents' community of origin.

The first languages in our classroom included Punjabi, Urdu, Hindi, Spanish, Tagalog, and Farsi. Eight of the children described themselves as multilingual, speaking several languages. For instance, one child was fluent in Tagalog and Ilocano, another in Urdu and Punjabi, a third in Hindi and Punjabi. Eleven of the children spoke Punjabi and were able to communicate with each other in that language. Other cultural backgrounds included German, Polish, and Spanish. Although nearly two-thirds of the class spoke English marked with dialectical difference and several children worked with limited vocabularies, all the children used English to express themselves in the classroom.

Admittedly, at first I worried that the linguistic situation might limit the study's applications. I wondered what such uncommon diversity would offer we who were learning about storytelling. Then I realized the situation gave us an apt context for observing and learning about schools in Canada today. Its multilingual membership would draw strong attention to the uses of spoken language in school, as it could bring participants together in the shared task of learning. The situation was also pertinent to current interest in how multicultural languages, experiences, and stories can interact in school. A study with Linda's classroom might help all of us who are learning more about Canadian schools in a country where 27.1 per cent describe themselves as immigrants.

As I prepared to join the class, I made some decisions. I wanted as much access as possible to children's ordinary conversations in class. I had to develop the kind of relationship that would facilitate our interviews later. I deliberately established an identity that placed me outside the usual roles of adults aligned with school's authority. I did not want to be experienced as a teacher or adult-in-charge. To that end, Linda and I decided I would be named 'Ms Jo.' By using my first name I differentiated myself from a teacher, by using 'Ms' I acknowledged my adult status.

I usually arrived twenty minutes before class started, caught up on news, and received an agenda for the day from Linda. I asked for ways in which I could facilitate tasks of the day and usually performed these outside of classroom hours. We agreed I would *not* take up such teacher tasks as marking, monitoring behaviour, leading group work, storytelling, reading with children, or supervising activities. As much as possible I avoided positions that were teacher-like. This wasn't easy. As I anticipated, children frequently looked to me for direction, worried about my response when they had behaved 'badly,' and came to me for solutions for conflicts and the like. In response I usually directed them to Linda. Just as often, I directed the question back to the child. I needed to establish myself as not-a-teacher.

It made a difference. Certainly, as an adult, I could not enter the children's social world. However, because I was an experienced teacher, I could compare the kind of relationships I had in Linda's room and see they were unlike a classroom teacher's. There was a particular sort of ease of access, a quality of conversation and disclosure. Relationships were not complicated by the possibility of evaluation or anxiety about academic consequences. By the conclusion of the study, it was clear to me in student interviews that my not being a teacher offered me conversations of disclosure, personal thoughtfulness, and spontaneity that I did not experience as a teacher. My determined efforts were encouraged by experiences in which I was invited into children's talk about Power Puff Girls, the man in the garage next door, fights on the playground, hopes about soccer games, and the like.

During class time I wrote notes about what was happening, using a simple three-ring notepad. When I got home I could tear off the pages on which I'd made notes and return to class without the risk of losing or compromising other field-note sets. On one day I would focus on the room layout, on another I'd study the organization of books or children's postures during listening. As time stretched across the weeks, I kept finding new aspects of our experience in school to focus on. These included the felt interruptions in a school day and questions about the roles of holidays in shaping school experiences.

My written observations helped me to pay attention, remember, and study later. Always I was careful in my writing and records to use pseudonyms for children's names and avoid details that might identify a particular child. Over the course of days and weeks my notes helped me to recognize patterns of interaction and sets of references, and to follow unfolding stories. Classroom observations drew me into deeper acquaintance with the life in the room, and the work of observing taught me to listen. At the end of classroom research I had fully annotated and recorded observations of thirty full schooldays. On other days I visited the class to obtain an interview, watch a program, or help with decorating for a school event.

Sometimes, children sitting beside me would be curious about what I was doing. They would look over my shoulder and ask me questions. I was surprised at how well children accepted my diligent recording of everything that happened in the room. More than once a child asked me to write down something they did during a study or activity. I did so. Occasionally someone would pass me a note with questions, comments, or funny pictures. I did not respond to these in the midst of the school day, but always at recess. I did not hide my work, ever. I allowed their attention but did not nourish talk about it. Any personal remarks or reminders I made for myself I noted during recesses on the backs of pages or in coded reminders on the side.

My observations were written up within a day or two of every school day observed, as I knew that time would diminish my capacity to accurately and fully record the vivid and marvellous intensity of a school day.

4 Landscape and Soundscape

A Powerful Participant

When we think about storytelling in school we need to include the landscape of the event: the classroom. As Leslie Silko wrote, 'stories cannot be separated from the actual physical places' in which they are told (1981, p. 69).[1] That 'place' is a classroom – a powerfully influential 'participant' that directs the tellers and listeners in their choices and conduct. It shapes the language, meanings, and applications of the story. In many ways, the classroom affects participants' expectations during storytelling and their interactions with each other during it. Afterwards, it affects participant's applications and understandings. In this chapter, I describe 'school' as a physical place, but also as a cultural site. It has its own language, social rules, materials, and values. This is significant to understanding what's happening during a storytelling in school. It is also important to our thinking about the uses of storytelling there.

When I came home from Linda's classroom that first day of school in early September, I wrote about the day. The scenes of crowded hallways, anxious children, and bustling teachers filled my journal that evening. The following description begins our introduction to the landscape where storytelling happened:

Tuesday, September 3.
First day of school! The neighbourhood pours into the school yard. It's a crowd of parents, grown-up friends, older brothers and sisters, relatives with children. Some children come alone, but most are with siblings and friends. The grown-ups enter the school yard taking up their children's

hands or letting them go. Someone adjusts a baseball cap, another quickly grinds out a cigarette. The halls fill with people. The usual smells of a school, made of books and institutional cleansers, mingles with home smells, spices, strong laundry soaps and perfumes. A mixture of languages floats through the hallway. Snatches of English suggest that people are talking about their work hours, childcare, home lives, and school teachers.

I'm here too. We make a bright quilt of colour spread between the walls: suits, skirts, tunics, ties, and saris. I see a parent adjust her child's t-shirt to hang straight and brush sand off his jeans. One girl in my class is wearing a green velour dress with exquisite lace edging; another is in a skirt covered with gauze, embroidery, and sparkling beads. Even when the clothing seems casual, the crisp edges and fresh colours suggest children are wearing new clothes for a new year.

The air is full of anticipation and anxiety. Some grown-ups urge boisterous children to behave. Others murmur urgently to worried little faces. Grown-ups talk about whether their children will be in a class with friends. They are talking and wondering whether their children will get 'a good teacher.' People peek into the open classroom doorways with undisguised interest. They look at brightly decorated bulletin boards, the waiting clean desks, shelves of books, game boards, and all the other materials of a classroom in bright readiness.

When a teacher makes her way through the hallway, we all recognize her without knowing who she is. Her clothing and self-assurance, her armload of paper separate her from all others in the hall. As she walks briskly through the crowded corridor, people make way for her. A woman jerks her stroller out of the way. One man removes his cap. The teacher is greeted respectfully, even with a kind of deference. She smiles, nods, slows down a little here and there, but determinedly makes her way into the classroom.

Most of us are quite familiar with the scene I described. The room furnishings of desks, boards, and charts are known to us. The ways we are allowed to move around in the hallways make us smile or grimace a little. We know what it means to 'go to the office' in school. We can instantly imagine the paper-scented storage room and the smell of the locker room. We know the rules about walking and talking in the hall or library or gym. We know the prescribed procedures for going to the bathroom. We know about the playground outside that fills and empties with the rhythm of the schoolday from Monday to Friday, the jubilant noise of broken restraint that fills the air for brief measured periods.

Isn't it surprising how well we know this place? I have travelled a lot over the years. Anywhere I go, I can recognize the school. In Sierra Leone or India, Holland or Afghanistan, Canada or Mexico, there are profound differences of language, architecture, social customs, and material culture. In spite of this, schools are uncannily alike. The configuration of rooms, the squared architecture, offices, school materials and furnishings are similar across differences. The ways we behave and what we do in the building are nearly identical in spite of other strong variations.

'School' is a resilient culture. It is globally instituted and has all the entailments and markers of 'culture.' It has its own material artefacts and rituals specific to it. Rooms are furnished with rather predictable furniture, and books, paper, and pencils are extremely important. Being in school demands certain skills for interacting with technologies, materials, people, and certain rituals. But school is not only characterized by its materials and classroom configuration. It also entails a particular language: communicating depends on print and demands such social protocols as turn-taking and hand-raising. There are certain patterns of behaviour that are appropriate to school. Being in the classroom requires compliance with rules about how to behave and socialize. Students submit to a well-developed hierarchy. Children who go to school learn how to move, behave, talk, and think in school-ways.[2]

School is a presence during storytelling. Sometimes it nudges the children quietly, often brazenly. It suggests that storytelling participants conform with its ideas about movement, talking, and thinking. Participants gradually learn what's important there. Ways of making meaning of information, explanations, or narratives are prescribed. In these and other ways, the classroom affects what happens during a storytelling. As readers can imagine, 'school' determines the choice of stories told and how they are shared. Some jokes are appropriate, others are not. School directs the intentions for storytelling, suggesting the applications made afterwards. Stories are used to teach and explain subject matter on the syllabus. The classroom presence imposes understandings about the meaning and significance of a storytelling event. A storytelling is done to get children to write or think about something.

The physical presence of school matters. Imagine that you are reading and thinking about 'school' while you sit in a storage room, at the kitchen table, or on a balcony overlooking the sea. The engagement you have with the topic, the understandings you make, are related to your circumstances. As we think about tellers, listeners, and stories told in school, we need to include the fourth participant, the classroom, which does not merely host storytelling but nourishes, suggests, discourages, and sometimes prevents the storytelling experience.

The Classroom

In Linda's classroom I took up an ordinary student desk and chair among the other students. This hard, plastic, moulded grey chair behind a metal-and-Formica student desk wasn't as comfortable as my accustomed teacher's chair and desk. But as I looked around I noted that many desk-and-chair pairs weren't suitable for the other occupants either. Grade 4/5 children are of widely varying physiques. Zara's thighs were against the underside of her table. Kate's feet didn't reach the floor. Natisha's desk surface was at chest level. Azun simply hated sitting, caught between a chair back, a seat, and a desk top. He spent as much of the day as possible on his knees on the seat or standing behind it.[3]

Linda's classroom was quite crowded. The students filled the portable classroom from front to back and side to side. Twenty-eight people spent six hours a day in a space of about 24 by 30 feet, about the size of a large living room. Few adults would host even a sedate social gathering of so many in so snug a place. During all my months in Linda's room, I felt like the room was too small for what we had to do there.

There were few options for sitting or lounging, besides using the chairs and desks. There were no cushions or carpeting. When children worked in groups to chart or discuss a topic, they lay or sat cross-legged on the floor. The room would suddenly be packed by lengths of bodies. Children leapt for the opportunity to change positions. Although the change was welcome, at least nine different children told me at various times that they 'didn't like sitting on the bare floor.' It was 'cold,' 'uncomfortable,' and 'dirty.' Yet their desire to change positions and have 'something new' meant they took up the chance to work 'wherever you like' with alacrity.

The children went in and out of the room, to the playground, hallway, library, and bathrooms. They ate, worked, and played in one space. The traces of their activities – dirt, dust, paper, food bits, and so on – collected in and out of the classroom. One caretaker, working very hard, looked after our school. This space occupied by four hundred and fifty people was tidied mostly by one man with a student helper. It is a staggering idea for anyone who has merely looked after a household.

Impressively, teachers participated in their room-cleaning needs. They cleaned windows, washed desks, and dusted.

Comfort in the room was vulnerable in other ways. The class was lit by fluorescent fixtures that always hummed and sometimes flickered. When the sun shone through the windows and poured over the thin walls, the room got quite hot. When it was cold, the furnace added a pervasive hum to that of fluorescent lights and the noise of classroom life. The air quality was affected by damp conditions and poor circulation: because it rained often and autumn's damp chilliness penetrated, windows were usually shut. Once, in November, we were so overpowered by a pervading stink that we had to move to the resource room while maintenance workers searched for its source. It took nearly a week before they found the dead rat that had sought shelter near the pipes under the floor.

Some of these problems are particular to a portable classroom. Linda's school had four of these joined together to make a small complex just behind the school in the playground. Such classroom facilities are common in British Columbia, as they are across Canada. Linda's room was just one of the twenty-one hundred portables reported by school districts to the Ministry of Education in 2002. As Glen Seredynski of the British Columbia Ministry of Education told me, the ministry knows 'portables are not desirable as a learning environment.'[4] They supply immediate needs. Several tens of thousands of children in Canada, and in the United States for that matter, attend portable classrooms much like this one.

Sometimes being in a portable classroom entails another discomfort. Previously, when children needed the bathrooms they had to leave the portables, cross the yard, enter the larger building, and walk two dozen meters more for relief. However, to the teachers' and students' delight, over the past summer a set of boys' and girls' toilets had been added to the complex.

The physical features of the room, its 'voice' of humming light fixtures, a growling furnace, the packed rows of desks, the sounds of other rooms, the press of scent, sudden intrusions of the PA speaker or tromping of classes going by in the hallway – all are aspects of being at school for the children's in Linda Stender's room. What do these aspects of a class space teach?

Inescapably, they say something about the value we place on educational activity. It is sobering to consider the place we regularly design and assign for children's learning. Young minds and bodies are prepared for participation in our shared culture in places like this. Because I have supervised student teachers in many classrooms in Canada and the United States, I know that many schools are challenged by overcrowding, poor furnishings, and maintenance. Chronically, education budgets are too small, and if there is some money left for discretionary spending, it is not commonly allocated to enhancing the space of learning. Little priority is attached to the effect of the landscape on the learning life of children.

In spite of all this, wonderful things happened in this classroom. It was a happy place to be in. As the following pages will show, children exercised creative power and engaged in skilful social manoeuvring and witty and clever interactions with their environment. Their teacher decorated the room, brightened it, and created centres of interest. Although it was easy to imagine the effects more space and better furnishings would have had on the quality of life in the room, the classroom was a pleasant place to be together, thanks to the energy of the teacher and the bright hearts and minds of the children.

Two Ways of Being Together

A teacher in the classroom has the task of bridging two cultures, or two ways of being with each other: the school way and the outside-school way. The phrase 'two cultures' oversimplifies the complex sets of overlapping cultures, ethnicities, and social groupings that meet in school. And compressing the sets of social expectations into 'two ways' doesn't acknowledge the great variation of home lives, schools, and neighbourhoods. However, it is fair to say that ways of being outside school and inside the classroom *do* manifest in two general sets of accepted social behaviour, materials, freedom of movement, and membership criteria. When educationalists and policy makers think about the neighbourhood in terms of economics, languages, or home habits that do or don't nourish abilities to read and write, they miss a common reality about an ever-present tension and juxtaposition. It manifests in what we call 'classroom management,' in which teachers are faced with a kind of tug of war between ways of being together. 'School' wants children to develop school ways of being with each other. It socializes children to accept certain values and customs important to a concept of how to learn together. The following entry from my journal shows these two ways of 'being together.'

Thursday, September 26.

The class meeting has finished. Children have finished recording the high and low temperatures and today's time of sunrise and sunset. Now Linda asks the children to put away their class meeting books and take out their writing journals. She also asks them to take out the picture books they got from the library last week. She tells the children that they will write in their journals about the library book they've chosen to read to their Grade 1 reading buddies.

'First write the date,' says Linda, firmly and a little loudly.

The class begins putting away books and looking for other books. Linda is looking for something in her desk. The class together shifts into about five full minutes of talk, play, and activity. While they shuffle through the stack of about 12 duo-tangs in their desks, conversations erupt everywhere. The room is full of voices rising, falling, and bursting out. When Zara pulls out her journal–duo-tang she pretends it's a bird. She waves it up and down, its cover pages swooping, and Zara is whooping with little restraint. Then Zara has her book-bird attack her favourite neighbor, Kreena. Laughing and eyes shining, Kreena slaps away Zara's book-bird while working to bird-ify her own duo-tang. Linda's look prevents Kreena from 'playing bird' back at Zara, and Zara, having seen the eye contact, quits.

Leon is trying to sharpen his pencil up to the eraser end. He's vigorously spinning his plastic pencil sharpener and pressing in the pencil. His pencil arm is rigid. While working on the pencil he is blowing the shavings off his desk at Buzz. Buzz gets mad and fiercely hisses at Leon to quit. Buzz hates speaking out in class, and his unusual response seems to energize Leon. Leon is grinning, sharpening and blowing, sharpening and blowing, sharpening and blowing.

Terry is feeling the African gourd that was passed around the class earlier. He puts his hand inside and seems to be thoughtfully feeling the surface that's not like the outside. Then he feels the difference between the carved out sections of the exterior and the smooth untouched surface of the gourd, the figures of elephants going around the gourd. He holds it between his hands and then smells it. He seems oblivious of anything else. He hasn't taken out his book.

Pender and Tych quickly snatched their books out and slapped them on their desks but didn't open them. The two buddies are in vigorous discussion. While they talk, Pender's foot is rhythmically bumping Tych's.

A few children are writing the date in their journal books.

'Okay,' says Linda, a bit more loudly and firmly.

More students write the date in their journals. When they are finished they look around. Now they see the bright picture books on each other's desks. A few children trade books with each other. But most of the class has turned to Linda. They are beginning to quiet down.
Linda firmly breaks in now. 'Okay! Okay, we need to write in our journals. Let's get ready. What are some of the titles of the books you've chosen?' Some hands go up and the directed classroom conversation starts.

On the whole, children in Linda's class seemed to gladly join in nearly all the activities she created for their learning. Yet over the course of the day, children opened up every possible crack in the routine for other interests. Released from one task to start up another, children burst into talk and movement. They talked, played, challenged, and retreated into personal activities. Leon happily irritated his neighbour in an energetic exercise of 'sharpening his pencil.' Books flapped, feet kicked, and children talked, hit, touched, and played with each other. Some children, like Terry, used the time between Linda's asking them to 'take out' materials and 'get to work' to retreat into the privacy of their minds.

This ordinary scenario happened every day, across the day, across the weeks and months, in infinite variation. When Linda taught something like graphing in math or a lesson on suffixes during language arts, children were mostly quiet and apparently attentive. They followed her directions; they did their work. But even then, in the midst of working, children snatched moments to make eye contact with each other, show a toy, or pass a tennis ball around the room. Someone would play-punch another person. Children leaned against each other across their desk borders. Sometimes they played small games, like copy-cat facial expressions, or mimicked one another drinking from water bottles in novel ways. These activities were mostly surreptitious and often slyly carried out. But from my desk in the room I could observe an extraordinary variety of small acts of play that escaped me when I was teaching.

Students also took time-outs, like Terry did. They retreated into their own thoughts and sensations. The clues were stilled postures, the focus of eyes, or attention given thoroughly to an object.

Whenever Linda released the children from their obligation to be attentive to her, the class almost always broke out into noise and action. If children were freed to leave their desks, they did so promptly. They sought out friends from across the room and sat under tables shoulder to shoulder. When they could read together in any way they liked, students promptly left their desks and lay on the floor, legs or arms touching. When the anticipated recess bell rang, almost all members of the class would rush for their snacks and coveted playground positions. They moved together, pressing and bumping against each other, patting arms, cuffing a head, gesturing with hands, stomping feet, and offering expressive faces. In these and other ways, children supplemented and substituted talk with touch, sound, gesture, and physical interaction to share feelings, intentions, reactions, and other meanings with each other.

On the playground, physical contact and noisy interaction were intensified. From the classroom window, I heard and watched children call others to join in forming great tangling heaps on the slide. They sat on each other's laps on the swing. I watched them collide joyously in soccer. They tussled on their way into the bathroom. When they lined up at the call of the bell, Linda's class leaned and jostled against each other while they waited. They usually stood, impatiently, arms around each other, playfully wrestling, shouting out names and taunts and standing close together. The child who was not in the thick of the line-up or part of the colliding, cuffing, copy-catting, and calling was noticeable.

At school, children knew they were joiners in a culture that entailed another language, movement, social rules, values, and interests. They acknowledged its directing presence. For the most part they complied with school culture's rule. But children took up any opportunity to engage in more physical, vigorous interactions.

This high level of physicality is restrained by school culture. Physical expressions of affection, pleasure, and conflict are controlled by educators. Generally speaking, Linda did not encourage 'vigorous' physical and verbal interactions. When a child hugged her in a spontaneous affectionate gesture, she received it warmly but withdrew as soon as was socially possible. Linda communicated delight and displeasure with her eyes, voice, and gesture, but rarely with touch.

Children learned this too. They knew they were at an intersection, in transition. They complied with school cultural expectations for their expressions of irritation, delight, affection, or anger. For instance, direct contact between players in physical education classes is prohibited. In regular class children had to obtain permission to move about. They sat in desks and participated in teacher-arranged social groupings. They had to ask to go to the bathroom. Quarrels were resolved by discussion. When Linda noticed a friendship that 'got in the way,' desks and friends were separated. Children had to keep quiet when protest or delight or a memory leapt to mind. They raised their hands and waited for acknowledgment before speaking.

Physical interaction was also restrained by the use of materials to facilitate communication. Children used written instructions, books, charts, and reference materials rather than asking, telling, getting up, or looking around. Linda's talking and instructions were regularly supplemented or substituted by paper handouts, projected images, posters, blackboard writing, and books. Children used pens, papers, or keyboards to 'talk.' In all these ways interpersonal interactions, which usually demand voice, gestures, and social contact, were quieted. While Linda's classroom was a place for talking, it was also a place in which children learned to use a specific way of listening, interacting, and printing to learn.

Like most teachers, Linda worked hard to subdue the slapping, singing, taunting talk, and activities typical of the playground and hallways. She worked hard to help children behave in classroom ways. This was a challenging task. Indeed, a room full of ten-year-olds can be a very noisy, rambunctious place. As Linda once said, 'I cherish two gifts ... most of all: *attention* and *silence*.' The emphasis was hers. She worked hard to restrain students' usual responses and ordinary impulses in the classroom. Children worked hard too. They were learning how to be in school, becoming members of school culture.

Paying Attention and Making a Quiet Class, or the Sound of School

Being in school has a lot to do with 'being quiet.' Yet silence was a rare commodity. Part of this was due to children's need to talk with each other. Another large factor was the construction of the portable classroom: it amplified sound. Uncarpeted floors over a hollow crawlspace intensified small sounds like a dropped pencil, footsteps, or the movement of a chair. When children worked in groups, low chatter quickly escalated into loud voices as groups tried to communicate in the midst of others talking. Teachers developed compensatory strategies for this. For instance, Linda cut holes in tennis balls to fit them to the feet of children's chairs. All the chairs in the room were socked in bright fluorescent-green balls to muffle the sounds of their moving.

Indeed, the day's fabric was permeated with a symphony of sound. Children swung their feet and rummaged in desks. Restless fingers drummed, snapped, or played with toys. Water bottles were squeezed, sucked, opened, and closed. Papers rustled; books snapped open and shut. Pleased with the noise, a child did it again. Paper was added to a duo-tang. Paper was ripped out of a duo-tang. Paper was folded, torn, crumpled, and tossed to thud into the garbage bin. Dozens of small murmuring conversations went on. Little bursts of laughter or hissed noises punctuated the day. Children got up to ask Linda, or someone else, a question. The grinding, grating noise of the pencil sharpener marked someone's excuse to stretch a bit. Add to this the sounds that came from outside the room. The public address speaker crackled into sudden loud directions or announcements, people knocked on the door, children shuffled past our room in the hallway, and another jet followed the invisible pathway just south of our roof.

Children were aware that Linda's expectations about talking and moving conflicted with their preferences. The classroom has a clear code regulating sound and movement. Parents, teachers, and passers-by expect a school way of being. 'A quiet class' is a signal that children are paying attention, learning is happening, and work is getting done. The following incident vividly illustrates the contrasting sets of ideas about how to be together, and that children knew what teachers want.

Wednesday, October 30.
It's Halloween. The classroom and children are transformed. The room is crowded with bats made of black paper and pipe cleaners. Lurid pumpkins grin from bulletin boards. Plastic spiders hang from stretched polyester fiber criss-crossing the room. The fake webbing is also stretched across some of the windows and draped over the blackboard.

The children are waiting for noon, when they get to put on their costumes. All their regalia is waiting in jammed lockers or stuffed in bags at the back of the room. Everyone anticipates the 'big parade.' The school will have a Halloween assembly at which all the children line up and show off their costumes while admiring each other's.

Bekkah missed hearing the directions and is in her ladybug suit. Her arms and legs are in brown and fluffy stockings. Her back is a large oval red pillow marked with black spots. She can hardly move with all the padding but takes every opportunity to get down on all fours to play ladybug. Buzz has a huge plastic axe on his desk. Leon has a white skeletal mask which he puts on every time Linda's head is turned. He pretends to pick his nose through the breathing holes, to the amusement of his neighbours. Spencer is wearing a tumbling black beard. He says his mom put it on and he has to keep it on because if he takes it off he won't be able to get it on again for the parade. The room thrums with noise and barely contained excitement all morning. Linda is clearly tired.

When the children come in from recess they are further energized by bags of candy and games enjoyed outdoors. They're excited by costumes and plans and parades. The stomping, shrilling noise of their entry is tremendous. They've been let in by another teacher and Linda is not in the room. I'm guessing she took a few extra moments of peace. The children all come in. They notice their teacher's not there yet. One of the students, Mila, screams at the class: 'HEY!!! HEY, LET'S MAKE A SURPRISE!! MAKE A SURPRISE!! MAKE A *QUIET* CLASS! A *QUIET* CLASS!!'

They all know what she means. Her best friend Layla promptly jumps up to stand on her chair and help. Violet jumps up beside them. They shout instructions. '*Sit down everybody. Sit down! Be quiet!*' Mila is rushing about pushing children towards their desks. A screaming, heaving, happy fracas is unleashed. They fight and force each other to sit, fold hands, and be quiet. They hoot, rush about, shout orders, joyously defy each other, and shove each other into desks. All this time Kreena is posted at the door watching for Linda.

Suddenly Kreena pulls her head out of the hallway to hiss fiercely into the room: '*She's coming! She's coming!*' The call is taken up in fiercely spat whispers: 'She's coming! Shut up! SHUT UP!! SHUT UP!! She's coming!'

A sudden dramatic silence coats the room.

Linda's shadow hits the door frame and she enters the class, she finds them frozen in an attitude of perfect student attention. They sit, silent, hands folded, eyes demurely fixed on Linda. 'Oh!' says Linda, 'That's wonderful!'

The cherished silence lasts less than a minute.

The Sounds of Being Together

As we think about storytelling in school, we include the qualities of sound and presence as media that amend meaning. Sound signals meaning and invites specific kinds of participation. We've thought about the mechanical sounds and physical presence of the room. We've included the ordinary talk and motion of children as these comprise life in the room. Think of how the sounds of school can be heard in the many different 'songs' that happen through the course of a day. Sometimes activity orchestrates all the sounds of participants into an expression of 'what's happening.'

The sounds of children on the playground, working through a math lesson game, doing social studies group work, or busy in the gym are dissimilar. Each has its own song. Children knew what kinds of noise and motions could be made during a certain sort of activity. Gym, math problems, social studies discussion group had different orchestrations. Children enlisted, established, and participated in activities, clued and directed by the sounds of the event. Participation in the soundscape was a mutually nourishing experience of who we were together.

I think of the times I sat in the empty classroom, eating my lunch and writing up notes. The noise of children on the playground poured in through the window. Such a marvellous concert of voices, a complicated melody of clamouring and calling. Glad exuberant shouts, sudden shrieks, and quarrelsome bursts were punctuated by the beat of feet running, walking, and jumping. Balls bounced, ropes slapped pavement. Voices wove together a lovely song of we-ness. This sound – the calling, laughter, and protests – were the song of being together, playing.

Noise is touch, being together is interaction. In the same way that children slammed into each other during soccer, looped arms, and kicked friends, they used vocalization to reach and touch, slap and stroke each other. They used gestures to complement talk. A shrug, a middle finger slid along the side of a desk, a complicit smile, raised eyebrows, vigorous nodding, facial expressions, and body postures of non-participation were all part of being together. The sight and sound of people physically together joins them into a sort of singleness of entity: a song of us.

This has an effect and quality specific to itself. Sound pours into the body, whether it comes from behind, below, or above a listener, outside or inside the classroom. The presence of others, gesturing and holding eye contact, in living solidarity or quarrelsomeness, demands constant participation. This is significant to thinking about what happens during a storytelling. Participating is a matter of being with each other. Children and the teacher in a classroom share talk, gestures, and responsive interactions. They enter a sphere of sound and physical presence that is a storytelling.

So many scholars, writing about teaching and learning with stories, routinely describe reading as listening, writing as storytelling, and 'conversation' as an interaction between authors. In this book, one distinction is critical: print is *not* the same thing as presence.[5]

Storytelling depends on presence. This contrasts with the solitary space of reading or writing. Educators' efforts for children's participation in school are much dedicated to reading and writing work. Reading interactions depend mostly on visual skills. They demand a very small area of focus; the classroom landscape needs to shrink down to the page under the reader's gaze. Thin lines on a page break open into language inside the reader's mind. While children sit, packed in a room with people and jostled by the sound of life there, school culture requires participants to shut these out. Students must be able to enter into silent interactions with absent writers and into silent conversations with print, not people.

This presents a kind of clash between two ways of being and two reasons for being together. As children move from Grade 1 to Grade 5 and onwards, their work is increasingly more solitary and individual.[6] At the same time the geography of the classroom forces children into close proximity. They are at each other's elbows. And while school culture attempts to cultivate the ability to think with print in solitary interactions, the classroom is noisy and punctured by interruptions and intrusive noises like the PA, the furnace, doors slamming, and traffic at the door. Noise and crowding intrude on children's attention for a quiet page before them. Complicating this, many children are physically uncomfortable.

Finally, while teachers emphasize how important it is to internalize learning,[7] the environment thoroughly externalizes subjects of engagement, procedures, and activities in posters, charts, books, and the like. The environment of the classroom insists always on a visible print alliance with subjects of study. Charts, books, blackboards, bulletin boards, agendas, and so on insist on outside traces to capture or guide learning and thinking.

As later chapters will show, the place of storytelling, the school, is inhospitable to many kinds of storytelling activities. We'll see that it took a determined teacher and a room of interested children to make lots of storytelling happen. In addition, school culture subtly makes storytelling feel like education is 'going off track.' It's not quite part of the song of being in school.

Storytelling is an event that happens in the intersection. It is a living space in which children's ways of being overlap with school expectations. During storytelling children brought their 'outside' lives into the classroom. Talking and listening to each other, being present to each other, participants shared stories in school and thought about life outside its walls. This demanded an ability to weave together the circumstances of life in the room with a story for meaningful interactions. 'Getting it' depended on this.

5 What Is a Storytelling?

Over the months I spent in Linda's room, a lot of stories were told; I tallied more than five hundred. They were very different: They were long and short. There were stories about a bit of news heard on the radio or taken from the newspaper. They were about movies and spectacular hockey goals. Children retold home gossip and recounted playground fights. While teaching, Linda told stories for math problems or used one to illustrate a point in social studies. Sometimes she told the children a long folk tale.

All these stories were dissimilar in content, vocabulary, and expression. They served different purposes and had very different conclusions and applications. Some of the storytellings were planned, others were spontaneous. Some were told by Linda with no interruptions at all; others depended on various tellers taking parts. Some took as long as it takes to speak a sentence and others took as long as twenty-five minutes. And they felt different too. The experience of a story told in the midst of a lively conversation didn't feel like the silent intensity of a folk tale.

At the end of my participation in Linda's classroom, I sat down with all my notes and transcriptions. It was time to learn more about what happened during a storytelling. The first great challenge was to organize, or 'make something,' of these radically different events and expressions. The variation confounded me. My experience insisted they were all storytellings and shared something important, but on paper they bore little similarity.

I began with all my known ways of thinking about how to organize the recordings, notes, and transcriptions I took from the classroom. In my first attempt I worked at a kind of chronological account of storytelling in Linda's class. Although this made for a very interesting description, it did not capture what seemed important. I went on, over the course of the next two months, organizing and reorganizing, again and again, the materials and experiences using different methods and frameworks. Each of the ways promised an interesting and informative means to help us think about classroom storytelling.

I categorized storytellings by the story subject. I organized them by the circumstances that inspired their telling. I rearranged them by the sort of lesson or subject study in which they played a part. I reorganized the data to show how a storytelling illustrated or contextualized information and again to show how it motivated writing. At one point I organized all the storytellings by participant: listener or teller. Another time I considered contrasting oral story engagements with written ones. Finally, I considered writing about storytelling as one subset of 'narrative conversations.' Children's talk and play and Linda's casual by-the-way stories were part of a discourse or a style of talk in which stories lurked and occasionally surfaced. Then, the more extended folk tales and stories Linda told would be the (real) storytellings. This idea fit more snugly with current thinking about stories told in school. It also helped me to explain how a 'story' of simply one line told during conversation was related to an extended event of twenty minutes. As some readers will know, the organizational frameworks I've just named are usual, but also helpful for teachers and storytellers.

Still, none of these ways of organizing the storytellings resonated with my experience. In the first place, none of these methods acknowledged the evidence of great variation. How come they looked so different when we were doing the same thing? I also remembered Linda's long-ago question about a 'structure underneath.' I struggled to discern what unified or held all these events together: the situation? the stories? the intentions? or perhaps nothing at all?

Perplexed, I studied the variation again. I wondered about the stubbornness that drove me to persevere. Why was I so sure that the disparity was not difference? I abandoned my papers and qualitative data analysis software program. Recalling that storytelling is an experience imprinted on memory and senses, I tried simply remembering. What was the same about all the events? I realized that part of what I knew about storytelling depended on having been there.

Then I realized what was the same about all the storytellings: a pause.

Whenever someone would start to tell a story, the stream of talk or activity was interrupted. This was true when children thought of something that happened, when they told the story of a book, when a joke popped up, or when Linda gave an illustration or shared a story about her growing up. Whether it was the teacher teaching, children socializing, or the midst of group learning work, a storytelling created a break in the stream of talk and action. Usual movement, noise, and ways of interacting changed. During extended storytellings the pause was dramatic. Children sat in uncommonly still postures, not speaking or moving. But even in shorter storytelling moments, like in the midst of a conversation or a lesson about graphing, other talk and movement halted. It was a tangible signal, felt, heard, seen, and cognitively experienced.

I had noted a 'pause' in the first week of my study – unaware that I would (much) later come to think of the pause as a story's signal of its entry and its dam-like effect on the flow of other kinds of talk and motion in the room. In my reflective journal I wrote:

Friday, September 6.
Linda is leading a conversation about safety on the playground. They've discussed the role of playground monitors and the teacher on duty. The conversation shifts to about what happens after school hours.

Tych said, 'Last night there was a fight at the football field. These guys who were playing football first …'

At once the class fell silent. He had moderate attention when he began, but now nearly the whole class turned to look at him. They all turned fully towards him and everyone looked at Tych, waiting for more. At first Tych faltered under the intensity of attention. He stopped momentarily, his voice cracked, and then he plunged on. 'Two guys got this little kid …' He seemed suddenly heartened by the attention he got. He spoke more loudly and filled in spaces between phrases with gestures.

I'm just new in the classroom. But I wondered what happened? Everything changed as Tych told us about the little kid who was beaten, the big football player who rescued him, and the police who came. He finished rather abruptly and awkwardly, 'So, uh, we just went back.'

We all stopped to listened to Tych. The class wasn't exactly noisy when he started talking. But suddenly everything hushed. No one whispered or rummaged in their desks or turned pages or was swinging her feet or tapping his fingers or dropping things or crumpling paper or moving things inside the desk, et cetera, et cetera!

When Tych finished his story, there was a kind of breath, like a sort of collective intake, and everything went back to 'normal.'

One might first think that the exciting subjects of a 'football player and fight' were the keys to catching children's interests. Perhaps students were quiet because Tych brought something of shared interest into the conversation.

But further consideration showed that the pause was a usual effect of a storytelling. It happened during class meetings when someone would tell about his uncle's experience on the Pakistan–India border, when the principal dropped by to talk and began telling the class about an experience he had on the playground, when a child told others about a time she fell into the river, when Linda started telling the tale of Rumplestiltskin, and so on. So, although 'shared interest' could explain the sudden moment of silence Tych created with his story, it didn't account for every time the class paused and turned to listen, or the visibly changed postures and attentiveness that marked the event off from previous activity.

A storytelling created an odd little hiccup in the stream of talk. We changed the way we were thinking and talking with each other. That 'pause' marked a change of language. In our effort to participate in the communication, we shifted from one way of talking, listening, and thinking to another. We changed how we used words to make meaning. We switched languages to make sense of what the other person said. We took up story-language.

This is a bit tricky because story-language looks so much like the language we use just before and then after a storytelling. So, let me explain this further with the familiar story of the rabbit and tortoise that race each other. The rabbit taunts the tortoise about his speed, and they agree to have a race. They meet at the starting line, and the rabbit bounds off while the tortoise begins plodding. Midway in the race, the rabbit has a snooze, wakes up with a start, and catches up with the tortoise, who has just crossed the finish line ahead of him.

Now, as we know very well, this story is not about animals or even about the best strategy for cross-country racing. It's actually about us. It's about tenacity, arrogance, and finding one's heart's desire. And it's neither historical nor factual, but it's still very true.

The language of a story is symbolic. In story-language, the images, events, characters call on us to think using symbols. The meanings of the words of the story can't be understood literally. A dictionary offers only the thinnest possible assistance; meaning-making depends on associations beyond the book. Listeners, participants in a story, make their meanings by linking their remembered experiences and knowledge with the story features. They make connections with and substitutions of the characters, events, and images they hear about. The language of a story depends on the listener's memories of experiences, other stories, and facts to make characters like the tortoise meaningful and relevant. Participation in story-language demands the listeners' mental activity of regular substitution. Thus, whether it is about turtles, a bullying football player, or Rumplestiltskin, a story is always about us: our shared experience in the wide world.

This is true even when the story seems to be about real things and real people. Story-language entails our making connections and associations. The story of the football player is about all of us scared on the field and threatened by someone really big. When we hear the story of Anne Frank or Terry Fox, we confirm, challenge, or just think about what we know about human behaviour and experience. We enter the story, participate, and think of other examples and situations. That's called 'getting' or 'getting into' the story. Only by making personal connections do we actually engage with the story.

This means that story-language is soft to every listener and apt for every age. The listener who hears 'The Tortoise and the Hare' in Grade 4 or in her final year of studies at university, or when she ruminates over her life near its end, finds pungently apt and new understandings. The story is relevant all over again. The flexible language of story continues to yield new or deeper meanings. When we were in school, we called this language 'metaphoric, symbolic, or allegorical.'[1] This is exactly the case. But what we don't do well in school is acknowledge that the language of story demands a different way of participating and thinking. We make meanings of a story in ways that contrast with the way we understand an explanation or information. We use a system of story-semantics.

Listening to a story, we loose our minds to it. We enter it to experience the story, not to know its facts. It snags attention and interest where we find connections and interesting associations. Afterwards, a good story-teacher helps students nourish their connections and find other ones. Teachers help students plumb their own memories for experiences and linkages that give the story meaningful resonance.[2] If the story and listener don't meet personally in an intersection of experiences or meaningful images, the listener won't 'get' the story and can't get into it.

It's difficult to understand how this symbol-language works. It's mysterious. Imagine: we make these 'substitutions' with such ease we don't even think about it. And to pay attention to them in the midst of listening is to ruin the story. Interestingly, at the youngest possible age children show a high degree of facility with stories. While they are learning to express their thoughts and experiences, they demonstrate natural and eager abilities to listen, tell, retell, play, and work with stories.[3] Only rarely does a child need to be told that a dragon isn't real, that she won't need to sew on a loose shadow, or that he needn't wait for the Polar Express train bound for the North Pole.

Time in the backyard or playground soon shows us that children spend most of their early social interactions using the language of story. They explore possibilities and discuss their lives in a medium that is flexible and deeply engaging. Young readers relish the images and events of Dr Seuss, Roald Dahl, E.B. White, or J.K. Rowling not because they are fantastic, but because they aptly express those readers' experiences and understandings about the world. Children's unrestrained, intensive use of story-language is the ground on which linguistic abilities are developed.

There are several other ways in which story-language communicates meaning differently from languages that explain or inform. We might think that telling a story is the long way to make a point. However, it is also the shortest way there. For listeners of the fable of the tortoise and the hare, understanding the point of 'tenacity' depends on being there for the whole story. Getting the story requires us to take the full journey from the first steps, through the long stretch that ends elsewhere. It's not possible to get the story if one enters at the midpoint, takes a short cut, or never reaches its ending. A listener has to be there for the whole thing. This again suggests why attention is given to a storytelling immediately: the beginning is the invitation and opportunity for getting in and getting it.

This doesn't mean stories must be chronological. The story is orchestrated in such a way as to convey its meaning, make a point, or share an experience. When we seem to start at the ending, or leapfrog about between characters or even travel between times, we are still on a steady path to our destination. Breaking the story's wholeness jeopardizes our ability to realize or 'get' the story's meaning. Listeners enter at the beginning and ride the words to the conclusion. Only the complete story-experience offers the listener its point. And listeners value the promise of that gift. Their shared understanding of story-language accounts for the lack of interruptions during a storytelling: they want to continue the journey to its ending.

I've mentioned the two main ways in which story-language isn't like other talk or writing: its demand for symbolic thinking and the necessity that listeners go from the beginning to the ending. There are other aspects. The content of stories is a knowledge body particular to itself. Stories are about the inner world of human experience. They communicate personal and social values ranging from ideas about relationships to life's meanings and the significance of an experience. And story-language depends utterly on imagination and emotion for engagement.

So, when Tych said, 'Last night there was a fight at the football field. These guys who were playing football first ...,' we all switched languages. We scrambled to join him, alerted that a story was starting. The pause was a tiny moment in which we leapt from one way of thinking into story-thinking. We wanted to share in the story.

6 Talking, Thinking, and Imaginating with a Story

When I looked over my journal and remembered all the storytelling that happened in Linda Stender's classroom, I found that we used our story-language in three main situations. In other words, we took up one of three kinds of participation during a storytelling. I have named these participations 'talking,' 'thinking,' and 'imaginating.' I'll briefly explain what I mean by each. After that, we'll look at an example.

The first one, *talking with stories*, was most evident in the midst of conversations. Participants remembered, recounted, and shared stories with each other. The children and the teacher were keenly responsive to each other during such storytelling, watching and listening. They all depended on each other's responsive presence and included one another in their experience of hearing, telling, and understanding a story together. While talking with stories, participants were in social awareness of one another.

Thinking with stories was more evident in the ways Linda used storytelling to direct children's lessons. Storytelling helped students understand something 'else.' That is, the stories were told as illustrations of a point, or concrete models for abstract ideas. Sometimes a storytelling gave a context for information or explained a statistic. Another aspect of this was the teacher's use of a storytelling afterwards. The remembered storytelling became a place to revisit or use for further learning. Children would think with stories on their own too. They used storytellings to understand an issue or concept or to put information in context. They made connections and drew conclusions about experiences while participating in a storytelling. A listener who is thinking with stories is much less aware of the others who are listening. He or she actively interacts with the story and teller and excludes other listeners. Thinking with stories, participants were in mindful interaction with the storytelling.

The third kind of participation is *imaginating with stories*. 'Imaginating' is a word coined by Layla, one of the children. It was most evident during the longer storytellings, like a folk tale or myth. During the storytelling listeners gave themselves up wholly to the experience. Such participation was visible during the telling of longer stories, ones that were artfully constructed and more fully developed in terms of characters, setting, and plot events. Almost always, this kind of participation occurred during a clearly defined event: Linda called the children together to sit on the floor and told them she was going to tell a story. Children promptly prepared themselves to 'get into it.' They rushed to sit on the floor, quieted themselves, shushed each other, and began the work of imagining their way into a storyworld, an intense activity of deep imaginative engagement. During this time, not only did awareness of each other dissipate, so did the listeners' awareness of self and the storyteller as a person or teacher. Children slid into a storyworld.

Each of these storytelling participations could stand alone and complete. Each develops abilities and knowledge specific to the activity. However, a wider lens shows an interdependent and complex relationship held or developed across participations. They are in complementarity; together they create a pedagogy of storytelling that spans three ways of listening, telling, and being with a story out loud. Talking, thinking, and imaginating with storytelling, children grew understandings and abilities only developed during that event. In later chapters I describe and explain each participation in detail, and in my concluding chapter I draw them together again to describe a pedagogy of integrity.

The following example, of Leon listening to Linda tell a story, shows all three participations entered into during one storytelling. As Leon demonstrates, each of the three can be experienced during a single storytelling without losing the integrity or full enjoyment of the event. And in later chapters we'll see that participants sometimes only talk with stories or think with stories. Or it may happen that one listener thinks with stories while another is fully aware of his company, busy 'talking' with the story. Finally, listeners may also participate in any number of the three ways during one storytelling. This is common.

Leon Listening

I wrote the following observation on the day Linda told one of the Grimm's folk tales, 'The Three Golden Hairs.'[1] The children sprawled over the floor in front of her. While listening to the story with the children, I gave as much attention as I could to one listener, Leon. I watched him begin his participation in awareness of himself among others; then he offered a few clues to suggest he was thinking with the story. Finally he tumbled into the storyworld offered by the story telling. He was imaginating with the story.

Thursday, October 10.
The class is sitting on the floor in front of their teacher. Most of them are sprawled out, leaning against each other, legs along legs, shoulders touching. Linda is telling the story of 'The Three Golden Hairs.' I'm off to the side, on the floor too. I've got my notebook and pen as invisible as possible.

Leon is not visibly attending to Linda or working with the class to participate. He's at the edge of the group. By now I've realized this is his usual mode of 'being' in the classroom. I am guessing he positioned himself as much as possible out of Linda's sight. But I can see him very well.

He looks around at children near him. They don't look at him. Then he attends to his running shoes. He first picks dirt out from the treads of his shoes. Then he pulls up his pant legs over his knees. He pulls his ankle socks up as high as he can get them to stretch. He pulls his pant legs down again. He takes an eraser out of his pocket. He smells the eraser. He begins erasing parts of the floor. He breaks off bits of the eraser and sticks them in the treads of his shoes. He pulls his pant legs up over his knees again. He runs his hand up one side of his shin to his knee, circles his kneecap and then down his shin, up and down, again and again. Then he tugs his pant legs down again. He curls his fingers around the desk leg beside him and runs his hand slowly up and down it. He plucks at the plastic casing at the base of the leg.

In the meantime Linda is telling the story. During this time, more and more frequently I see Leon's eyes flick upwards at his teacher. I'm not sure if it is interest or whether he is simply checking to see if she observes his 'inattentiveness.'

Now Linda is about five or perhaps even seven minutes into the story. She is telling about the king's fury and horror at discovering that the youngest, 'stupid' son of the farmer had just been married to his daughter. She says quite loudly, 'The king roared, "I don't want my daughter to marry someone so stupid and slow."'

At that moment, Leon seems to slide out of himself, out of the present place and far away into the story. His movements cease and he sits, perfectly still, one knee up, foot flat on the floor, the other leg lying crookedly over the floor. His head is cocked, lolling slightly to one side. His body leans against a desk leg. His eyes are fastened on Linda but not focused on her. Within this moment his absorption resembles that of the other children.

Like all the children now, he's oddly stilled. It is hard to describe Leon's posture. Words like 'trance' and 'rapt' come to mind, but like the other children, he is strongly focused, deeply attentive, and concentrating. The children seem to hang on Linda's words. Shadows of their responses to the story-events chase across their faces.

I wonder what snapped Leon into the story. I don't think I will ever know. But I do know that, like me, he went on to follow the young man in the story: a loser, a boy who was stupid and slow. But that boy beat a giant, tricked a king and ghost, and won riches, a good wife, friendships, and a throne.

In the beginning, Leon's attention was given to the strategy of his seating arrangement, his personal comfort, and things around him. He showed that he was aware of the other listeners and the teller's presence, and felt himself among them. He experienced himself as part of a whole circumstance of people, sounds, and sights in the physical place of the storytelling moment. He was participating in the 'dialogue' of persons and place during a storytelling. So, we can understand Leon to be talking with a storytelling.

The second kind of participation, thinking with the story, was not as visible. However, because he eventually became fully absorbed by the storytelling, it seems certain that his experience included listening to the story with more attention than his actions indicated. He participated from the beginning, gradually moving from a position of awareness of others and himself during the story, to thinking with it. His regular glances at Linda and his silence suggested he was listening while his hands and body were busy touching and playing. If he was not listening with 'half an ear,' we cannot account for his ability to attend to the story, which had advanced by at least five or seven minutes. He must have absorbed enough of the story's setting, cast, and dilemma, as these were necessary to understanding and getting into the rest of the story. As he gradually excluded the presence of others and began giving less attention to himself and what he was doing there, he may have begun a kind of dialogue with the storytelling. Leon, or any one of us listening to Linda's telling, might have mentally interacted with such responses. He might have thought something like I would have:

I don't know if I'm really interested in this. That guy in the story reminds
me of someone. I wish that she wouldn't look at me when she talks. I saw
a movie that was kind of like this story. Huh, it's just not possible that
king would let his daughter just marry just like that ...

In this way, thinking along with the story, the listener remembers,
connects, and mindfully interacts with what's happening.

Finally, at some indefinite moment, Leon forgot about himself, his
present circumstances, his knees, eraser bits, and trouser legs. In fact,
he seemed to pay no real attention to Linda either. He was thoroughly
absorbed by his experience inside the storyworld. He was inside the
story experience, deeply lodged in a space beyond the room we
shared. Led by the storyteller, he was imaginating with the story. Although he participated with a stilled and oddly slack posture, he was
fiercely engaged with a furious king, a river rife with water-ghosts,
and the task of getting those three golden hairs. As the children's later
interviews testified, they were aware of neither themselves nor each
other while inside deep imaginative engagement.

Thus, Leon's participation began in social awareness. He was talking
with the story. Increasingly, he gave the story his thoughtful participation. Gradually he became deeply involved with the storytelling experience. As he more deeply engaged with his imagination of the story,
he was tugged loose from the classroom and entered his storyworld.

This progression is not invariable: it is possible to participate in just
one or two ways with great satisfaction. It is possible to think with a
story or remain aware of others throughout any storytelling. However,
the tumble into the storyworld, being able to imaginate the story,
seems to demand such a progression. It begins with an awareness of
self among others, goes on to demand thinking with the story, and cul-
minates in being inside storyworld life.

Linda Listening

Here is another example of three participations during one storytelling. This account is from Linda's journal, where she wrote about hearing the author-storyteller Mem Fox. Linda describes all three ways of
being with a story. Notice how initially Linda was aware of herself
among others. That's what we mean by 'talking with stories.' Then she
went on to describe her mindful interaction with what was going on;
she was thinking with the stories and about storyteller Mem Fox. At

the end she alluded to the experience of imaginating. That's the place of the deep engagement story-listeners hope for: the 'calm' of a story.

Sunday, September 22.
Mem Fox was fabulous ...

I noticed our settling in as Mem prepared to speak, the whispered rustlings of all those bodies as we sought physical comfort now so that no external bits would later interrupt our concentration. Rather like the way you arrange yourself in your seat before a long plane journey.

And then that 'charge,' that energy that seems to be exchanged between teller and listener just before the story begins. And Mem Fox didn't disappoint. She shared her personal story, punctuated with wonderful loving tellings of her picture book stories, layer upon layer. And when she shared her picture book stories, she told them. She didn't read them. She held the text in her hand, but never once did she divert her attention from us to sneak a peak at it. She knew her story. She had painstakingly crafted each sentence, writing and rewriting until the 'tune,' as she described it, was absolutely right.

How often in school do we encourage repeated tellings and retellings so kids can appreciate the 'tune' of a story? How often do we allow them to linger over a much loved and familiar tale? I'm certainly going to slow down with that picture book project we're preparing for the grade one buddies. Mem Fox also demonstrated, with great humour and charm, the difference between a story told as an act of love and one told as an act of education.

Another thing to be mindful of: not to interrupt the flow in order to satisfy our own compulsion to teach. Let the story do it, for heaven's sake. Well, good thing I went to Mem Fox, as there hasn't been much story in class on which to reflect. When things get crazy busy, the first thing to go is the calm of a story.

Linda's reflective journal entry shows the progression of participations. She began by describing herself as 'settling in' to listen. She was keenly aware of herself among others who were whispering among themselves and making noise. She tried to get comfortable in order to listen. Her time of 'settling in' and establishing her 'physical comfort' was in 'preparation for a journey.' She began her listening participation in social awareness.

She went on to recount her mindful interactions with Mem Fox. She writes about her thoughts about the teller, books, conversations with me, and ideas she had about storytelling. In this participation, she seems to let go of the earlier social, physical considerations of her participation. She actively, personally engaged herself with the story and teller in the second kind of participation possible with a story. Finally, she alluded to her goal, why she had come to the event. She had embarked on a 'journey' that she hoped would reach 'the calm of a story.' She wanted the deeply imaginative and curiously restful but energizing engagement with a story. It was a beloved place.

7 Three Participations, One Pedagogy

When Leon listened to 'The Three Golden Hairs,' he moved from an outer circle into an inner circle of quiet where he sank into the story. He went from experiencing himself among others with a story to thinking about what was happening. Finally, he sank into an inner place, imaginating with the story.

It's tempting to consider Leon's shifts of participation as he moved from awareness of himself to submersion in the storyworld as a logical, prescribed progression. We might say he went from paying poor attention to paying better attention. But it's important not to understand it this way. In these pages I hope to show that the three participations are not levels, nor are they a three-step advancement. Each participation has its own abilities, knowledge, and effects. Whether the storytelling happens within a stream of talk, during a thinking interaction with the story, or from the vivid place of deep imagination, each is an experience of integrity. Learning is happening; social, linguistic, and cognitive abilities are developing; and a body of knowledge nurtured. Together, the three participations are complementary and interdependent in a pedagogy. Although I've concluded that one can rarely, if ever, enter a story without going through both of the other participations, the idea of progression subtly assigns an incorrect purpose and value to ways of telling and listening to stories. The classroom stories that follow this chapter will illustrate this point.

The Three Circles of Storytelling

Because mine is a rather new idea about what is happening during storytelling and how we can organize storytelling events, I've

Figure 1. The three circles of storytelling

developed a model to help us think about it and communicate the concept more easily.

Storytelling events are 'round,' or, more accurately, spherical. This claim has two aspects. First, a storytelling creates a kind of bubble in the midst of other activity. When a story happens, participants 'pause.' The event is distinct from conversation or teaching or usual class activities. Later we can remember 'the story' or storytelling distinct from other talk, lessons, or activity. The other reason that I think of storytelling as round is the way participants gather round during a storytelling: people stand, sit, and interact in ways that are less linear.

Figure 1 shows three circles presented as one bounded sphere. Together, they constitute a unified way of teaching and learning. Storytelling participants sometimes talk with stories, sometimes think with them, and other times are inside them. During one event, one participation, participants locate themselves in any, some, or all of the circles. Each circle entails abilities, knowledge, story genres, and experiences particular to itself. As participants move from one to another way of listening and telling, they acquire abilities and develop understandings specific to storytelling in each circle. All together, the circles comprise a way of teaching and learning, a set of abilities, and a body of knowledge that is storytelling. Thus, it is a pedagogy.

Talking with Stories

In the first circle, the outer ring, tellers and listeners are talking with stories. They tell and listen in awareness of each other; they experience themselves as in the midst of their gathering. This influences their participation with the storytelling. They are, in general, responsive or attentive to the circumstances that are part of storytelling. This way of being with a story includes the situation, others' presence, and an awareness of oneself in company. These all bear on the meaning and the applications made of storytelling. This first circle of storytelling is

Figure 2. First circle: talking with stories

much more permeable to life outside the circle. For example, interruptions are tolerated and even incorporated into the experience with some ease. Notice too that there is hardly an idea of a teacher or a storyteller in this circle as contrasted with the other two. It is an event that is all-of-us.

Thinking with Stories

In the second circle, participants are thinking with the story. They are in a mindful interaction with the story and teller. The storytelling event calls up an active dialogue between the listener's mind and the story's content, associations, or relationships with a task at hand, personal memories, and so on. Thinking can be directed by the listener or by the storyteller. It can also be provoked by associations the listener makes with the story. This typically happens within the mind of the participant, but it can happen out loud.

Figure 3. Second circle: thinking with stories

This boundary is less porous. Unlike participation in the outer circle of talking with stories, this interaction is threatened by interruptions, shifts of subjects, or intrusions. In this circle of storytelling, partici-pants lose keen awareness of the others. As the diagram shows, partic-ipation is an interaction between a listener and the story(teller).

Imagining with Stories

Finally, in the centre, a listener is alone. In a deep imaginative engage-ment, listeners exclude the circumstances, the teller, and other listeners from their experience with a story. Although they depend on the story-teller to open up the storyworld, the imaginator's focus is just beyond the teller. It is held by storyworld life. This participation is not perme-able. For the listener who is inside, in a deep imaginative engagement, the experience is jeopardized and even destroyed by interruption. In the diagram, the listener sits within the borders of the storyworld.

Figure 4. The centre: imaginating with a story

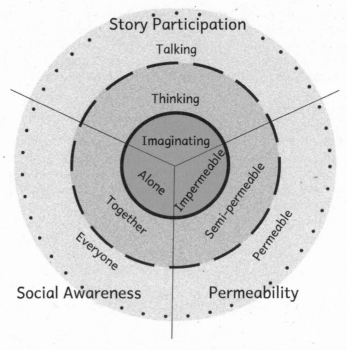

Figure 5. Pedagogy of storytelling: participating with a story

In the following chapters I'll discuss each participation in greater detail. Each chapter offers a full description with accounts from the teacher, tellers, and listeners about what was happening during storytelling. A lot of learning work took place during each of the participations. In the next chapter I'll describe and discuss what happened when the class talked with stories. I'll go on to describe imaginating with stories, and conclude my description of storytelling participations with chapter 10, in which I examine how children think with stories.

Some readers might wonder why I'm discussing the three participations out of the order given in Figure 1. I do so to emphasize the interdependence between participations. Most of the literature on storytelling in school exclusively concerns the middle circle, where children think with stories. But Linda's classroom shows that the language, facilitating relationships, and experiences necessary to thinking with stories are developed in the other two participations. In story-talk, listeners develop the vocabulary and relationships they need for thoughtful interaction. Imaginating with stories develops the abilities necessary for conceptualizing, connecting, and understanding a story's meaning, implications, and applications.

One more thing: this model is about participation during a storytelling, but it is possible to make other applications of it. Reading stories is the first possibility that comes to mind. We could think about the self-selected reading time that happened in Linda's class: every day, the class had a half hour in which they read books together. I saw and heard children talk, think, and plunge inside stories in ways somewhat similar to storytelling. However, I leave this connection to another time, another book, another writer. Here I give full attention to the distinct experience of a story in the air. It is significantly unlike one on the page.

A story, told by heart, unleashed the pedagogy of storytelling in Linda's classroom. That pedagogy is embedded in the medium of experience and memory. It depends utterly on human relationships held together by storytelling. A story's meaning is not merely elaborated by the presence of others; it is made in that presence. In each other's presence children talked with stories, thought with stories and imagined their way into stories. The sounds of words, the light of eyes, and the hook of a story drew them into a learning event with its own rich trove of knowledge and empowering abilities.

8 Talking with Stories

Class Meetings

While math books were being put away and social studies papers were pulled out, a buzz of talk erupted in the window of opportunity between subject studies. Children turned to neighbours or hissed for each other's attention from across the room. During group projects or peer editing, children also took opportunities to divert discussion from the assignment to a new video game, plans for recess, or a recent outing. In the hallways, bathroom, and during lunch time children gossiped, taunted and teased each other, and traded stories about what was happening. In short, most children seized any and every opportunity during the school day to connect with others in the room. As any teacher can tell you, this is pretty usual at every level of schooling and in nearly every classroom. All the spaces in the corners and cracks of instructional blocks of time are conversational pockets jammed with stories.

In this chapter we'll think about talking with stories as *storytelling*. These are specific events during which participants talk and listen to each other with a story. Admittedly, when I began my study in Linda Stender's classroom, I didn't think of these brief, vivacious exchanges as 'storytellings.' I thought about storytelling as a performance event, much like the account we read about in chapter 6 entitled 'Leon Listening.' I thought of the sprawl of limp listeners fiercely hanging on the storyteller's words.

However, when Linda identified herself as a storytelling teacher, she thought first of the children talking with stories; about the stories scattered and held in conversations. She called herself a 'storytelling teacher' because she nourished this kind of storytelling event. In her classroom she made time for such conversation.

ME: You call yourself a storyteller; what do you mean by that?

LINDA: Well, I don't know if I do …

ME: When I told you I was looking for a storyteller-teacher, you said, 'That's me!' (lots of laughter)

LINDA: Well, I think it is someone who tells stories and someone who believes in that form for learning and thinks it helps kids make meaning. I want to get them to tell their own anecdotes and get them to refine the anecdote so that other kids will pay attention to them. So that they can create listeners around them and get them to, to … to …

ME: It sounds like you're talking about getting children to tell their own stories, sort of gaining a voice that's clearer?

LINDA: Yes. And I am enjoying creating, recreating experiences, and recreating incidents and sharing them.

(She pauses)

I want them to notice what's a story in what's around us.

A storytelling teacher is someone who believes it is a 'form for learning.' It is the language used to make meaning of experiences. She hoped children in her class would learn to tell their stories and notice 'what's a story' in their worlds: sharing experiences, being attentive to each other as storytellers. For Linda, these were valued abilities and experiences.

Linda said such storytelling happened in her class

when we share. Whenever the kids bring something from themselves into storytelling. Like when they bring something [material]. For example, our class meeting has an 'arts report.' Often they'll bring some kind of little artefact. And they'll tell about that. That will be a storytelling event. Or, when we try to solve a problem.

ME What do you mean? Social problem or a math problem or …?

LINDA Social problem. That's a storytelling event too … You know, that 'one o'clock thing' (said with emphasis). They've been out, now they come inside …

[She's talking about troubles from the playground that need resolution or mediation; and I don't get it immediately.]

ME Oh? I don't …

LINDA Don't forget about that, Jo! Those things are all there! It's not all just sitting there telling stories to each other. We get, 'He did this and he did that and she did this and she did that.' (She mimics the sound of quarrelling children.)

ME And that's all storytelling?

LINDA Yeah, definitely. They listen to each other. Because that's probably half of it, isn't it? The listening.

Linda had noticed the importance of the many small storytelling interactions that happened across the day. When children 'brought things in,' 'reported on' something they saw, or stood quarrelling with each other, they were telling and *listening* to each other. She wanted this 'sharing' to happen more often, but with guidance and intentionality. To that end she developed an event called 'class meeting.' In it she 'creat[ed], recreated experiences, and recreat[ed] incidents' in which children could tell their own stories. She opened a venue for teacher-sanctioned conversation.

The class meeting was scheduled twice a week, first thing in the morning. All children had a copy of the classroom meeting agenda pasted in their notebooks from the first days of school (reproduced in appendix C). It was also printed on poster paper and hung at the back of the room, within eyesight of the chairperson, one of the students. In the order of the agenda, the chairperson called on the others to tell a world news item, some personal news, school news, and sports items; one child would give a book talk and another reported on the weather. When it came to the weather, the whole class pulled out pencils and charted the high and low temperature of the day as well as the sunrise and sundown times in their classroom meeting notebooks. Then a child would tell us a fantastic fact he or she had discovered, and someone else would give us the joke of the day. At the end of the meeting, Linda tacked up new names beside each agenda item. Those students had to prepare for the next meeting.

On the morning of the class meeting, Linda did a quick check to ensure everyone had their item ready. If they didn't, there were resources in the room from which children could select what interested them. A newspaper was regularly delivered; there were joke books and other books available for the fantastic fact of the day. Preparation included writing up some notes for their contribution to the class meeting; they would sit down and write intently for fifteen minutes. If students prepared at home, they were allowed to clip the item out of the paper or magazine and glue it in their books. However, they had to know the story well enough to talk about it. Linda checked everyone's readiness before the meeting. For the first three to four weeks of September, children often forgot their assignments and asked for the newspaper or help finding a book. As the weeks piled up behind us, children were almost always ready.

Before we go on to look at several examples of class meeting talk with stories, let me describe the meetings a little more. Linda assigned roles in such a way that almost every student in the classroom contributed to at least one meeting a week. One of the most coveted roles was that of the chairperson, who directed the whole meeting. At Linda's invitation he or she rushed to the front and got in the 'spinning chair,' Linda's desk chair. Linda would ask if they wanted 'a spin' to get their brains activated. Most children said 'Yes!' emphatically. Linda would give the chair a good twist and the student enjoyed a few moments of glorious movement.

The chairperson called on students in the order they were listed on the poster at the back of the room. Then he or she also called on others who had their hands up during the meeting. Often there were comments, questions, additions, and stories added to the mini-presentations. One by one, children took turns talking and telling. They shared something from home, brought in a mystery object, re-told a book's plot, or recounted a movie. When the student gave out the times of sunrise and sunset with the high and low temperatures, a great rustling ensued and everyone charted the figures in their note-books. Once in a while Linda asked students to write down some-thing else that came up during the meeting. For example, when they had a conversation about stickleback fish, they made a reminder note for themselves to use when they went to the computer lab later.

The meeting was a conversation shaped by a set of topics general enough to allow a wide range of possible choices and common enough to get nearly everyone's interest, or at least everyone's easy participa-tion. During world news, children often chose news items that re-lated to their home countries. We learned about the border issues between Pakistan and India, protests on the streets of Manila, and crime-fighters in Atlanta. For sports, there was one child who always brought news about motocross racing, another gave us hockey news, and another told us about Highland fling dancing competitions. The talk was characterized by free association. The stream of conversation carried many 'that-reminds-me-of' stories, impulsive opinions, and other comments. Students asked each other questions, shared similar stories, and added new information. They had a high degree of free-dom to speak or not speak, express interest or uninterest. Most of the children participated with visibly given attention. All the faces and postures of children suggested to me that the class meetings were re-ally enjoyable for all of us. There were lots of interruptions, laughter and snorts, sudden sharp pauses, and animated faces. Children usually raised their hands to speak, but there were times of blurting and spontaneous talk. When they were interested, they participated energetically. When they weren't, the conversation sagged and children found other ways to occupy themselves. Then Linda promptly directed them to a new activity or topic.

Within two weeks the class understood the routine and clearly looked forward to this time of sharing, talking, and listening. For me, as an observer and learner in the room, these were lively times. A lot happened; I had to listen and watch closely. Topics of conversation developed quickly, took sharp turns, or were dropped.

As Linda says, some items sparked lots of talk and storytelling:

Like the Terry Fox Run ... like those kind of events. Uh, events, like ... a lot of it comes from the newspaper. You know, like the nine-elevens, items about the destruction of the World Trade Center. That sparks things. I remember I had an Iraqi kid in the class. Two years ago his uncle was killed by Saddam Hussein, and his dad and he fled, fled Iraq. And so that, those kind of events, world events, trigger stories from these kids.

Like Remembrance Day, Anne Frank's story ... I think real-world events trigger children's stories. And a lot of kids have stories too. Whatever happens out there, connects to the class.

This is good for the kids to do; by sharing those stories they are learning something.

Although the chairperson directed the conversation, Linda was plainly present, guiding as unobtrusively as possible. Sometimes she stepped in to steer a topic into development. For instance, when there was talk about acceleration and speed, or about national border, Linda took the opportunity to develop an authentic learning opportunity. She pulled out maps, asked children to elaborate, sent someone for a book to help us, or drew diagrams to clarify an idea. There were times in which she offered her own little story to inspire more student storytelling. So she talked about once golfing while it was getting dark; another time she told us about her experience of not being able to speak a language. Other times she halted a stream of conversation by asking the chairperson to take up the next agenda item.

During these meetings, many storytellings were sparked. Typically, the stories were short, impulsively offered, and sketchily put together. Yet this was the most common kind of storytelling activity in Linda's classroom. In just thirty days of recorded observations during class meetings, I counted about 235 storytelling moments. Compare this with the more formal storytelling events, like the one of 'The Three Golden Hairs.' Linda gathered the children to hear her tell such a story only twelve times in five months. I counted 36 other, shorter storytellings during instructional time given to illustrate something or teach a concept. These were storytellings to work through a math problem or explain an event or more abstract concept. For instance, she described the effects of 'occupation' with the story of Anne Frank and clarified 'proportion' with a baker's making of cookie types. (These statistics are elaborated in appendix E.) By sheer number of stories and time given to storytelling, talking with stories was most emphasized in her room. As we read earlier, Linda said that *this* practice was what made her a 'storytelling teacher.'

This certainly isn't a usual way of thinking about a storytelling teacher. Another exception of which I know is Vivian Paley's work.[1] Like Linda, she calls herself a storytelling teacher and believes in children's storytelling as the vital means to her teaching and learning with kindergarten children. Each of her many books, written over 37 years of teaching, opens the door into the talk-with-stories happening in the midst of her classroom. Sadly, the understandings that guide Vivian Paley's work rarely cross the hallway from kindergarten class into the other levels of schooling. And, ominously by my thinking, they are being pressed out of kindergarten in a climate of nearly panicked urgency about 'reading first.'

Of course there is talking in every class. And there are pedagogical reasons that prompt teachers to include children's talk to nourish learning. Strong theoretical and research-based rationales support Linda's practice and other professional educator's uses of talk for learning.[2] In most language arts classrooms we find the understandings activated in responsive reading conversations, literature circles, grand conversations, or book clubs. (Two good examples of work done to guide teachers' activation of children's conversations are Arthur Applebee's work *Curriculum as Conversation* [1996] and Harvey Daniels's work to help teachers include literature circles of guided talk about books [1994, 2002].) But beyond literature-centred talk, there are few models for and little help in using the rich, nourishing ground of oral language for learning. As my college textbook says, there is very little 'available for guiding the development of a curricular framework for effective oral language instruction' (Reutzel and Cooter, 2008, p. 49). Although educators know that 'talking matters' in children's learning about language and content, we do not have much help in putting our knowledge into practice. As we go into Linda's room and participate in classroom meetings, it is important to keep this in mind.

Linda's practice varies from that advocated in the literature about conversation in school, most of which entail firm ideas about defined roles, topics, accountable participation that can be assessed by worksheets, checklists, and children's writing. There are not many examples of or curricular directives or professional supports for the kind of practice we will encounter in Linda's room; but I expect that the account in these pages will suggest the vitality and significance of learning facilitated by the kind of talking with stories that happened in that portable school room. Talk was mostly led by children's ideas of what was interesting, not the teacher's. It was fully centred on children's personal interests. The content and the children's participation were directed by curiosity, social interest, and personal memories. The agenda functioned only to help stories flare into life; the talk with stories was the main impetus to learning. The activity was both process and outcome, the object of the lesson. As we will note by the end of the chapter, there is a significant pedagogical difference between, on the one hand, work that advises talking with books and, on the other, Linda's practice of talking with stories.

Friday, October 4.
Azun might be smaller than any of the other boys, but he's certainly as energetic as, or more than, any of them. Although he was born in Canada, his first language is Hindi and he thinks of Fiji as 'home.' His reading skills and command of English vocabulary are limited. However, his lively interests and social skills make him a welcome participant in anything that's happening. Today, Azun came in before school started. He is responsible for 'current events' in the upcoming class meeting. He knows Linda will have a newspaper ready in the classroom for students who need it.

She offers him the *Vancouver Sun*. The paper's headlines are about a topic soon to be studied in health class. Linda tells him this and suggests that the article is perfect for what he needs. She clearly hopes he'll choose the front page to discuss. This would direct conversation to the health facts and implications of smoking. Linda helped him read the headline before class began. Azun practised reading it twice. Later, after the meeting at lunch time, Azun told me he selected the front-page news item because he liked the picture.

When it is his turn in the class meeting, Azun comes to the front. 'I brought this,' he says. He reads the paper headlines firmly, articulating each word: 'Young girls who smoke face higher risk of breast cancer.' Then he shows the large front-page photo of two girls aged 15 and 16 to the class. The picture takes up a full third of the page. Two young blond girls are holding cigarettes and looking at the photographer rather mischievously. The class studies the photo with interest. 'They are smoking,' says Azun.

A conversation ensues. Children often speak without waiting to be acknowledged. They don't actually interrupt each other.

'My cousin goes to sleep late every night. Very late. And so he does bad work.'

'My cousin is 14 and he smokes all the time. All his other friends too.'

'My auntie smokes and wants to quit.'

One of the children, who has visited a jail several times, asks, 'Are the girls in the picture in jail?' Linda interrupts, 'Why do you ask that?' 'Because she is wearing an orange shirt like they do in jail.'

'There's a girl in Grade 10 and she just started smoking.'

'It will make you die.'

'Some people say that if you eat soy products it helps. My mom had breast cancer but she's better now. She can even run now.' There is a swift hush, a pause after Mila's contribution.

The conversation goes on. Tumbling sets of stories about aunts, cousins, a boy in Grade 6, and a sister's disobedience. Linda interrupts several times to ask about and bring attention to the details of the report with its grim statistics.[3] Finally, she steps in and directs the conversation to the next item on the agenda, although children were still vigorously engaged. Children wanted to tell their own family cigarette-stories and demonstrated no interest in the abstract and generalized facts about health. I also sensed Linda's growing uneasiness with a conversation that brought vivid and perhaps rather private bits of home life into the classroom.

In this small picture, Linda illustrates a rather common intention of a teacher using discussion. She wanted to teach her students the facts about smoking and health: the legal aspects, the effects of smoke entering the lungs, and the figures warning smokers about the likelihood of getting sick. The newspaper article was the introduction to this. As she hoped, children's attention was strongly engaged by the issue. But, as the example shows, using conversation that invited storytelling initiated two common threats to her purpose.

First, the line between children's home lives and schoolroom culture was threatened, creating a potential for breaches of home privacy. This danger is implicit in every classroom, where teachers strive to maintain a firm boundary between what's okay inside and outside the classroom, or between personal and public shared knowledges. When boundary, or Linda's professional sense of it, was crossed, she interrupted and redirected the conversation.

Secondly, the conversation veered sharply away from Linda's intentions. She wanted to draw attention to the dangers of smoking and to evidence of its destructive effects. The stories suggested these in a sideways fashion; but there was so much personal sympathy and sense of dilemma in the conversation that the 'facts' were submerged. The class had no interest in the statistics offered by the newspaper report, nor in the documented health hazards. Instead, children brought together their personal, diverse, and strongly felt connections with the subject. Linda's health lesson became a complicated network of anecdotes. One child thought about the disturbing details of his cousin's life, another about a relative in jail, and another was anxious about her mother's health. In these ways the danger of smoking was understood through children's experiences and shared interests. Smoking was not abstract; it was entangled in the personal.

Letting go of the conversation meant unpredictability. A jostling, stream of experiences, interests, and ideas was created by children together. If we think about this conversation as 'delivering' curriculum, it's hard to know what was taught or learned. All the small stories emphasized the dangers and repercussions of smoking but none were developed, elaborated, or even generalized into applications. Participants moved from contribution to contribution, using them like stepping stones across the surface of Linda's study topic during the conversation.

It wasn't until the next week that Linda could use this conversation for her starting point to develop the health lesson. She drew the statistics into view and focused attention on the lesson she wanted to teach. In this, she did what educators generally do with conversation: use it as a springboard to learning about smoking and its dangers. This learning strategy hooks children's interest and engages their fuller participation. Teachers use the platform of children's existing understandings to build more knowledge or abilities. This process is usually described as scaffolding (Wood, Bruner, Ross, 1976).

However, that is not quite what happened during conversations in classroom meetings. As we saw in the preceding example, talking with stories is not easily amenable or to creating a clear stream of conversation used to teach new information or syllabus content.

Skinny Stories Thicken Language Arts

Let's listen in at another class meeting to learn more about what is happening. In this class meeting the chairperson, Kyla, has just asked Kate to come and share 'personal news.'

Monday, October 7.
Kate stands in front of the classroom. She is a thin girl with long black hair, often uncombed. Her thick bangs reach her lower eyelashes. It's her turn to give personal news at a class meeting. She stands, steadily regarding the class, waiting until she has everyone's attention. Linda has encouraged this approach, but less than half of the children are able to do this. She is tougher than her quiet and seemingly shy demeanour might suggest. When she has the children's attention, Kate says, 'Yesterday I went to the river. I caught 15 fish and sold 8 and I got 2 dollars.' She has a soft voice.

'What? What?' demands Tajo, 'What did she say? I couldn't hear.'

Kate repeats herself, this time a little emphatically and with a little more volume: 'Yesterday I caught 15 fish and sold 8 for twenty five cents each and I got 2 dollars.'

Tajo promptly bursts out, 'How come you sold them for just twenty-five cents?' The whole class is nodding. They are all thinking that twenty-five cents for a whole fish is not much money.

'They were only this big,' Kate answers. She holds up her hand and spans a space of about five or six centimetres between her thumb and index finger. Her intensely dark eyes and expression are unsmiling. 'The fishes they were in shallow water and I could just scoop. I just scooped them out with my hands like this' – Kate makes a dazzlingly swift but graceful arcing scoop with her hands – 'and sold them.'

There is a pause. Terry's hand is up. Kyla, the chairperson, acknowledges him: 'Yes?'

'In the summer time' – he pauses, and plunges on – 'me, I, we – go and I have a net to get fish,' Terry finishes his sentence in a rush. He is usually a methodical, careful, slow speaker. When he speaks I usually have a sense that he pronounces each word internally before speaking it. Not this time.

Violet interrupts, 'When we go to Kelowna, last summer, we all had nets.'

Linda asks Kate, 'Were they minnows that you caught?' Kate says, 'Yes.'

Tajo, blurting before being recognized to speak, says, 'What do the people do with them, the people who buy them?'

'They keep them for pets,' says Kate.

Spencer's hand is waving. When acknowledged he says, 'One time, me and my friend we were walking by the ditch.' He waves vaguely out the window. All the children know about the nearby ditches. These are in place all through the neighbourhood to manage drainage on a flood plain between the Fraser River and the Pacific Ocean; they are quite wide and surprisingly deep. Several children nod. There's a swelling murmur while children confirm the ditches they know and what they've seen in them. 'They're called, those fish, they're sticklebacks,' says Spencer firmly at the end.

Linda responds, 'When we go to the computers this afternoon, let's look that up.' She writes 'Sticklebacks' on the board. 'And let's find out about minnows. I'm surprised about the sticklebacks because I thought they only lived north of here by the Queen Charlotte Islands.' The class looks blankly at her. Two or three children are writing 'sticklebacks.'

'Taza?' asks Kyla, taking back her leadership role.

He says, 'Somebody fell in a ditch and drowned. He died last year.'

Linda says firmly, 'Mila has some special news …'

We can notice several things about the children and the conversation. They shared things they knew and told stories. They participated as they wished. Violet, Spencer, and Taza responded to Kate's and each other's stories by sharing their own highly condensed stories as they were sparked by the event. They depended on common knowledge about the ditches and the nearby river. There was flexibility about who participated and how. We also found out a few things about Kate, about the river, and a little bit about fishing. Some students waited to be acknowledged before speaking; others blurted out of turn.

Other aspects of this conversation can't be known to my readers. Kate showed remarkable composure and courage when she stood and spoke at the front of the class. Usually she stayed within the safety of her desk and nearby friends. And Terry spoke! That is remarkable because he seldom did. He rarely answered questions and almost never volunteered to talk. We also notice some of Tajo's irrepressible nature. In the class he interrupted often and apparently had tacit permission to do so more often than his classmates. Then there is Taza's story about the drowning accident in the ditch. This is part of a theme common to most of Taza's storytelling. He seemed concerned by or interested in death and dying. Linda's experience taught her to stop him and prevent a new stream of stories that would likely be sparked by Taza's contribution. Significantly, these understandings can only be derived through my extended experiences in the room.

As I said much earlier, it's hard to think of Kate's, Spencer's or Taza's anecdotes as storytellings. They are what Linda called 'skinny stories.' They were more like fragments or suggestions of stories, thin in detail and with skeletal plots. They were part of a thick tangle of talk, action, and shared histories. The stories can't be quite understood outside the stream of social exchanges and the moments during which children remembered together. Making meaning of the story depends on the larger complex of events, understandings, and relationships children and their teacher shared in that precise moment. There, the teller depended on listeners' abilities to fill out the story with experiences and memories. When Kate talked about fishing and Taza mentioned the ditches, listeners nodded and responded vigorously. They expanded and filled in the story with images and events taken from their own memory banks. Recalling the Fraser River and the small pools collected near the shores as well as the ditches criss-crossing their shared landscape, they stretched the skinny story into a larger one of detailed images, histories, and significance.

Most of us are familiar with this kind of storytelling. It happens wherever a group of people who know each other get together. Tellers and listeners rely on knowledge from beyond the story's spoken words. They use the elaborations of presence. In class, Kate showed how she caught the fish, she didn't tell it. Her listeners put the story together using Kate's words, hands, and face. They took shared situations, private and collective understandings, and the teller's presence and wove them together into the story. Thus, participants made the story together.

But this talking with stories happened in school. We expect an educational intention to direct the talk rather than the blowing wind of unplanned connections and shared impulses. What was Linda teaching? As we saw, Linda did use talking with stories to lead into subjects of study. However, I rarely saw this happen in obvious ways. Even when students were asked to record and look up 'sticklebacks,' only three or four students used computer time to do so. I must say that subjects brought up in conversations rarely led to such traditional classroom outcomes as further research, notes, writing about, reports, graphs, and so on. In conversations like the one led by Azun about cigarettes or Kate about fishing, the story talk seemed to run away with the topic or even lead far away from it. There was no clear path between the conversation and a study subject or learning outcome as you might read about these in educators' work mentioned earlier. At the same time, we can be sure that Linda Stender, an experienced, highly valued, and successful teacher, was a purposeful educator.

Linda freed the purpose of talk from a school idea about 'topic.' When I talked with her about this, she explained how the free-flowing conversations 'created possibilities for children's storytelling as language exercise.' In a class where more than half of the children did not speak English at home, this was especially significant. It helped children 'gain confidence to speak English in front of a group of listeners.' It offered them an 'opportunity to hear and learn new vocabulary in contexts that give meanings to the word.' They could 'practice pronunciation of new or familiar words.' When students recounted personal experience or displayed an ability, like Violet's dancing or Taza's cricket bat swinging, they 'created options and variations for talk.' Those options and variations were built into class meetings where children tried out varied genres such as jokes, riddles, book talks, personal anecdotes, recounting of current events, and reports. The invitation to tell a story inside the structured ease of these meetings 'freed children to experience the flexibility of language.' Encouraged by telling their own stories and listening to each other's, they grew more 'daring' and 'more experimental' in their uses of English.

During talk with stories, Linda listened to her student's oral abilities. Over the course of the year she listened for children's language development. Class meetings facilitated this in a real context. She looked for growth over the course of the year. By the end of a year of talking with stories in class meetings, she could make some assessments. As she explained to me before school started, listening to talk during class meetings

helps me to see that there's growth. I want to know that [after they've spent] a year in my class, they are going to be more expressive. And they're going to be a little more careful in their talking than they were in September. You'd want that to happen.

Her hope was realized even over the five months I spent in the class-room. From September to January, I heard children recount stories from books, tell jokes, and retell news items with increasing confidence and ability. They demonstrated growing fluency and improved vocab-ularies and language abilities. Children grew increasingly comfortable and even 'daring' in speech. Kate stood in front of class, and Terry spoke. Other students, like Jack and Alt, spent the first month wrapped in the safety of silence. By November Jack, as the narrator in a play, retold a complex folk tale, and Alt told the story of his grandmother suffering from Alzheimer's disease.

Terry offers us a good example of potential language development through the use of talking with stories. In September his limited Eng-lish vocabulary made him reluctant to speak, or even read and write. Gradually he developed what he needed in a classroom where much talking and listening happened. In the following account, written by Linda in her journal, she describes how Terry's progress showed the power of storytelling to develop vocabulary. After she told the story of 'Sody Salaratus,'[4] the students were to retell it with each other:

Saturday, November 30.
For me the highlight had to be hearing Terry use the word 'skittered' as he described the little squirrel's journey to the stove. Terry paused, con-ducted a quick inner search, found the word, and then said with great confidence: 'He skittered out the door and down the road to the bridge.' That's real engagement for Terry, who in September seemed quite absent from all classroom goings-on.

I'm sure if he'd been prescribed a hundred vocabulary worksheets and dictionary drills he would never have come to appreciate the power and delight of finding just the right word to convey a thought or idea, the way he did when he proudly and consciously and correctly produced that particular word.

With the attention he gave to the initial telling of the story and then the repetition that preparing the story for performance allowed, Terry was able not just to tell the meaning of the word but to use it in context. This again speaks to the importance of storytelling as a tool to enrich vocabulary.

In Linda's class, children learned that understanding new words demanded more than finding so-called equivalents or learning a denotation in a dictionary. Indeed, meanings move reluctantly and inadequately across languages. For example, one September morning Taza was telling the class about his grandmother and himself in his old home in Pakistan. His grandmother was telling him a story. They were together on the *manji*. He told us that it was his very own *manji* that she made for him with her own hands for his birthday. Taza wanted us to know that it was 'very, very nice.' He paused and seemed unable to speak for a few moments. He visibly swallowed. It seemed Taza was moved, remembering his grandmother and his lost 'manji,' something not in his new home. Then Linda asked on behalf of herself and others who looked puzzled: '*Manji?*'

Punjabi speakers in the class nodded understanding and encouragement for Taza, who stood suddenly silent with his hands in his pockets. They began suggesting English equivalents, and spoke in bursts, out of turn: 'Bed! A bed!' 'Couch!' 'You can sleep there.' 'In the temple too!' Perhaps Taza couldn't think of an English word. More likely, the so-called equivalent was wholly inadequate to his meaning. 'Bed' didn't carry the fullness of his feeling about it, nor the exactness of its identity. It was something more familiar, a dear and usual place for sitting, lying, and talking together in the house.

Later that night, as I thought about this incident, I remembered being in grade 1 in George McKillop Elementary School in Lethbridge, Alberta. My teacher asked me how I helped my mother. I said that 'I always do the *stoff-ziuger*.' The class and teacher looked at me perplexed, or was it pityingly? She briskly called on another student. When I looked at Taza's face, I vividly remembered the bottomless well into which my word fell more than forty years before. In that Lethbridge classroom, I had felt mortified about being tricked again: *Stoff-ziuger*, a vacuum cleaner (literally 'dust-sucker'), was another one of those words, another thing that belonged at home, not at school. For a long time I was reluctant to open my Dutch home to school. And it restrained my willingness to talk at school.

In a classroom where the majority of children did not speak English at home, Linda's urgency about the uses of conversations with storytelling was lead by that consideration. She encouraged Taza to go on: 'please go on and tell us more about it ...' We all wanted him to tell us more. And he did. He had a supportive environment and the means to untangle this complicated learning about languages and words. He was encouraged to risk doing this again: a key to learning dispositions.

In another instance, Tajo was telling a story about his sister riding a tricycle in the house; she crashed into the *madhami* and broke it! With bright eyes and laughter, he waited for us to be horrified. But his punchline fell limp when the most of class looked at him, bewildered about what had happened. Together we went on to discover that there is no 'Canadian' word for this common and important Indian kitchen implement, a kind of butter-and-yogurt-making churn. Like Taza, when Tajo had to explain it, he briefly lost his pleasure in the story, but regained it under our attention. The next day he brought in a small wooden model of the *madhami*. In both cases we learned about language, gained a new word, learned more about each other and the wider world around us.

Telling their stories helped children value their own traditions and histories. As Linda said, children were learning 'pride.' 'They're finding out that where they come from is valuable.' Children worked on personal identities and their collective social identity. They developed ways of knowing and being with each other in the classroom. As Linda said, conversations helped children share memories and get to know one another:

> They gain appreciation of and honour their own stories: the stories of their families, their uncles, their aunts; and they see how that shapes who they are and now who we are. These are the stories about who they are.
>
> I hope they ... tell stories ... so they don't feel shame about those stories. That can happen, you know. Or that they think that those stories aren't worthwhile anymore. That they don't have a place in their new life in Canada. I would like them not to feel that. ... It's still pretty critical to who they are.

Sharing stories between parents and children about growing up doesn't happen in every home. From my own experiences, I know that a divide can develop between parents who grew up outside Canada and their children who are growing up in the new country. Parents and children have different languages in which they comfortably express themselves. They have deep familiarity with dissimilar landscapes, cultural materials, and social life habits. They have contrasting and even conflicting experiences of childhood. The shared set of reference points is limited. Differing accounts and understandings about 'growing up' make conversation difficult. In some cases parents are uncomfortable sharing stories of the other life, outside Canada. They have established a new home and intend to improve on previous circumstances. Thus, for some, the old life of other customs, concerns, and lifestyles feels like an embarrassment or at least anomalous.

The growing gap between experiences as well as 'embarrassment' might both be reasons that some parents and children don't talk together very much at home. There are other reasons. In some homes, storytelling is dangerous. Adults may not wish to have their former lives and work made public. Consider that in this classroom some children's families came from Afghanistan, Argentina, and Pakistan with in the last ten years. While children did not talk about the particulars of this, anyone who listens to the news will understand that families may have left because of social, religious, political, or economic oppression or other uncertainties. Revealing their stories may threaten survival; they may risk unwanted discoveries. Family stories might also recall too much pain, loss, and terror. There may be homes in which people do not wish to remember.

This is not only true for those who have relocated across cultures, languages, and geography. Families where parents have divorced, families who live in the midst of social or economic struggle, and homes where people are recovering from personal tragedies also do not easily tell and share stories. Unresolved conflicts and unhappy memories are not easily brought into the present. Families who are 'making the best of what they have' keep their memories at bay. Such stories impede or derail efforts to accept the present situation as endurable or pleasant. In all of these ways, a gap can be opened between children's and parent's social languages and bodies of experience. This affects possibilities for storytelling at home.

Opportunities for talk are also challenged in homes dominated by the presence of television and electronic stories and games. Linda reflected on this after a set of parent – teacher interviews. She found herself talking again and again about the need for children to do their homework. At one point she met with a parent who expressed his struggle and frustration, trying to share in his daughter's learning. He burst out, 'He no listen a me!' Linda wrote in her journal

> This certainly gives me insight into the 'other' lives of the kids. Again, I'm amazed at how many parents shared [the] father's complaint about his daughter that 'he no listen a me.' Many parents expressed powerlessness in their ability to regulate the amount of time their kids spent watching TV and playing video games. They seemed unwilling and unable to take control and set limits in this regard ...

It may also be that many of these families are necessarily occupied with the business of making a living, which often means both parents working long hours at two, sometimes even three, low-paying jobs. Parenting may be left to extended family members. Aging grandmothers and aunts may welcome the children's attention to TV so they can get busy with other household chores, and tired parents may appreciate the passive zombie-like state that too much TV arouses.

A colleague and I were discussing all of this in the staff room. A parent confessed to her that his child watched as many as ten hours of TV a day on weekends. Whenever he threatened to turn the set off or to hide the re-mote, the child tantrummed so hysterically that the frightened parent gave in and turned it on again.

Makes me wonder if any talk happens at all in many of these homes, highlighting the importance of lots of opportunities for the oral sharing of all kinds of story at school.

The cry of the father about his daughter is poignant. Talk in the home is not muffled only by language abilities, but also by the din of technology and other electronic storytelling entertainments. Video games, television, movies, and computer time create walls between cultural ways of being together in such homes.

The importance of establishing identities, developing relationships and human values, is one of the reasons Linda encouraged personal family storytelling. Each class meeting obliged one child to prepare a 'personal sharing.' Making space for these stories in school entailed some risk. Linda could not know what story might be told or antici-pate what might happen afterwards. In kindergarten this invitation opens the door to awkward disclosures. But Linda's students were ten to twelve years of age. They had developed some social aware-ness, ideas of appropriateness, and personal restraint. They chose their stories and determined their own degrees of personal invest-ment and disclosure. Students showed varied abilities to choose suit-ably and use sensitivity to a classroom circumstance. The stories were varied. There was a story about winning a medal for Irish dancing, about a cherished Beyblade (a Japanese top), a new family portrait brought to class, a trip to the pyramid in Vegas, and motocross dirt-bike racing. We also heard a child's story from about court proceed-ings and her divorcing parents.

In every case, children chose how they participated when they prepared their contribution before class. They had to have a written account in their class meeting notebook. None of these compromised or threatened home privacy. Following these stories and presentations during a class meeting, Linda let the conversation take its direction from children's contributions as these created and inspired connections among listeners.

However, as the last examples showed, the planned storytelling of one child often inspired sets of 'skinny' stories. Children's prepared storytellings were considered. They thought about the content and chose the risk. A prepared storyteller thought about the appropriateness of a disclosure. However, when children responded to these, in the midst of company, sparked by sudden memories and jolted by interest, they didn't consider their responses. The small breaches, threats to privacy that Linda fielded, nearly always happened in the context of those response stories. When one story sparked another child's memory or association, tumbling sets of disclosures and personal memories followed each other. That was visible in the talk about smoking. This was the risk Linda took when she gave children the space in which they talked with stories. Significantly, she also knew how to gently or firmly interrupt and redirect the conversation. She was a storytelling teacher.

The children's talk with stories was unified by Linda's educational intention. Children's telling of family stories helped them learn the words and ways of the English language while honouring and keeping first-language roots of meaning-making, bridging identities and extending them. This went both ways. The whole class learned about each other's words, worlds, and ways in authentic interactions. The strong emotional engagement and momentum of talking together with stories helped speakers continue when overcome with uncertainty about language, not meaning. The process encouraged growing sets of associations, strategies for expression, and new vocabularies. It increased children's confidence and made risk-taking possible. Over the course of five months I saw children become increasingly comfortable in their search for words and in using them. Class meetings nutured language learning.

Linda organized the conversation to move through a wide range of subjects, from the weather to sports, news, home stories, and arts. Thus, children's English vocabulary and usage were developed across the variety of genres and knowledge bodies. Class meetings helped children participate in what Linda called 'formalized conversation' and 'elevated discourse.' Conversation in the classroom was more sustained and considered than it is on the playground, in hallways, or in most kitchens. This matters especially when English-language practice is limited, as it was in many homes around the school.

Readers who are teachers will recognize Linda's classroom meeting practices as inquiry-based instruction. She sparked possibilities for curiosity and self-motivated studies. Such conversations facilitated learning across curricula. All these are significant educational benefits. Encouraging such conversations in class nourishes language learning.

Weaving Ourselves into 'We-ness'

Talking with stories developed vocabulary, expressiveness, and knowledge. But it also wove a sturdy social fabric that supported learning together. The students grew familiar with each other. Talking with stories helped them get to know each other well enough to work with each other.

Talking with stories isn't 'tidy' teaching. Many times I listened to conversations that veered about wildly. Students didn't stay 'on topic.' Personally made connections, inspired associations, sparked social interactions, and allusions made a confusing menagerie of topic items, abrupt shifts, and erratic bits. Apparently meaningful connections made by children popped up and promptly disappeared. Talk swerved in seemingly unrelated directions. The following example illustrates what commonly happens when a conversation is freed to children's direction.

Tuesday, October 22.
It's been a very busy start to the day. Linda wants to get 'the day going' so she takes up the chairperson's task until Tajo comes back from the office. The class meeting has just started. There is a moment of silence and then Linda asks, 'World news?' Azun comes forward, to the front, to give his news.

He stands until the class is still again. Then he says, 'They caught the sniper.' Linda, perhaps a little impatiently, says, 'Yes, that was our world news yesterday already. But you were so sick yesterday.' Smiling at Tajo, 'Still, your news sure does make us feel better, doesn't it.'[5]

Kate has her hand up. Linda says, 'Yes, Kate?' In a breathless bit of a rush Kate says, 'At a university? They said that somebody is shooting people at a university. I think in France and there was this gas and people died.'

Taza's hand snaps up. Linda says, 'Yes?' 'I will go home to get my math at lunch.' Linda nods a bit blankly. I think she has forgotten the discussion they had before class started about his forgetting to bring in his home-work for her to check.

Linda acknowledges Jack, whose hand is up. 'Okay,' she says to Taza, and then, 'Yes?' to Jack.

Jack says, 'I heard about in Russia they put gas in buildings and thou-sands of people died.'

Kreena interrupts now, 'In the sky train somebody was bad and they put gas, a kind of gas, into the train so that he would get out and lots of people died.'

Linda firmly stems this apparently disjointed flow of bits of talk sparked by rumour and misinformation. She recounts the news from Moscow in which Chechnya rebels held more than seven hundred people hostage, and the Russian military finally stormed the building using gas and guns in response to the execution of several hostages. The loss of life resulting from the gunfire and gas was 90 persons.

She is just finishing when Tajo bursts into the room and takes the 'spin-ning chair' at the front. He is the chairperson and has just rushed in from bringing attendance sheets to the office ... he must have run to the office and run back!

Urgently and enthusiastically, Tajo demands, 'Where are we, Ms Stender? Where are we? What now?' He is settling himself into Linda's spinning chair with visible pleasure. Although the class watches expectantly, Linda doesn't 'spin' Tajo. She has forgotten. Linda says, 'We are at personal news.'

Tajo, undaunted, says with a firm authoritative voice: 'Personal news?'

Jack's hand goes up. Tajo waves him to the front but Jack stays in his seat at his desk. Everyone waits while he half rises, keeps his knees on his chair. Jack says, 'This morning my mom told me that an Indian lady who is 21 is missing.'

Linda asks, sharply, 'Here, in Queensborough?' Jack shrugs, 'I don't know. Maybe in India.'

Tajo says with a strong voice, acknowledging his friend whose hand is up, 'Azun?'

Azun says, 'Yesterday I kept on throwing up for about 5 minutes and I couldn't sleep because I was throwing up.'

Tajo nods and then turns to another student, 'Layla?'

Layla says, 'Uhm, my aunt? My aunt just got a job as a nurse ...'

I feel sure any experienced teacher reading is by now sighing or chuckling. This kind of talk is familiar. Perhaps, this is precisely the sort of conversation most teachers do not want. Allowed to 'just talk,' students tracked through a jumble of horrifying news events and ordinary family-life stories of illness and employment. Apparently disconnected topics, rumours, and suddenly urgent personal sharing or inconclusive anecdotes popped up and promptly disappeared. One story inspired another with no expressed or easily deduced connections. Linda looked at me anxiously at least twice. 'What do I do with this?' was the unspoken message. Linda's anxious look signalled that the conversation wasn't conforming to our understanding about how conversation should be done in school. It was 'off-topic' talk.

But the students gave no sign that this conversation was 'messy' or incoherent. They were fully engaged. Every new speaker had others' attention and interest. Children turned to listen to each new speaker. They showed not the least confusion about shifts of subject. No gesture or physical attitude indicated that a speaker was out of turn, off topic, or uninteresting. Participation was complete, in fact uncommonly so.

This is significant. Such sustained attention and interest suggested the conversation had an integrity of form and purpose that eluded me. While the apparent subject changed briskly throughout the conversation, attention and interest did not waver. As I looked around the classroom it was clear to me that my experience wasn't the same as the children's. Their attentive postures, facial expressions, and steady flow of contributions suggested they were engaged and satisfied with how things were going.

I had to assume they were doing what they wanted. After all, the children were experienced, competent communicators; they could say what they needed and listen to satisfy personal interests. They knew what they were doing; participation was purposeful. I had to consider that something significant unified the conversation and held their collective attention. It would be a subject that was common and important. It had to be so flexible and inclusive it could apply across dramatic shifts of content and contributions.

The answer was simple. The subject was 'us.'

Children were talking and learning about themselves. They were busy exploring and establishing their presence amongst each other. They were developing understandings about one another and learning about themselves as in the midst of others. They brought up world events and family or hearsay stories not so much as information to share but as small declarations of presence. They sent out connecting lines into the group. They webbed new understandings about each other and themselves into growing identities of self and class. This idea of participation and 'subject' is critical to conversation and storytelling.

As we saw, Linda used storytelling in conversation in many ways that are familiar to teachers. Conversation developed vocabulary, offered language practice, and helped children develop confidence to speak about and share experiences. Students made connections between facts like those about smoking and health, addiction and its costs. Conversations with stories created strong engagement and motivation for further studies. However, it's doubtful that children themselves participated for those reasons. Rather, they asked questions and told stories in order to establish and puzzle over their own presence among others.

Talking with stories created a community of companion-learners out of a group of children who were thrust together as a class list in September. A group of people are brought together simply on the basis of a similar age and the happenstance of location. There is not much else that helps them cohere. They come from different ethnic, religious, and social backgrounds; they speak different languages; they have widely differing interests, abilities, and life experiences; their parents don't know each other. Coming from hugely varying circumstances and experiences, children find themselves sitting together in a classroom for days, weeks, and months.

Learning depends a lot on being comfortable and happy in the room together. Children need to be able to work with each other and for each other, learning from one another. They need a sense of personal and social safety so that they can be freely curious, active, and engaged with their learning work. To make this happen, members need to know each other well enough to be comfortable. It was storytelling in talk that made this possible. As the weeks passed, stories piled on stories. Every new layer of stories, new connections made between stories, grew a collective identity: who *we* are in the room. The stories about a sister throwing up, worry about a missing woman, trips and accidents, helped us find out who we were with and how we could work together.

Because of class meetings, no one was left out of this process. Even though children like Leon or Tych did not tell stories from home or about growing up, they accrued sets of stories from events on the playground and in the classroom. Typically, things that happened in hallways and class projects became stories that let us know about each other. Rumours and hearsay of neighbourhood events, gossip amongst children about each other, shape children's identities. Many such storytellings didn't happen in Linda's presence. This is why class meetings were so important. They helped those students who would otherwise only be known through gossip and hearsay. The meetings demanded that children develop more nuanced understandings of each other. Teacher-sanctioned conversation was a forum for sustained talk with stories. Thus students grew complexity by layers of stories and by the many threads of connections. All children participated in developing the story of a particular individual and in the creation of their shared identity as a class.

The growing knowledge about each other became tangible in such things as the sudden pause that followed Mila's mention of her mother's fight with cancer when they talked about cigarettes; in the collective indulgence for Tajo's regular blurting; or their support and encouragement of Terry's taking the narrating role in their play. Storytelling softened labels and stereotyping that so often has the power to prevent real participation. Talking with stories developed the characters in the classroom into fullness.

I think of someone like Taza. One of his first stories was about listening to his grandmother in Pakistan and about moving to the United States and then to Canada. He was a newcomer, and homesick. In September his tense face and almost alarming alacrity when he followed instructions suggested anxiety about doing the right things. Over the months, story added on story. He was a boy who played cricket in Stanley Park, kept to the Ramadan fast, had a reckless bicycle accident and a bold encounter on the playground. By telling and listening, he became complicated enough in the minds of others for everyone to find a connection with him, somewhere, somehow. The class developed understandings of him and affection for him. By the end of November he had situated himself comfortably enough to make an occasional 'smart remark,' talk about his religious practises, and not show misery about incomplete or incorrect work.

Children established their places in the classroom in different ways and times. For instance, Layla began the year with her Beany Bears lined up on her desk. She told bold and quirky stories about them, and demonstrated Highland dancing for us. But then we heard about her desperately nervous stomach before competitions, and learned that how she appeared was not the full story. Her boldness took on a new aspect and snagged empathy, developing into admiration. Another student's stories of an acrimonious divorce that plunged the household into pain might have cast her as a figure of pity. But other of her stories, about funny encounters with a neighbour, figure skating, and crazy play on the playground gym sets, insisted she was much more than a victim. Layers of stories developed complications, nuances, and possibilities about who we were.

Stories in conversations gave rise to more flexible understandings of each other, open to new aspects. All the 'skinny stories,' fragments and bits of them, created ways to know each other well enough to learn together. This created a community that facilitated learning together; it became a much better facility than the portable itself. When Linda and I talked about this, Linda immediately thought of Bekkah. In the following transcription, I had just asked her why classroom conversations were so important. She exclaimed:

> Acceptance! Now that we are halfway through the year, when Bekkah tells one of her bizarre little things, nobody teases her about it anymore.
>
> (Linda pauses to think. Then she says thoughtfully) You can't change your life, you've got to accept it, don't you, Jo? She can't feel crummy about her life. If she … before she can go on … her life has to give her confidence, even if it seems like a strange or crummy life. You don't need somebody to say your life is no good. You have to have your situation validated. Then you can move along … you can't have secrets about who you are.

Bekkah's stories and my observations of her life and place in the class confirmed Linda's point. Bekkah's slow movement from the outside to the inside of classroom social life took quite a long time. In September, she had puzzled the other children. She was socially independent; she seemed to feel no need to fit in with the others or participate when she was not interested. She played with a child from another classroom in a younger grade during recess and noon hour. Her interests were baffling to her classmates, who loved BeyBlades, Power Girls, the Olson twins, and Spider-man. Her own passionate interests were historical: Houdini and Florence Nightingale. She could not interest anyone else in the classroom in her books or stories. When she presented her interests at two separate class meetings, for instance, her classmates were unresponsive and frankly uninterested. Contrast the following two excerpts from my classroom observations in September with what happened later in December.

Tuesday, September 10.
Bekkah tells us about her book about Florence Nightingale. She showed us her 'Lady Bird Book.' She pointed at an illustration at the beginning of the book and said, 'When she was a little girl, she would look after her dolls and pretend they were sick.'

Bekkah's face is intense with needing to let us know what a wonderful book this is and what an important person Florence Nightingale was. Although she looks at her book, her eyes regularly flick upwards to look hard at the class. Her cheeks are flushing. She is talking but I can't hear what she is saying. The children are restless and the room is full of the rummaging noise of uninterest in her talk.

And:

Wednesday, September 25.
It is during a class meeting. Bekkah has just finished 'showing' us a magic trick that failed. The rope, the tying of it, all of it was to no purpose anyone can see. Children stopped watching or listening long before she was finished. While Bekkah packs up her things, Linda says, firmly, to the chairperson: 'Okay, Kate?'

Kate says, 'Any news?'

Bekkah says, still standing at the front: 'One thing. Just one thing. Every month, Houdini would lower his bath temperature two degrees so that he could stand very cold water.' She steadily looks at the class. 'Just in case.' This is said with a kind of ominous tone. Children look at her blankly, it seems to me wearily. She picks up her things and goes to sit down.

Linda says, 'We are missing our newsperson, but I have something here. The anaconda at the aquarium just had 19 babies. As soon as the baby snake is born it can survive on its own.'

Leon says, 'I was looking for snakes and I found a whole bunch of eggs.'

Such responses and other rebuffs did not diminish Bekkah's steadfastly eager participation at class meetings.

Physically, by dress and appearance, she also stood apart from her peers. She wore bright long dresses, vests, and unusual things. Her long fine brown hair, that reached past her waist, was carefully braided or prepared every morning, but gradually gave way to dishevelment through the day's course. Her glasses, perched on her thin nose, seemed to emphasize her astonishing reading and vocabulary abilities, determined to be at about a Grade 10 level. She was known for tart, critical remarks and for dramatic, surprising stories. When she was interested in something, her face flushed, her voice shook, and she would take off her sweater because she 'was too warm.'

At the same time, she had a disconcertingly streetwise knowledge of rough language and sexuality, more common to older children hanging out at the local grocer's or on late-night street corners. In her talk and life in the classroom, steady hints of somewhat atypical home life and ideas of play intruded. She seemed very happy about her school life. She told me at least three times how much she loved 'our class' and preferred being at school to being at home, where there was 'nothing to do.'

Over the course of three months, Bekkah's storytelling in conversation and her work with other children changed her place among the children. This example was taken from a class meeting three months after school started.

Monday, December 2.
Violet is chairing the class meeting. She has just invited Daniesh to give the 'Fantastic Fact of the Day.' Daniesh comes forward and says, 'I was reading that there is a plant that can eat insects.'

Bekkah's hand shoots up, straight. Violet nods her permission to speak. Bekkah says, 'My dad has one.'

Violet nods to Mila, who had her hand up too. Mila says, 'I think I saw one in a movie or something.'

But children are still looking at Bekkah. Terry, who is sitting near her, interrupts Mila and asks, without putting his hand up, 'What's it like?'

Bekkah answers, 'Well, they have this glue stuff inside. The fly goes in and it gets stuck then the Venus flytrap closes.' As she says this she speaks slowly and clearly. Her face is beginning to flush. Her flair for the dramatic loosens her body to augment the storywords. As she says 'then the Venus flytrap closes' she demonstrates with her hands, her wrists against each other, cupped palms moving slowly towards each other, fingers like teeth moving towards each other ... then suddenly snapping together and interlocking. She then makes a gleeful kind of smack with her mouth when she closes them. The class is fully silent and attentive. They are all listening intently, faces turned to her. Bekkah concludes, 'It's just on the windowsill to eat.'

Daron repeats after her, 'On the windowsill?'

'That's where the flies are. To get them.' Bekkah absorbs the full attention of the class, which is clearly intrigued.

Linda asks, 'So, that name, "Venus", do you know what that might have to do with this?' When she asks the class about the name, I wonder if she is trying to move this conversation away from Bekkah's home experience and the story's oddly morbid overtones.

Kate's hand goes up, and Linda acknowledges her. Kate, known for her love of reading Greek mythology, says, 'She was ... like really, really, really pretty. She is kind of like Aphrodite.'

Linda responds, 'Yes, she was so beautiful that men would be attracted and get into trouble. That's why this plant is called a Venus trap.'

Violet takes back her role as chairperson. 'Bekkah?' she asks immediately.

Bekkah's hand was up through all of this. The attention of the whole class is turned to her again. 'Sometimes my dad will put a cup overtop the fly and then smoke inside the cup to stun the fly. Then he takes a tweezers and picks it up and puts it in. In the winter my mom cuts off the rotten parts. Once I found a fly that had five legs and I felt sorry for it so I helped it get away.'

This incident contrasts with the earlier examples of her participation. Children now listened to Bekkah. Even when Mila, one of the most influential children in the class, connected the plant to a movie she saw, she drew no visible response or attention. Neither did Linda's determined redirection or Kate's beginning story about Venus swing the interest from Bekkah. Typically, a reference to a beautiful woman, men, and attraction would have diverted all attention to that subject.

When Bekkah said her dad had the plant, children wanted to hear about it, from her. Class protocols for speaking were dropped. Unlike in the two examples of her earlier contributions, children didn't shuffle, play with something in their desks, whisper with neighbours, or sip from water bottles. They listened. Certainly the fascinating, macabre aspect aroused children's curiosity and imaginations. But, importantly, her storytelling over the course of weeks and months knit her a place within the classroom community; it was the vehicle of connection. Over the weeks the children shared stories with each other, they learned to hear her and she learned how to talk with them.

Bekkah's storytelling helped her acquire a more complex identity, in the room. She became less of a 'puzzle' and more a piece of us. She gained definition over time and made connecting points over the course of storytelling that began with Houdini and went on to include stories about playing golf with her dad, rolling down a dirt hill, being in a neighbourhood fight, and rescuing a fly from a Venus flytrap. Bekkah and her classmates acquired body of shared experiences; their lives now overlapped. Every skinny storytelling was like one thread in the making of a classroom community, weaving the class into we-ness.

I came to realize that when children talked with each other during a class meeting, they didn't take part to find out about fishing, plants, the hazards of smoking, or what happened with the rebel hostage-taking in Russia. They participated to be acknowledged as present and find connections with the others. They wanted to know about each other and wanted others to know about themselves. It was the process of talking with stories that helped them figure out how they fit together. They were making a 'learning community' in the small space they shared six hours a day and five days a week. Thus, while talk with storytelling encouraged language learning and opened new topics of study, perhaps its most vital function was to establish children's presence in the room and nurture a sturdy complex of connections among them. Talking with stories made the room a good place to be together and learn with each other. In each other's living presence, children paused and turned to listen when a story was told. They learned about each other and themselves among others, making a space in which they could learn together.

Story-language made this possible. Children listened to each other's stories in a way markedly different from other sorts of listenings, when a child answered questions with information, gave fantastic facts, or explained something. The quality of attention changed when Mila told about her mother's illness, or Taza about conquering temptation and keeping his Ramadan fast, or Marcus about going out onto the hockey rink to play with his youth team between periods. Students stopped their movements, looked at the teller, and took on postures of leaning and turning to face the teller. This was a regular pattern, even if the story consisted of just a sentence or two. Over and over, I was struck by the reliable recurrence of this response, even when the stimulus was as slim as Spencer's 'we caught fish.' Indeed, all of us are familiar with the kind of storytelling I've been describing. We know when we can and can't interrupt or elaborate with a personal anecdote.

By themselves, the stories were not memorable, or not in the same way other stories are. For instance, I easily recall 'The Three Golden Hairs' or 'Sody Salaratus.' But if I hadn't written down what happened in Linda's room, I wouldn't easily remember those little bits of stories in talk. Yet these latter storytellings are also distinguishable from the rest of the conversation. I can say, 'Remember when Bekkah told us about the Venus flytrap?' or 'Remember when Kate went fishing and sold her minnows and earned two dollars?' The respondent says, 'Oh yeah!' and neatly separates the story from the rest of the event. Those events form the encircling ring of storytelling pedagogy. The tellers, listeners, story, and situation comprise the learning events activated there, in each other's presence. Students talked with stories and learned.

Talking-Stories: Riddles and Jokes

Until now I have described storytelling within a circle of social aware-ness as it happened during conversations in class meetings. I've used the classroom meetings to help tease out the important learning inter-actions that happen when the storytelling occurs. Talking with stories is an event that unifies the story, the situation, and a participant's awareness of himself or herself among others. These are orchestrated for teaching and learning together. Children learned about themselves, developed expressive abilities, and created sturdy learning relation-ships. However, that didn't happen just in the stories drawn out by classroom meetings. As we learned in chapter 6, when Linda listened to Mem Fox or when Leon listened to 'The Three Golden Hairs,' talk-ing with stories isn't just relegated to openings in conversation.

There are many other ways in which story-talk happens. For in-stance, when children chant together or sing in the middle of a story-telling, the story is opened to include the voice and presence of all-of-us. Listeners can make sound effects, do story-actions, chant responses, or make comments to each other during a storytelling. In this, the inclusion of each other's voice and presence fills out the story. Tellers and listeners are aware of themselves, others, the storytelling, and their circumstances.

Tuesday, October 29.
The class has finished the story 'Scary, Scary Halloween.' Nearly as one person, they burst into 'Trick or treat! Trick or treat! Smell my feet!'

Thursday, September 5.
Linda is telling the story of Rumplestiltskin. 'The girl asked, "Is your name Bob?"' Linda waits and looks expectantly at the class. The pause is a bit long. Tentatively, a few children say, 'No.' Linda nods.
'Is it Dandy Legs, then?' asked Linda on Rumplestiltskin's behalf.

Now, with great relish and looking at each other, the class shouts, 'No!'
'Well then, is it Bandybush?'
'NO!' shouts the class with gusto.

In these examples children opened the story to each other's voices and presence when they shouted in unison. They played with Linda, with each other, and with the story in a single participation.

Talking with stories isn't confined to conversation. It is also formalized in traditional storytelling genres. It can be noticed in stories that include chants, action, and choruses; comments and questions a teller might direct to listeners in the midst of a sustained story; and in storytellings where participants share the telling role. Traditionally, people who talk with stories together have developed genres of storytelling that meet the learning and teaching needs of each circle of the pedagogy. Before closing this chapter, I will give several examples of a formalized way of talking stories: riddles and joking. While these genres might not be considered 'stories' by some, they do have an established place in bodies of oral narrative traditions.[6]

Up until now, we might have thought that talking with stories was tantamount to creating the peaceable kingdom in class. It's important to emphasize that talking with stories admits diversity and complexity. Participants need ways to test social boundaries, bump into differences, challenge hegemonies and hierarchies that are present in the classroom. They need a means to express competing positions in the classroom and let children challenge each other in safety. Riddles and jokes, long-time members of oral tradition, do this. They are part of a tradition Mikhail Bakhtin called 'laughing words.'[7] Parody, ritualized insults, satire, and taunting games are all part of an oral language genre that gives children permission to test each other and the borders of what is permitted.

The class meeting agenda included a 'Riddle of the Day.' Although children were asked to prepare a riddle, almost half of the contributions were jokes.[8] Children did not distinguish between the two. The difference between a riddle and a joke lies in the role of the listener. In a riddle the listener is challenged to supply an answer. In a joke the answer is inside the teller's story. In both of them, the teller's success depends on listeners not knowing the punch line. The pleasure of telling is in the flaunting of wit. Both present puzzling situations, verbal twists of meaning, or conundrums for which, hopefully, only the teller has a key.

I suspect this genre of storytelling was more common on the playground than in the classroom. Although the teacher made room for riddles and jokes during the class meeting, I heard them more often outside the room than inside. In hallways and from my perch on the back stairs during lunch hour, I heard jokes, language, and talk that didn't happen in class. In fact, children cut off their talk as soon as they noticed an adult was within earshot. They protected their personal teasing and derogatory jokes about turbans, Chinese food, and other similarly ethnic or cultural slurs. They kept the more violent, sexually explicit riddles and stories to themselves. I heard ritualized forms of slanging or insulting addresses like 'you motherfucker' and 'hey you, gay guy' outside the room, but almost never inside the school.

Once I was unexpectedly privy to an exchange happening ahead of me in a line-up returning from a fire alarm practice. The boys suddenly discovered I was behind them in line. They realized I'd certainly heard one of them say, 'So, you just got to bitch slap him!' One of the boys immediately and elaborately explained to me that 'bitch really means a dog' and, anyway, 'the slapping is just pretend.' Children distinguished between the kinds of jokes and riddles they could do in the classroom and those that were inappropriate. This did not need to be articulated; it was 'understood.'[9] One exception was Leon. There were several occasions at which he showed that he had not read the cues or submitted himself to the unexpressed boundaries. He once told a joke about a girl without underpants who was convinced to climb a flagpole for a nickel while the boys below enjoyed the view. But during the joke, which was obviously known to some children, the class was awkwardly quiet, and there was no laughter when it was finished. Cued by the response, Leon didn't make this kind of mistake again.

Such an incident was remarkably rare. Most children had a strong sense of talk that was sanctioned by school culture and talk that wasn't. As I have said, children restrained themselves in the classroom.[10] Even so, students surreptitiously challenged classroom norms. They selected for appropriateness while coming as near as they dared to the edge of what was 'okay.' Making everyone laugh was a coup, and involved startling or surprising the audience. Carrying off a good joke depended on the teller's being complicit, cleverly challenging norms, and displaying boldness of wit and words. This was a good recipe for winning the coveted wave of laughter.

Thursday, October 31.
'Ms Jo?' Layla has come to my desk. She inspects my lunch and then says, 'Ms Jo, you missed a good joke, yesterday.'
   'Oh NO!' I say.

'I can tell it to you,' she offers.

'Oh please!'

'Okay,' she says. 'Once there was these three boys and their names were Pooh, one was named Pooh and the others names were Manners and Shut up.'

'Oh yeah,' says Alt, 'I know that one.'

'I heard it before yesterday,' interrupts another student. 'I knew it already.' Children are gathering around or leaning in to listen and be part of this.

'NO!' says Layla. 'I'm telling it.' She glares down any competition for her prerogative-by-first-come to tell me the joke. Layla goes on, now.

'Pooh was skateboarding and he fell down. Manners went to help him up, and Shut Up ran to the police station because it was nearby right there. And he says, the police officer said, "What's your name?" and he says "Shut Up." He says again, "What's your name?" And he says, "Shut up." And then the police officer says, "Where's your manners?!" and he says, "He's around the corner picking up Pooh."'

'EEEWW'WW!' shout several children. The story finishes in the midst of laughter.

Formalized genres have strongly developed formats and deep understandings about significance and meaning-making. As jockeying for the right-to-tell suggests, telling a joke entails an element of privilege. Notice how children challenged Layla's licence to 'tell it.' Her response was adamant. Her insistence on her right to tell the joke merely by seizing the moment and being first is part of the protocol of joke telling. She started it, she gets to tell it. It was a way of establishing or rearranging social power lines in the group. Jokes and riddles were verbal tug-of-wars and 'king-of-the-castle' games. Her triumph was amplified when she challenged the school's power over her language. Layla and her friends were delighted by the opportunity to say 'pooh' right in the classroom.[11]

Jokes offer the opportunity to challenge social structures. Earlier I mentioned Leon's joke that failed to elicit laughter or match the classroom's idea of suitability. It's significant that Leon sought opportunities to tell riddles or jokes and did it often. This was noticeable for several reasons. In the first place, he exerted little social influence in the room. He was often alone. I did not see him in the regular company of any classmate. Several times a week he left the classroom for 'help,' as the other children called it. He was accepted in study groups when he was assigned, but he was rarely chosen by children. His work was usually incomplete, and he was apparently indifferent to the marks he got or the way his work looked. However, when it was his turn to give the 'Riddle of the Day' he was always prepared and eager to present his riddle or joke. In the following excerpt from my class observations, Leon had quickly left his desk when his class meeting turn came up. He took up his position at the front of the class:

Tuesday, November 5.
Leon stands at the front, short red hair framing his pale freckled face. He is grinning. 'Why do birds fly?' he asks. Kate puts up her hand. Leon nods his permission,
   'Because they have wings?' Leon grins wider. He says emphatically, 'Uh-uh' [no].
   Kreena has her hand up and Leon nods his permission. 'Because if they don't fly they can't go anywhere.' Leon is clearly pleased. It's another wrong answer. 'Uh-uh,' he says.
   Now Leon nods to Tajo, who asks, 'Because they hate to walk?' Leon shakes his head vigorously, 'no.' He is still grinning. He's had three wrong answers! He says 'Uh-uh,' with undisguised triumph.
   Linda intervenes. The rule is three wrong answers and the riddler wins. She says, 'Okay, three strikes, they're out. What? I mean, why?'
   Leon laughs and grins widely. He says, '"Cause the airplane costs too much money. If they went on an airplane.' Leon very slowly walks back to his desk.

Leon tested his challengers' wit and ability to snatch his triumph away from him. A struggle ensued in the room while listeners fought to supply an answer. It was a test. The outcome would be straightforward: triumph or defeat for each combatant. In this case, Leon won. The class was defeated. The delight and disappointment for each was visible. Class laughter was a rueful groan. Leon was brightly energetic for quite a while afterwards. I suspect he was especially tickled to realize that he also beat his teacher. Children's emotions were plainly etched on their faces in these cases. This was true in its reversed situation:

Tuesday, September 10.
Natisha asks, 'What do you call two banana peels?'
   Alt shoots off without raising his hand: 'A pair of slippers!'

Natisha, clearly deflated by the fast ending to her riddle, rushes back to her desk, not speaking or looking at anyone in the class, her lips pressed together.

This happened early in the school day. Natisha did not put her hand up or supply answers in the class until after recess. There are many examples of riddles told in which a member or several members of the class shouted out the answer or promptly supplied the key. In all of these cases the teller was visibly disappointed. In some cases, as with Natisha, the deflation seemed to be experienced long after the exchange.

Some riddles and jokes needed two persons to carry them off. These were the most popular of all retellings. Children seemed to take special pleasure in sharing a telling:

Monday, December 2.
Layla asks for a volunteer. She chose Kate to come forward. 'Okay,' she says to Kate, 'Okay, just answer my questions. Okay? Okay.' Kate is nodding yes. The two of them are standing shoulder to shoulder, looking at the class.
   Layla asks, 'Do you know who I am?'
   'Yes,' says Kate.
   'Would you remember me in a day?'
   'Yes.'
   'Would you remember me in a week?'
   'Yes.'
   'Would you remember me in a month?'
   'Yes.'
   'Would you remember me in a year?'
   'Yes.'
   'Knock, knock.'
   'Who's there?' Kate gives the familiar response of a long series of knock-knock riddles.
   'HEY!' says Layla putting out her bottom lip and giving a bit of a stamp with her foot. 'I thought you said you'd remember me!'
   The class laughs. The girls go back to their seats, smiling broadly.

Here's one more example of a tandem joke-telling:

Monday, October 7.
Terry and Azun return from their conference and practice in the hall-way. They have prepared and are now ready to 'do' their joke for the class meeting.

'Okay,' says Terry, 'Okay, see, I am driving.' He says this to the class. He is holding an imaginary steering wheel and turning it this way and that. Azun is standing somewhat stiffly beside him, mimicking a passenger.

Azun says, 'Turn left! Turn left!' He uses a high voice, imitating a woman. The class laughs, delighted.

'No, right,' says Terry emphatically.

'Turn left, turn left!' says Azun again in high tones, from his passenger seat.

Terry pretends to slap Azun with gusto: 'Who's driving, you or me?'

Terry says, 'This is scene 2.' Terry puts his arms down and relaxes his posture to show that he's not driving anymore. He turns to Azun and says, 'Make chicken, make chicken.'

Azun answers 'Make beef!' He is exclaiming in his imitation of a woman's voice. The class laughs.

Terry says, 'No! Make chicken, make chicken!' More laughter.

Azun pretends to slap Terry and exclaims, 'Who's cooking, you or me?'

Terry says, 'Okay, scene 5.'

Azun says, 'What about 3 and 4?'

Terry pretends to slap Azun again and again: 'Whose joke is this? Yours or mine?'

The class heartily enjoyed this, laughing at Azun's voice imitation and Terry's impassive and steady delivery. The mock slapping was noisy, exaggerated, and appreciated. The joke was a huge success for both of them. Terry and Azun left the front slowly, both smiling. It was replayed during lunch hour several times by different pairs.

Children clearly relished being part of these word-plays of banter and jockeying with each other. They delighted in complicit acts of social daring right in school. Like Layla's joke about three boys with funny names, the boys' joke challenged school ideas about correctness. Gender roles and violence are two issues on the immediate surface of this joke. I noticed Linda's slight wincing that matched my own. Linda generally called for the next item on the agenda promptly after such contributions. Afterwards, at lunch or on the back steps, I heard both jokes repeated several times in weeks afterwards.

The laughing words brought children together in play; it unified them in the classroom and invited a high degree of participation. But such jokes are not unproblematic. Was the boys' joke appropriate? Do such jokes nourish sexism or ethnic stereotyping or sanction violence? Conversely, do they acknowledge variations in life outside the classroom? Do they later provide the example in a social studies discussion, and a safe concrete example of abstract social issues? Do they provide formal language participatory structures for children who otherwise might not talk? (It was quite heartening to see and hear Terry at the front, speaking and playing.) The answers to all of these questions are far more complicated than educators admit. I doubt there is a single answer, and I will not attempt one here.

As we have seen, Linda's inclusion of riddles and jokes in class meetings helped children to connect with each other. She allowed the development of a common language of 'laughing words.' My observations suggest this offered a significant opportunity for some children, like Leon. Children learned about each other, and tested and challenged social positioning. Aware of each other as adversary and friend, complicit and excluded, they used jokes, laughing-word stories, to bridge the spaces between themselves. They solidified relationships and social circles. Students confronted structures that felt limiting or restrictive. At the same time they developed social sensitivity and acuity. Jokes and riddles challenge tellers to accurately weave a complex of understandings into a concise, pungent verbal form.

Talk with Stories

So much happened in the outside ring where tellers and listeners talked with stories. Children laughed, quarrelled, remembered out loud, touched, gestured, and turned curious faces towards each other. They grew confident in expressing themselves. They developed oral language abilities as well as a deeper understanding about the language needed to share information, themselves, and their experiences. They explored the edges of social acceptability and the strictures of school culture, and plumbed identity. They reached into their memories and experiences with one another in order to make connections with one another and with their study subjects. They made meaning of events, experience, and images.

In the outer circle, participation helps children develop the language and relationships needed in the other two circles, where children and their teacher share stories out loud with each other. In all of this, story-talking children wove the room into we-ness. They made a sturdy learning place. They learned about themselves, a community who share a classroom, and each other as persons with homes beyond the school walls.

9 Imaginating

The Uncommon Gift

Once in a while, Linda Stender asked the children to come up to the front and sit on the floor for a story. She did this 12 times in the five months I spent in the classroom. That is not often, but it was often enough for children to know how much they liked it and what they had to do. They usually rushed out of their desks and arranged themselves with uncommon promptness. Some children leaned against each other; others lay on their stomachs, feet stretched out behind them under the desks. Some children braced their backs against desk legs or sat alone, cross-legged. Once or twice Linda stood to tell the story and children listened from their desks. Most of the time she waited until everyone settled and then sat in the 'spinning-chair.' She made sure she could see everyone, and sometimes redirected a student to sit in another spot. Soon afterwards, within a few minutes of the clamour and relocating, the class had hushed itself into absolute quiet around their teacher-storyteller.

Every time Linda told a story she began by briefly introducing it. Sometimes she showed the book the story came from. Sometimes she explained where she first heard the story. Always, she gave her reasons for telling it. For instance, when she told 'Rumpelstiltskin,' she said it was a great story for helping us think about names, since we were studying them. Sometimes stories related to the season. At Halloween she told 'The Boy Who Learned to Shudder,' and around Remembrance Day she told the story of Anne Frank and the folk tale 'The Field.'[1] When the class was in the midst of a language arts unit about heroes, she told the Greek myth-story of 'Theseus and the Minotaur.'

Most of the stories she told were connected to other things we were do-ing, but sometimes a story was told just for the enjoyment of it.

She looked directly at the children during her telling, and used ges-tures and expressions. Sometimes she changed her voice a little and al-tered her volume to suit the story's characters, tension, or movements. Once she played a ukulele, to the children's huge delight. During her storytelling, her face and body were animated by the life in the story. Generally, the storytellings lasted between 20 and 35 minutes. In spite of the sustained length of the story, children were very, very quiet. They hardly moved or talked. Their stillness was a striking aspect of these storytellings, when we consider the noise and activity that nor-mally characterized the classroom.

Linda chose folk tales for most of her storytelling. She had strong reasons for choosing them:

> Folk tales are as significant to the study of literature as the number system is essential to the study of mathematics. When I *tell* the folk tale I'm hon-ouring the tradition in which they are rooted. When children are told a story rather than read a story they seem to feel much freer and more con-fident in retelling the story to someone else. In that way the children too become honourers of the tradition.
>
>   Therefore, as Alan Purves commented and I told you before, folk tales form an ideal canon. The stories also pose moral and ethical questions, the response to which helps shape our values. They teach lessons about hu-man behaviour that are common ... can be enjoyed and understood at dif-ferent levels. They're ideal for the inclusive model of education that we practise today.

Readers who have read or studied traditionally oral stories will know there are many good reasons for choosing to tell them. The themes of folk tales resonate powerfully with common elements of human experience. Stories are led by ideas, actions, characters types, and dilemmas that people have found important and entertaining over centuries of listening and telling. Their longevity is due to their pungency and aptness of meaning and expression for listeners. To-day, in books and other media, these stories are told over and over again.[2] They are also the best stories for telling out loud: they were crafted to be *told* over and over again. Developed over generations of tellers and listeners, they are perfectly shaped for participation and remembering by their strongly patterned content and form. Because they have repeating events, motifs, choruses, and stock sets of characters, they are easier to remember.

When Linda told these stories she never used a book or notes to aid her: She told the story by heart, or from memory. I do not mean she memorized the words; rather, she remembered the story and used her words. Even so, as readers can imagine, she had to know the story quite well in order to give a twenty-five minute telling with no written aids. She had considerable commitment to her task, and was driven to tell the stories by her personal interest in them. This practice distinguishes Linda from the great majority of teachers in grade 4–5 classrooms.

Although story-talk might be common in many classrooms, sustained telling of a traditional or crafted story is not. Thus, Linda's students had an unusual experience. Not many teachers do what Linda did with regularity, and far fewer teachers do it at all. After all, such storytelling is not a required teaching ability, nor is it even encouraged by professional educators or institutions. In fact, no education program mandates storytelling practice, and only a few colleges offer the opportunity for student teachers to learn how to storytell.

Linda included this kind of storytelling because she knew the pleasure and significance of the experience. As my experience also confirms, imaginative participation during a sustained storytelling is profoundly felt. Uncluttered by pages and not screened by text, the story-experience has keenness and intensity. Enjoyed in the company of fellow travellers into the story's world, the experience includes a sense of camaraderie and lodges deeply in mind, remembered easily and relished long afterwards.

I write these words before taking us into the circle of listening because the experience might not be shared by some readers. If you have not had this kind of experience, a time during which you listened to a told story, imagining your way through the adventure and images sparked by a storytelling of 20 minutes or more, then some of what I describe below may be puzzling. You need to have been carried into a story on the heart and the words spoken by a storyteller to understand best how it is different from having a story read to you or reading one yourself.

Linda's main reason for storytelling was her desire to present her children with a 'gift.' She believed her storytelling offered her class 'something of beauty.' Because she was a storyteller, she felt she had an obligation to tell them stories for that reason alone.

The storyteller has responsibility to give pleasure or to share something of beauty, to give a gift. That is enough. The gift is enough.

Over the course of several months I observed her offering such gifts. Listeners received them during the telling, creating islands of pleasure in the midst of the day's stream of activities. They explored storyworlds brought to life in the storyteller's words. The children visibly affirmed the delight of the activity. They rushed to ready themselves for storytellings and listened, sitting quite still and undistracted, for the entire duration of its telling. They usually emerged saturated and jubilant with the effects of being inside, of imaginating within, their storyworlds.

This aspect of storytelling, the value of the experience, of giving, receiving, and enjoying a gift, superseded Linda's other intentions. This is not to say that she did not incorporate other and more usual educational intentions. She often integrated her storytelling with commonly held curricular goals for language arts teaching. Storytelling sometimes launched a unit, motivating children to read and think about the subject of study. It facilitated different kinds of writing work: response writing, story writing, opinion, and commentaries. She told stories to develop children's communication abilities and language arts knowledge and skills. Indeed, as she and other storytelling teachers know, storytelling is a sharp teaching implement to get children reading, writing, and talking. As I will elaborate upon in the next chapter, such practice is well supported by an increasingly large body of professional writing about using storytelling in school. Writers such as Bob Barton, David Booth, Kieran Egan, Shiela Daily, Ellin Greene, and Claire Jennings, among many others, encourage the use of storytelling to nourish learning in language arts and other curricula.

It is important to realize that Linda was fully committed to provincial curricular objectives, and that these led her to use children's responses to storytelling to help her assess children's language development.

There needs to be a response to that gift [storytelling], you have to ... (pause) make sure. It's your responsibility to see that children are clear about what they've been given. I need to make sure that they're learning something.

As we enter this next circle of engagement with a story, we must begin with the understanding that Linda chose to use storytelling to meet some of her curricular goals; but she chose *storytelling* to do this. While it is a method or tool for many teachers, storytelling itself was a primary outcome for Linda. It offered an experience of such intrinsic value that sometimes other outcomes were not necessary to establish a reason for her storytelling. Writing, vocabulary work, or reading assignments after a storytelling had the potential to contaminate or intrude on the experience. It was precisely this felt value of the experience that drove Linda to include the 'freed' gift of storytelling in her teaching.

This is true about my classroom work and true for every storyteller and storytelling-listener I know. I urge the reader who has not experienced immersion in a storyworld to seek out a storytelling. Perhaps you will be an exception and not find the deep pleasure so many participants describe with gestures and words; but it is more likely that you will discover a new way of engaging with a story that offers significant learning and a longing for more.

Two rationales, varying in expectation and purposes, generally guide storytelling in the classroom. Some teachers do what Linda did: they offer storytelling as an experience of intrinsic value. Many others always and expressly link storytelling to reading, writing, comprehension, and vocabulary work. To do what Linda did demands confidence in the educational value of storytelling. It also takes some courage in an educational climate that tolerates but does not encourage such practice.[3]

In the following pages, children describe their experiences of listening to a story. They guide us to appreciate the significant abilities and learning that happened inside the circle of imagining. These words may persuade more educators to value the experiences children describe with so much pleasure and wistfulness.

Inside Out

Children came in from recess 15 minutes ago. They have cooled down after playing hard for those few minutes, and are settled back into working. They need to finish up tasks begun before recess. This included writing up the measurements of Mount Everest and a lesson on bar graphs. Linda's getting ready to tell the story of Abiyoyo.[4]

Tuesday, September 24.
Linda says, 'Okay, I want you to clear your desks of everything. Right now we are doing language arts.'

From across the room I hear a student say to her friend, 'Why do we call it arts? I always wonder about that.' I don't think Linda heard the comment, but I am struck by it. While the class fills with rummaging noise and talking, I think about it. She's right. 'Language arts' sure doesn't look much like 'art' class. But there is a lot of 'art-work' connected to it.

Right now our 'language arts' work concerns children's selections of picture books to read to their Grade 1 reading buddies. Students selected their books a week ago. They have written about their remembered experiences with the story and a summary of the book. On one bulletin board, several children have already hung their colourful posters about their chosen stories.

Linda is insisting that everything except water bottles has to go off the desks. The room is full of shuffling and small conversations starting up. Linda says, 'One thing, when we read our stories to Grade 1s, we really have to know the story very well. How many of you have read your story several times?'

Leon's hand shoots up among the others. He says, 'I read it about 10 times. I know it very, very, very well.' 'That's great,' says Linda. She goes on to recognize other children who raise their hands to tell about the books and stories they are working with and know well. After about 5 minutes of interaction, Linda says, 'I'm going to tell you a story, then I'll show you the book. This is what you can do too when you tell your story to your Grade 1 buddy. You can do it in different ways. You can have the book and read it, or you can tell it and show the pictures, or you can just tell it without the book. Then they have to make it in their heads.'

Some students seem to have stopped listening after she said 'tell you a story.' Students get up to go sit in the middle, but Linda motions them to stop and says, 'You can just stay in your desk.'

I am not sure, but I feel like there is a ripple of disappointment. I have seen them go up to sit in the room's centre area with enthusiasm when Linda tells a story. Usually they sit on the floor in front of her. Later I find out that she wanted space for her ukulele and her own movement while telling. She was also experimenting with storytelling, to see how it worked with children in their desks.[5]

Linda starts after introducing the story by name. 'The story I'll tell you is called "Abiyoyo." Later on, I'll show you the book it came from.'

'Once in a little village there lived a boy and his father …'

I notice there is still activity going on. She started before she had everyone's attention. Linda doesn't have all the eyes of the class on her. Perhaps just more than half are really looking at her. Daron is studying his Beyblade, a new Japanese top he's brought to school today. Kreena had her shoe in her hands and is now putting it on again. Zara is doing something with her hands in her desk. Azun is turned completely away. He is looking at the chart on the back wall; it looks like he is checking to see what he has to do in the next class meeting. Pender and Leon have some kind of interaction happening between them. I'm realizing that getting children come sit on the floor in the front takes care of this sort of problem.

Linda goes on telling the story. She looks pointedly at Pender and Leon, who immediately stop talking. But she does not pause the storytelling. She goes on: 'So, Abiyoyo's father is a magician but people are annoyed with his magic tricks. For instance, when someone sits down to drink lemonade, he comes up from behind and ZAP! ZAP! He turns the lemonade into hot tea!

At the sound of 'zap zap' or the word 'magic trick' Leon and Pender stop their surreptitious interactions completely. They both turn their heads and shoulders fully to face Linda. Pender then leans his head on his arms, which are crossed on his desk like a pillow. He looks at Linda first with a kind of inquiring attention. Soon afterwards he seems to look at her without seeing her, focused dreamily beyond her face.

In the opportunity made by the laughter of his classmates, Jack leaned over to talk to Terry; Terry looked back at him blankly. Linda looks at Jack warningly. She is telling the next magic trick in the story. The father goes out of town and meets the townsmen working: 'There were all the woodcutters, working hard with their axes and … ZAP! ZAP! All their axes and saws become needles and thread.'

This creates laughter in the room. Linda is going on with the story: they all go back to town. The townsfolk are all irritated with the father's tricks. Now it's evening. 'A man goes to sit down on his easy chair – ZAP! ZAP! No chair!' There was much more delighted laughter about this last trick. Linda made some of the motions of the surprise and imbalance of suddenly finding your chair gone.

Now, except for bursts of laughter or such wordless responses, the entire class of children is quite still. No shuffling or rummaging. Every student is looking at Linda, or towards her. Kreena stopped taking off and putting on her brand-new, stylish black sandals with thick cork soles. Off–on, off–on went her sandals earlier, but now her feet are still. Daron left his Beyblade in his desk and rests his head on one hand, elbow on the desk. The other arm is splayed on the desk limply. He steadily looks at Linda. Taza has slowly moved his seat, without looking at his chair or others, bit by bit to see Linda more easily. He is now on his knees on the chair, holding the back of his chair with both hands. He is sort of looking at Linda, perfectly lined up and motionless in a position that looks quite uncomfortable to me.

Linda is telling the next part of the story: 'And the son was also different from the villagers too. He had a ukulele.' She walks over to the shelf by the window and picks up her ukulele. 'He had a song he liked to sing, "Abiyoyo, Abiyoyo, Abiyoyo, Abiyoyo …"' Linda sings and strums the ukulele. Natisha is smiling. So are Violet and Tajo and Mila and others.

'Another thing he liked to do was, he used to like to stand outside the school window and sing, 'Nyah, nyah, na-nyah nyah! You have to go to school! Nyah, nyah, na-nyah nyah! You have to go to school!"' She does this in the familiar, taunting, sing-song voice heard often on the playground. Children laugh. They seem to love this last song even more.

The story goes on. Jack is deeply attentive now. He gave a delighted snort to hear Linda sing out the taunt, but he seems unaware that he even made any noise, nor does anyone else seem aware: no one looked at him or seemed to notice his funny sound. Leon takes a drink from his water bottle, but his eyes never leave Linda. He puts the bottle down gently, carefully.

Linda goes on to tell the story. The father and son are banished. They are too disruptive to village life; people are fed up with their play and tricks, and so the town sends them away. Sadly they go to the other side of the mountain. But it's dangerous because of a giant who lives there.

'One stamp,' Linda stamps, 'the giant makes a lake … huge. One step and he can cross a valley or climb a mountain. He's huge. And if he steps on the village he'll kill everyone.'

Linda continues, 'One day, it's morning time, but there's no light. People get up to find out what's the matter. It's the giant. The giant is blocking the sun, he is getting ready to step over the mountain. The boy and his father know that the village is in danger. They'll all be killed under the giant's foot.'

She tells about how the boy and his father bravely go to where the giant is. The boy sings with his ukulele, 'I am Abiyoyo, you are Abiyoyo, we all are Abiyoyo …' Linda is singing and strumming her ukulele.

'The giant loves the music. He stops in the middle of taking a step.' Linda sings Abiyoyo's song again. 'The giant lies down.' Linda sings the song again. A few students join her, singing the song.

'The giant falls asleep.' Linda goes on singing the song. Now most of the class is singing with her, with increasing gusto. Finally Linda puts the ukulele down. The singing falters and fades. When it's quiet, Linda says, 'Then the father takes his magic wand and ZAP! ZAP! The giant disappears.'

The story continues. Linda tells how the village people beg the father and son to come back to the village, and how no one gets mad anymore when the father changes lemonade into tea or zaps wood-cutting tools or makes chairs disappear. Then she tells about the boy, who still doesn't go to school. But now, when he sings his taunting song outside the class-room, the teacher and children all go out to sing with him. She finishes up singing: 'Abiyoyo! Abiyoyo! Abiyoyo!'

The story finishes. There is a kind of heavy pause at the ending of the story. Then children start moving, Tajo and Azun get out of their desks.

Tajo says, 'Hey! Hey! Ms Stender, hey! Ms Stender? That song is about us, you know! Nyah, nyah, na-nyah nyah WE have to go to school.' Linda nods.

Now the class is in a kind of tumult. The boys in the back row, Alt, Azun, Leon, and Jack, are all now singing: 'ABIYOYO, ABIYOYO, ABIYOYO!' over and over again. More and more children join in with the song. Other children are singing 'Nyah, nyah, na-nyah, nyah!'

Children are talking, singing, moving about, and here and there con-versations start up. Linda is trying to get children to 'be quiet ...'

The tumult at the beginning and end of Linda's storytelling contrasts sharply with its centre, in which all the children were hushed and mo-tionless. The children's eyes were on Linda, but their gaze was some-what unfocused. Taza seemed unaware of his physical (dis)comfort and Jack of the noises he made. This remarkable quality of attention and posture, held by the whole classroom full of children, lasted 15 minutes (I discount the first five minutes of children's settling into the story). Some children, like Bekkah, Kate, and Alt, listened this way for the entire 20 minutes it took Linda to tell this story. During some stories, like 'The Three Golden Hairs' or 'Theseus and the Minotaur,' a similar attentive quiet reigned for nearly half an hour.

The still and intently attentive postures of the entire class give us a clue that an importantly distinct activity is occuring. Children's behav-iour during storytelling starkly contrasted with that of all other class-room activities and events, including movies, science experiments, and silent reading. Some comparisons might be made with their engage-ment during silent reading time, and more so during read-aloud times. However, even then the intensity of attention to the subject was neither as sustained nor as unanimous as during storytelling.

Perhaps this is self-evident. We all know this. In fact, we commonly refer to the phenomenon of stilled and limp children as succumbing to the 'magic of storytelling.' The phrase acknowledges just how astonishing the experience is. Usually active, noisy, and difficult to restrain, children are transformed into a unified, silent force of attention. Even students like Leon and Tajo sat uncharacteristically quiet, listening for the entire duration of the story. There were no other class time events during which I saw these boys sustain such attitudes.

Teachers love this usual effect of storytelling. Many educators who discover its power in their classrooms don't look back; their first use of storytelling is a life-altering moment. The startling and dramatic effect that leads to a kind of conversion to storytelling is a common theme among storytelling teachers. Beloved storyteller and writer Sheila Daily writes about her first time of storytelling:

> On an impulse I simply put the book down and told the tale instead. The effect on the students was startling. A look of deep, hushed attention came to their faces, and when the story was done, their interest in the art activity was higher than usual.[6]

Flora Joy writes:

> Walk into practically any classroom and say, 'Students, get out your textbooks,' and hear their moans and groans. Walk into the same classroom and say, 'I have a story for you,' and you will hear a completely different reaction. Teachers and storytellers need to empower themselves with stories to help them with practically every aspect of the curriculum ... and when they do, they'll watch their students' motivational levels soar.[7]

The theme of discovery and conversion runs through the growing pile of books written by storytelling teachers who transformed their practice after just one storytelling. They discovered a way of teaching that works. Full attention and interest were palpable during the storytelling, and children were excited about it afterwards. They loved it; the whole class loved it. The teller and listener enjoyed a deeply satisfying harmony of interests. Diverse children, competing interests, clamouring agendas merged in a profound unity. Children were hushed, fiercely attentive, and clearly enjoyed themselves. This was an uncommon classroom experience.

Let me reintroduce the question that led to my study in Linda's classroom: what was happening during storytelling? As we'll learn in this chapter, listeners were so busy with the story, so deeply engaged imaginatively, that they had time for nothing else at all. We should not be deceived by their quiet and stilled positions, for these masked a powerfully absorbing activity. They were stomping with giants, fending off angry villagers, and mountain-climbing. Feelings of delight, fear, triumph traced faintly over their faces, but it was only at the end that the experience exploded to the surface. Stomping, laughing, and crowing, they shouted, 'Nyah, nyah, na-yah, nyah!' Afterwards they talked animatedly about a place they clearly hadn't gone to and events that did not happen. They remembered their experience long afterwards with as much detail, intensity, and emotional attachment as they gave their personally held memories of physically lived events.

The experience was not only emotionally or imaginatively felt – was physically felt. Linda has written about the physically demanding nature of storyworld experience. When she attended the Vancouver Storytelling Festival for a weekend, she was so exhausted by her experiences of listening to stories that she needed to stay home the next day and recover. She wrote in her journal:

Monday, November 4.
Two days of storytelling! Delicious! But I felt so full and spent that I had to stay home on Monday. And I wasn't a performer! I was a listener who attended only six sessions (storytelling events) over a 48-hour period. It certainly affirmed my consciousness that storytelling listening is an intensely vigorous activity both intellectually and emotionally. Now I can forever let go of the worry that kids are doing nothing when they're listening to stories. And the stories I heard that weekend have been with me since. I've retold some of them to my family, and friends have enriched my understandings as I discussed them with [those] who accompanied me to some of the tellings.

The deep imaginative engagement demanded by listening to a story is so complete that while body and all other thoughts or inclinations seem stilled, listeners are vigorously engaged. The intensity of experience absorbs them wholly. The way children sat during 'Abiyoyo' and hung on Linda's words signals an intense mind-activity. We need to recognize this strong evidence for the singularity of experience: they are imagining.

Imagination

When I interviewed the children from Linda's class, I asked, 'What is happening inside your head when you listen to a story?' Many said that they were 'in imagination.' I asked them to explain that to me, to tell me what 'imagination is.' They described their experience as pleasurable, and had much insight into it. As their accounts and comments show, they were extraordinarily self-aware about imaginative life. They explained it to me with energy and interest.

ME: Did you ever hear the word 'imagination?'
LAYLA: Yup!
ME: What is it?
LAYLA: Well, imagination is making it up.
ME: Making it up? What are you making up?
LAYLA: Like a story or something. So you can't see it out there. So you make it up inside your head.
ME: How is imagination different from … thinking, then?
LAYLA: Uh … Cause, when you think, it kind of takes a long time but when … you're going like this: (Layla furrows her brow and taps her forehead, presses her lips together, making faces at me of trying-hard-to-think-of-something.) you're trying to THINK! But when you're imaginating your pen just moves and you have it on the paper.
ME: The story?
Layla: (Nods emphatically)
ME: Can you imagine without writing?
LAYLA: It's better with no writing. It just goes through my head. (Layla bobs her head back and forth at me. She's smiling.)
ME: Do you like that?
LAYLA: Yeah!

And:

KREENA: Imagination is like when you are thinking that you're … like … when you're growing up and if you wanted to be, like the queen, right? Like, my sister wanted to be the queen. My dad asked her, 'What do you want to be when you grow up?' and she's like, 'The queen.' And then she says 'Why can't I be queen right now? Why do I have to be a queen when I grow up?!' (Kreena is mimicking a pouting little girl, speaking in a high voice, and playing at it. We laugh.)
ME: So, imagination is like a wishing?
KREENA: Imagination is like, something like … I … you wanted to be something, then you just think, or you can be dreaming, the same thing, right? You're dreaming that you're a big queen or like … your imagination lets you.

ME: Do you think imagination is important? Like, do you really need it?
KREENA: Imagination *is* important. If, like, imagination … you need it because
   you can just be bored with nothing to do. And then, when you grow up you
   won't even have anything to do. So you should have imagination so that
   when you grow up you have imagination and you can tell other people you
   have dreaming to know what to do.

When I asked Tajo, he explained that imagination is 'thinking,' but in
pictures. He illustrated what he meant by retelling one of Linda's stories. He described the bear hiding under a golden bridge, like the one
he visited in India. Out of that conversation I asked him a question.

ME: So, it seems like you're saying [imagination's] different from thinking a
   mathematics problem or something like that?
TAJO: Different than about mathematics and imagining?
ME: Yeah?
TAJO: Okay! Okay, mathematics is like, is like, not like similar. Because you just
   do questions. You can imagine nothing from mathematics … Oh! Well you
   can imagine the numbers and plus and equals and answers. Yeah. And
   imagine it more. But, of, in mathematics you can imagine anything you
   want. You make them Beyblades, or you got boxers [fighters]. You can have
   anything you want, and it can happen too!

And Bekkah:

It's like … all of a sudden you're out in a different world and anything can
happen, in a story. It's like … it's not the same as reality. It's pictures in
your mind that you feel. Wouldn't it be neat if scientists actually know
how that happened?

Earlier, Tajo said imagination is 'thinking, but in pictures.' He and
others distinguished between thinking and imagining. Layla pointed
out that thinking was harder and slower to do. All of them indicated
that imagination lets you have 'anything you want' and can make anything 'happen.' It was satisfying as well as pleasurable.

Layla said imagination was something she did inside her head and
she really liked doing it. As she described it, when she was imagining
she was 'making up' experience. All three of these children talked
about the ability to make something up. They made 'pictures' in their
heads. As Bekkah describes it, the pictures were part of 'another

world' that was real enough to 'feel.' That substantial and affecting aspect is characteristic of the imaginative experience children have in listening to a story.

Children said they could make choices about making their pictures. Tajo could fill his math problems with strutting boxers if he wanted, and Kreena's sister could be the queen. For all of them this was a pleasurable aspect, that is, they could get and make what they liked; but it was also importantly useful. It was helpful to thinking about or to solve problems, among which is one of life's most important questions: What will I do when I grow up? According to Kreena, you need to 'have dreaming to know what to do with your life.'

Children knew about imagination, knew they needed it to learn, think, play, and grow up. It was something that happened inside their heads, not outside. It was real. Even though they made the pictures, it was a substantial and affecting ability. Bekkah pointed out this mysterious aspect of something experienced and valued, but not present in the room: 'Wouldn't it be neat if scientists actually know how that happened?' She and the other children tidily summed up the conclusions of researchers and theorists working to understand imagination and a teacher's use of it. Kieran Egan, for instance, writes in his *Imagination in Teaching and Learning*:

> It is generally agreed that imagination is a good thing and that it ought to be stimulated and developed in education. Two related obstacles stand in the way of our routinely achieving this: first, it is difficult to get a clear grasp on what imagination is, and, second, whatever it is, it does not seem the kind of thing that lends itself to practical methods and techniques that any teacher can employ in classroom instruction. (1992, p. 1)

Children had a lot of knowledge about imagination. Over the course of 24 interviews, they developed a description and confirmed an explanation of commonly shared activities and experiences during a storytelling event such as 'Abiyoyo.' They offered astonishing insights and unexpected abilities to reflect on and explain complex experiences. I regret not having the space in this book to fully develop all their comments, understandings, and ideas about imaginating their way through storyworlds. Here I will confine myself to a summary of five main points they made about their experiences during the hush of intense listening.

First, the story-telling world is a real place. It was experienced so keenly that it displaced the room where the children listened: it became substantive. Second, listeners had to 'make pictures' *in order to* get inside the storyworld. Layla called this 'imaginating.'[8] While I use this term to mean imaginating with a story, being fully inside the storyworld, technically she meant the work of making pictures to get there. Third, children showed that the worlds inside imagination and outside in Linda's classroom were organized in different ways. Time was experienced differently in the two worlds. This leads to the fourth point: the boundary of the storyworld is fragile. Interruptions from the classroom-world do not merely interrupt – they disrupt its life. The two worlds are based on two different ideas about veracity. The uses of detail to confirm truth in the storyworld are dissimilar from those in the classroom's world. And, fifth, the event is an experience of *Wonder*. These are the five aspects of imaginating with a story pinpointed by the children.

The Storyworld Is Real

As Linda and the children have already suggested, the storyworld is sensibly experienced. It is seen, heard, and felt, sometimes with vivid intensity. Listeners participate in events that provoke their feelings, thoughts, and understandings about themselves or other things.

ME: You know how when you are listening to a story, what happens when you go, like inside your head?

MILA: Yeah.

ME: What's that called, do you know what we call that?

MILA: Imagination.

ME: What is that? How would you explain that?

MILA: What you think about. Things that you imagine. But if you didn't know what 'imagine' was then ... I'd kind of not ... (Tapers off; she's thinking?)

ME: Huh. (I pause.) What does your mind do when you are imagining?

MILA: It kind of goes into its own little world.

ME: What do you see in that world?

MILA: Nothing what you're looking at. You just kind of think what you're thinking of and you just kind of don't look at the stuff around you. You can barely see, like I wouldn't be able to see the table (Mila gestures at the table between us) very much.

As Mila described it, when she was in the story she could hardly see the furniture in the room. Her experience was expressed by other students in different ways.

VIOLET: It feels like I'm in my own world instead of this one ... because when you are inside your imagination, it's like you're inside a different world, like you're on Pluto without anybody with you, or you're on your way, or somewhere else in the world, or on Saturn's rings looking over the world.

The storyworld screened out the room so well that listeners were 'in another world.' Listeners were away, busy in a landscape of objects, characters, and events created by the storyteller's words. These displaced the desks, the children, and the room where they listened. Bekkah talked about that earlier when she said, 'all of a sudden you're out in a different world ... it's pictures in your mind that you feel.' Linda also talked about this feeling during storytelling: 'You feel taken away. You know, you feel very detached from aches and pains.'

While imagining, listeners are inside their storyworlds, thoroughly engaged with events and a place that is elsewhere. That 'away-ness' is observable during a storytelling, where children sit in oddly stilled postures. In a story like 'Abiyoyo,' they were taunting schoolchildren, watching magic tricks done before their very eyes, scrambling over a mountain, and besting a dreadful giant with music. This involved emotional, physical, and lively intellectual participation. The storyworld was every bit as preoccupying as a classroom could be.

Pictures to Presence

The children went on to explain that until that sense of 'realness' happened, they had not 'gotten into' imagination. Until 'you can barely see the things you are looking at' and are 'inside a different world,' you haven't entered the storyworld. You are not yet imagining with a story. That was the ultimate goal. Getting inside, being sensible to its reality, was a highly desired experience. Listeners worked to get there. In this section they explain how they got into the 'other world.'

ME: Let's say someone was asking you, 'Taza, what's imagination? I don't know what that is! What does it mean?'
TAZA: When you, when you read and book ... and you, and nobody shows you the pictures and then you imagine the pictures that are in their minds.[9]
   ...

LEON: Like when you're reading ... without pictures, you can picture them in your head.

...

Kyla: You picture it in your mind, uhm ... You can picture, have pictures, you can see movement, you know?

...

BEKKAH: Your mind goes off to something else. You kind of picture a place, a picture in your head. Like someone says, 'Clouds swirl' and then you just get that picture of clouds swirling in your head. And, or clouds that look so good you could eat them.

Linda described her telling similarly.

LINDA: Okay, I'd say I do it a lot with pictures.
ME: In your mind?
LINDA: Visual images. And scenes.
ME: So, when you're telling a story do you move from tableau to tableau?
LINDA: Uh huh. Uh huh. Yes. What do you do?
ME: Well yes! Very much so. But I actually, it's sort of like a journey, I think. When I tell, I physically ... well, in my mind, I move.
LINDA: You move, you move, you're here, you go there, you're there, you describe and you tell what happens there, and then you leave there and you go somewhere else.

Earlier in our conversation, Linda said that she 'used words like a paintbrush,' painting what children needed to see 'pictures.' She watched her students for cues, signs that they needed words for clearer, sharper, more image-able pictures. Both she and her listeners described picture-making as a first step towards getting into storytelling. If her words painted the pictures well enough and children could imaginate them, they would find themselves in the storyworld.

The idea of 'making pictures' is part and parcel of what we usually mean when we talk about imagination. As Kieran Egan writes,

It may not be invariably true that imagination involves our image-forming capacity, but image-forming is certainly common in uses of the imagination and *may* in subtle ways be inevitably involved in all forms of imagining. (1992, p. 43)

Imagination goes well beyond image-making. For example, one may imagine the ringing of a recess bell, drinking from a grape juice box, or the sadness of a friend. One uses imagination to plot how to get the best computer in the lab or to anticipate which parent will come to pick up a child after school. In these examples, pictures aren't central to imagining. At the same time it seems to me, from my interviews with the children, that 'making pictures' is significant to the storyworld experience. It is a step towards the waiting world. This is an important point: although nearly all the children referred to imagination as 'making pictures,' it is not what they meant by 'being in imagination.' The erasure of the classroom happened *after* the picture-making.

Kate describes the process and difference very well. She answered my question using Linda's telling of 'The Field,' a story about a mother bird speared in the midst of a battle between two armies over a bit of arid ground. One soldier sees the dying bird and its nest of baby birds. He is filled with horror over the effects of their war and stops fighting. Risking himself and his career, he rescues the baby birds and leaves the battle.

ME: So then, what happens inside your mind when you're listening to a story?
KATE: Like ... well, like in 'The Field?' I see all these guys and they're all dressed in armour and some are not. And some have these long arrow thing-a-mah-jiggies ... but they're not ... they're not arrows – (she is gesturing with her hands)
ME: Oh. Spears?
KATE: Yeah! And a few daggers. Spears and daggers. It's practically all I see.
ME: And ... (I wait, then ask:) A bird sometime?
KATE: Yeah, I usually see a robin.
ME: And what makes you pop out of imagination?
KATE: When somebody pulls my hair. It's not usually their fault. Their hand usually gets stuck in my hair 'cause it's so knotty. Or they talk. Or something happens.
ME: What happens to your picture of the story then? When you go back?
KATE: I don't get the same picture. If I see a boy, like a real live-looking boy ... and then somebody talks or something and then I go into a cartoony kind of boy and then it takes a few seconds to go back into the way he looks.
ME: Oh! That's pretty interesting how you explain it ... (I pause rather lengthily, but Kate says nothing more.)

Kate describes herself imagining the story. She is deep inside the storyworld where she is among 'guys all dressed in armour and some are not.' 'Spears and daggers [are] ... practically all' she sees. An interruption pulled her out of the storyworld; as soon as possible,

Kate made her way back into the story. She made the pictures she needed. She first went 'into a cartoony boy.' We note that a 'cartoon' is deliberately drawn by hand. It is a picture of particular rigidity of form; even when it is animated it has a two-dimensional quality.[10] Kate used an inner drawing-hand to make what she needed to 'go back into' the story. Then the moment she hoped for happened: the boy went 'back to the way he looks.' He took 'a few seconds' to do this. When it happened, the cartoony boy took on, or rather regained, his storyworld life-form. Kate moved from making a picture of him to being with him, in his presence.

Her soldier was 'a boy,' not a man as the storyteller had suggested. Neither was he the 'cartoony' figure she first made. The storyteller did not say what kind of bird was in the tree, but Kate said she 'usually sees a robin.' The storyworld had its own life, conjured into reality by her listening and making pictures. As Kate explains it, the boy, the field, the birds had lives of their own. When she was 'back' in the storyworld, the story unleashed its own life. Images, details of events, and aspects of its experience were beyond the full control of the listener or teller.

Pender also described this process of going from making pictures to imaginating with a story. He showed a sophisticated meta-awareness of a process in which he moves from the outside to the inside the storyworld. As you will notice in the following transcript, I was initially quite confused about what he meant, but he was clear about what he wanted to communicate:

ME: What kinds of things make it easier for you to imagine?

PENDER: Well, uh … (long pause) when the person says it … and it's like a real little spot or something like that? Like they're in a room or something like that?

ME: Yeah?

PENDER: Yeah, well in the forest in the middle or something like that.

ME: The person telling you is? Or? … oh … explain it to me? I don't really get it. (I am completely confused about his meaning. Does he mean the storyteller or the story? Is he talking about a story I don't know?)

PENDER: Yeah. Well, you know … the person telling it; like, if they say, like in a small place or somewhere around like this (he gestures around the room where we are) … then, it's easy for me to imagine it. Not … not like flat land with trees all over it and streams going through, then it's hard from me to imagine. It's got to be quite small but not that small.

ME: Yeah?

PENDER: It's better if it's small.
ME: So you need the place to be small enough to see?
PENDER: Yeah! (His eyes light up and his voice grows louder – he's glad to see that I finally 'get it.')

Pender explains that he needs a concise, strongly outlined locale in order to imagine his way into the storyworld.[11] His 'getting in,' his ability to imaginate with the story, depended on being offered a well-defined space, 'small, but not that small.' If the place was boundlessly flat and confused by trees and streams going through he would struggle to construct it. Such a description wouldn't give him the specificity he needed; it would be 'hard … to imagine.' The starting place had to be 'small enough to see' and make, a sturdy entry point.

Tajo explains how he made the 'picture' piece by piece until it was ready for him to get into the story. He said his work was like making a puzzle:

ME: So, when you are going to go and listen to a story, and you sit down, what kind of things make it easier … for you to imagine? … So, like, in 'The Field' … what kind of things make it easier to get into the story?
TAJO: It's like, when she says the word, like when she goes, 'Once upon a time there was a field.' I imagine a field. And then she goes, 'It was with rocky and dirt.' So I imagine that on it. And then she says 'They wanting to fight.' So I put people on it who want to fight. And then when the guy wanted to save the bird I didn't want to imagine the field, I wanted to imagine the field behind the person and the bird in front of the person and … and then he picks it up, yah (sighs), and then he carries it home.
ME: Oh! I love the way you told that. It's very clear. It's like what happens: she says it and makes the picture, the picture starts getting bigger and you start moving around.
TAJO: Like a puzzle.

Tajo's use of the simile 'like a puzzle' was extraordinary. His second language, English, challenged his easy expression. But with clarity and eloquence he described his experience. He imagined the pieces he needed: the field, rocks and dirt, a tree, and 'people who want to fight.' He made pictures, one after the other, to make his way in. He fit them together until he'd made the puzzle, his way into the story.

Significantly, Tajo recounted the sequence of events and images of the story for which he made the pictures that led him into his experience in the centre circle with the story. Once he had explained what he did to 'get into' the story, he leapt to the story's ending where the soldier carries the baby birds in his helmet. Tajo went from the introduction of the story to its conclusion; he left out the confrontation of armies, their battle, the flight and death of the mother bird, the accident in which the nest fell from the tree, the conflict between the captain and soldier, and finally the soldier's defiant removal of his helmet. He simply explained how he got into the story and then concluded the experience.

The gap in Tajo's storytelling is significant. He also made a shift in the *way* he told me the story. In the beginning, when he was explaining how he 'got into' the story, he used his hands and explaining voice. Then he said, 'and ... and then he picks it up, yah ...' At that moment, Tajo changed the way he talked to me. His deep sigh and expressive eyes suggested that even in telling me about the story, he successfully moved from making the pictures to being inside a remembered event. He expressed himself from inside the soldier's pang of compassion and horror. He held the clutch of baby birds in his hands.

This phenomenology, this felt shift of experience is critical to our thinking about the aspects of imagination. Children clearly distinguished between two kinds of story-listening and imaginative engagement. They first made pictures and fit them together to make their way into the storyworld. In the second part of the experience they were imagining. Submerged and inside the storyworld experience, they had reached the state they worked for. Let me give a few more accounts from children to confirm the significant differentiation of experiences.

Layla used our shared experience of 'Sody Salaratus' to help answer my question about her experience during storytelling. It is a story of a bear that waits under the bridge to eat the four family members who come, one after the other, to get 'soda for the biscuits' at the store on the other side of the river. When they come back with the soda, the bear eats each of them in a lusty gulp. Finally, the squirrel that lives with the family goes to the store. He tricks the bear, making it fall down heavily. Out pop the man, woman, boy, and girl; a happy reunion ensues, and grandma bakes the biscuits.

Layla used the large table between us to illustrate her points. She gestured vigorously and used both hands. Notice too her rejection of my suggestion that Linda helped her 'get into imagination.' She did it herself!

ME: What kinds of things make it easy for you to get into imagination?
   What does Ms. Stender do that helps you to listen?
LAYLA: Like once she gets ... like, almost, ... like, say this! (She makes a sweep-
   ing motion over the table, pointing at the far ends of the table and indicates
   the space between). A story that is ... is as ... as big as this table. (She waves
   across the table space and then points at one end and says:) Then, that's the
   beginning. (She gestures at the other far end) and this is the end of the story.
   So, just about right here, up to the middle ... (She points with one hand to
   middle of the table. With the other she reaches short of the middle, coming
   up from the beginning edge of the story) this is the middle right here!
ME: Right. So before the middle?
LAYLA: So before the middle I'll start getting the picture.
ME: Ahh? Can you give me an example of that?
LAYLA: Like, say the house was over here (She reaches to touch and then cup
   her hand on the 'beginning' side on the table) and the girl in the story was
   talking, and trying to ... and she walked along, and she went to the store
   and then she went back (Her hand is slowly moving to meet her other hand
   that is 'waiting' at the middle of the table. Her hands join when she says:)
   and then she met the bear. That's where I started to get the picture.
ME: Oh. It does take that kind of little while to get that picture!
LAYLA: It's like watching a video. At first you don't get it? And during on you
   get it.

Layla's account isn't easy to follow on paper! But she was very clear
about what she wanted me to understand. She used the table surface to
give shape to something in her mind. She swept her hand through the
air, showing how the story was spacious. She pointed at the beginning
and end of the story on the table. It may not have been considered, but
she used the entire table surface, not its edge. The storyworld is roomy,
not linear. The characters, pieces of setting, and relationships were more
like tableaus of objects. She set these up, one after another, to fill the
table. Slowly the world filled and Layla 'started to get the picture.' When
she says 'get the picture,' she is referring to the experience of imaginating. She is inside the storyworld. In this way, her description is like
Tajo's 'puzzle.' Her use of a table surface suggests her need is similar to
Pender's. A table is a bounded space, 'quite small but not that small.'
   'Getting the picture' was a destination towards which children
worked with determination. Daron also differentiated between two
experiences with imagination. He described what it took to make the
way in strong enough to let him 'get into' it.

ME: What's happening, inside your head, when you are listening to a story?

DARON: I'm making pictures, yeah, like pictures in my mind.

ME: Do you know what you might call that? A word for that 'pictures in your mind?'

DARON: Concentration more ... (pausing) or, imagination!

ME: Yeah! Big words, Huh? Imagination. What is that, do you think? What is your brain doing?

DARON: I don't really know, like, it's hearing. Your nerves, they listen and they, like, tell your brain how to do that, stuff like that. So it's how you listen and, like, signals go to your brain from you listening.

ME: And what does your brain do for you?

DARON: Sends a picture. But, like, at first when she just starts you can't really get a picture. Once you get into it, like in the middle and stuff, then you start getting pictures.

ME: Can you give me an example?

DARON: Like 'Sody Salaratus,' if you were telling that story you would probably get a picture of that right away because it's a short story.

ME: How about a story like 'The Field' then?

DARON: At first I didn't get, really, like, the pictures, but then when I got to the part when they're, like, on the field and then when the bird is, like, struck down and then it started getting pictures.

ME: So, first you're just listening and figuring out and then your imagination takes over?

DARON: Yeah. And sometimes when I'm at home and I'm watching TV and I get right into it and someone starts talking to me and I don't even hear it.

As in other accounts, Daron subtly shifted positions. He went from 'making' to 'being in' imagination. When he first considered 'concentration,' I think he meant the effort of 'making pictures.' Then he corrected himself and said 'imagination' to refer to the experience of pictures flowing through his head. He described the difference when he said it is 'like ... hearing. Your nerves, they listen and they, like, tell your brain how to do that, stuff like that. So it's how you listen.'

Daron did not listen in his usual ways inside the storyworld. He used the idea of 'nerves' to help explain the difference. The different world demands a different way of listening that excludes the usual way: 'If someone starts talking to me I don't even hear it.' It was 'like watching' a video or TV. He received but did not make the pictures while imagining with the story. He was inside, listening with his nerves. Daron's account shows extraordinary awareness. He knows that he changed the way he listened and interacted when he was 'into' a story. He subtly gets at the changed volition he experienced or the sense of control he has during his deep imaginative engagement. Thus, when children imaginate with a story, it fills in its own life in the listener's imagination. Daron's change of pronouns emphasizes this:

> At first *I* didn't get, really, like, the pictures, but then when *I* got to the part when they're, like, on the field and then when the bird is, like, struck down and then *it* started getting pictures.

The pattern of movement from making pictures to coming into the presence of the story was 'familiar' to everyone. It was tacit knowledge. Interestingly, no child explained the moment of crossing. The hoped-for moment of moving from picture-making into imaginating went unnoticed. Children quieted themselves, listened to Linda's words, and made pictures until they found themselves inside the circle with a story.

My readers may recognize that this is something they do too. However, I never realized this until the children explained it. Working through the data from their accounts brought this understanding to my awareness. Children demonstrated abilities to consider their experiences of listening, untangle its aspects, and explain their ways into imaginative engagement. The commonly held and high value they assigned the experience prompted strong efforts to describe it to me.

These accounts might tempt us to think that a good 'setting' facilitates entry into the storyworld. But neither the children's accounts nor my observations clearly indicate what makes the storyworld come to life for listeners. Neither do they show that making pictures inevitably facilitates imaginating with the story. As we saw, it took about five minutes for children to settle into the storytelling of 'Abiyoyo.' In general, children took several minutes beyond a story's introduction before they assumed postures that showed they'd slipped into the storyworld. 'Going in' was facilitated by a variety of aspects that included the furnishings of the setting, but it also depended on children's interests and other experiences. They had to 'like' the story. Still, these accounts make it plain that a critical element of getting into the story is the specificity of the locale as well as characters or dilemmas that interest the listeners. Children need the raw material from which they can create the pictures to make their way into the storyworld.

Another aspect of children's 'getting into' the story concerns the storyteller. Linda's storytelling, choice of stories, and relationship with her listeners are some of the ways in which she facilitated children's imaginating. The story has to be told well enough to draw interest and with enough animation to help listeners make pictures.

Story-Time

Obviously, classroom life and storyworld experiences differ in many ways. Perhaps the most obvious is that one is visible and the other is not, or that one is physically shared and present to the children and the other is imaginatively held by individuals. In this section, I will discuss another specific aspect of the storyworld: the experience and ordering of time.

Recall how Layla explained how she 'got into' the story of Sody Salaratus: she used the table to show the 'beginning' part of the story where she made the house, its household, and the pathway across the bridge and the store. She indicated that the 'beginning' ended when the girl 'met the bear.' 'That's when I started to get the picture,' she positioned her hands on the table to emphasize what she said: she 'got into' the story 'just before the middle.' However, that moment was not in the middle at all. Layla's 'beginning' took up less than a seventh of the time taken to tell it. If I had pointed it out to her or asked about it, I am sure she would have acknowledged this significant discrepancy. She missed telling us about the three more people who had to leave the house, go to the store, meet the bear, and be eaten; the squirrel's decision to cross the bridge; and his talk with the store-keeper, return over the bridge, and confrontation with the bear. She doesn't describe the squirrel's trick or the emergence of the four family members. So, when she says she started to 'get it' when 'the girl met the bear,' she is describing a moment well towards the beginning of the story. Yet she'd said and gestured that she got into the story 'just before the middle.'

Layla described her entry as she felt it. While she was imaginating with the story, time folded up and shortened. She experienced its passage differently than while she was making pictures. This is a common experience. Layla's recounting was similar to Tajo's: when he described 'getting into imagination' he explained the first few moments of the story to me and promptly skimmed to its conclusion. Time took longer outside the story than in it.

Not only is time experienced as shortened, inside imagination it is organized differently. The rules of chronology, ideas about sequence, seasons, maturation, or cause and effect in the classroom world disappear. Inside the story, time dances. It can move in steps that are linear, cyclical, reversing, or folded over again and again. It flashes forwards and backwards. Inside a story characters' lives and events are unfettered from time's rule.

Listeners aren't confused by this. They fluently follow events without needing the kind of logic that binds other genres. This astonishing ability suggests a highly developed albeit also usual ability concerning facility with stories. Listeners know how things are ordered in a story. Story-time is ordered by the point of the story, to create a special effect. Time is organized to best share an experience or a point of view. It is the listener, rarely the teller, who determines the complex principle that guides and unifies the organization of time in a story. These aspects of time in a story are well documented.[12] Most teachers know about the ways in which time is reordered in stories because of all their work with written stories. However, the differently felt experience of shortened time during a storytelling or story engagement during reading is hardly mentioned in anything I have read.

When we later think about using stories to encourage writing, this point becomes very important. Taking a story experience into classroom time and language requires the teller to compact or fold an enormous time-space into the constraints of school time. Consider the following example in which Daron tries to tell a story. After seeing the movie *Spiderman* on the weekend, he enthusiastically began to tell how the high-school boy in the film first realized he had superpowers. Energetically he began:

Wednesday, October 16.
'Oh! Yeah, so, he was having lunch and didn't know he had superpowers yet. Then, well … he …' He trailed off and stopped. Children around him who had seen the movie nodded emphatically and encouragingly: 'Oh yeah!' 'Yeah?' Yeah?'

But Daron didn't go on. Held easily in his mind, he suddenly found himself struggling about where to begin with the story. He had to explain about the girl, the bullies, the accident with food trays, and so on before he could get to the fight that revealed Spiderman's superpowers to himself. Even after the fight there was a longer stretch of events and bewilderment before Spiderman realized his webbing, bounding, leaping, flying capacity. All at once the story was too long and far too much for Daron to tell.

In his mind, all the events, people, and things occupied a moment.
But in classroom time, he had to unravel all the parts and order them.
The table of tableaus, open to view in his memory, needed his recounting and ordering to bring the story into view. Daron realized how long
it would take for him to tell the story in classroom time. He suddenly
grasped how much he had to do. It was impossible. In the next chapter
we'll come back to this point. Writing a story carries more challenges
than teachers realize. Children find themselves frustrated by a flow of
images too vast for words. Or they find themselves stuck in a task they
can't finish.

The classroom and storyworld occupy mutually exclusive time
zones. No wonder people experience delighted relief when they have
both read the same book or watched the same movie. Too much of the
storyworld's life eludes the time frame of the classroom world. It is
more easily recalled than retold. When we consider the work of creative writing out of imaginative experience, this understanding demands our consideration and incorporation.

Storyworld, Fragile Borders

During our interviews I asked, 'What can break your imagining?' or
'What gets you out of the story, even if you are in the middle?' Children's answers were similar. The explained how they were in a deli-
cately bounded space. When the classroom world intruded with touch
or noise, their imaginating participation was punctured. In the same
way pricking a blown-up balloon bursts its boundaries, so the storyworld instantly deflated under the power of an interruption.

BEKKAH: Like sometimes, if a water bottle falls, and … I kind of like just lose it.
I go into a whole different world. When someone, like … when she goes …
like, she's right in the middle of the paragraph and she goes, 'stop that,' that
kind of breaks my imagination and I have to go, like, 'where was I again?'[13]

Children talked about different kinds of interruptions. These included a friend's asking a question, a touch for attention, someone
talking, something falling, the blurt of the PA system, a knock on the
door, or Linda's stopping the story to reprimand a child. Children's no-
ticing of these sounds contrasted with their usual tolerance for noise.
In fact, for nearly the whole of the schoolday children rummaged
inside desks, moved chairs, dropped pencil cases, books, and water
bottles; they chatted, whispered, and hummed. The day was further

punctuated when students got up to sharpen pencils with gusto at the sharpener screwed onto the shelf. Normally these sounds went unremarked, yet they leapt into awareness during storytelling. With new power, sounds or touch jerked children's attention out of the story and back into the classroom.

With only two exceptions, Leon and Buzz, all of the children responded with vigour to my interview question about 'interruptions.' Students had strong, negative feelings about being pulled out of the story. I found the accuracy of their memories and intensity of feeling remarkable. Even when the event was long past, it was freshly felt and easily recalled.

ME: So, what kind of stuff interrupts and stops your imagining?

SHASU: Like, people making noise. Their own noise.

ME: How do you feel about that?

SHASU: No! No, because then I stop imaginating.

ME: Oh?

SHASU: In one of the stories, somebody, like, I don't even remember who and then I looked at them and then I got, uhm … about five minutes to get back to the story and I missed the part.

Children ably and promptly explained what interruptions did. According to them, an interruption

MILA: … puts you out of what you are thinking.

~

VIOLET: … takes your mind away from the story.

~

KYLA: [makes it so] you don't know what's happening. She tells you a part, where you … but nobody hears and everybody's wondering what's happening and stuff like that.

ME: Tell me about that?

KYLA: I used to sit beside Violet and Danielle, then Violet used to start laughing and then Danielle would start laughing and I couldn't barely hear the story.

ME: And then how do you feel?

KYLA: I feel like telling them to be quiet. I want to YELL at them!

ME: You feel a bit awkward too, I guess (I am acknowledging that these three girls are also the best of friends). So, then is it hard to go back into the story or is it …?

KYLA: Uh–uh. Because you don't know what happens. What happened when
    you weren't, when you didn't pay attention …
ME: Is it like a hole in the story or what?
KYLA: It seems like the beginning of another story. It seems like she started
    another story already because you don't know what's happening.

~

PENDER: It's hard to get back. Well. How do I get back …? I concentrate
    real hard.

Children easily recalled instances in which their listening was interrupted. They suggested it forced them to use valuable time away from
the story and demanded strong effort to get back in. When they finally
did get back into the storyworld, according to Kyla it was possible that
the interruption had created something that felt 'like another story.'
Too much had happened in the meantime.

Interruptions not only broke up the story, but became memorable
events. The following interview was conducted well after Linda told
'Abiyoyo.' Terry had just finished telling me that 'people moving'
interrupted his listening and made him 'forget' where he was in
the story.

ME: So, do you find it hard to get back into the story?
TERRY: Yeah.
ME: Can you tell me about it a little bit?
TERRY: Once, I was, uhmmm, when she was reading 'Abiyoyo,'[14] she didn't
    show us the pictures or anything, cause she was telling it, and I was think-
    ing about how Abiyoyo looked like and Jack asked me a question and
    I was like 'what?' and he's like 'Is it Halloween Day?' We were … we were
    reading … Abiyoyo?
ME: (I am confused. It is nearly a month since Linda told 'Abiyoyo.' The last
    story Linda told was 'The Boy Who Learned to Shudder.' And it's closer to
    Halloween today. Linda had told another story much more recently, one
    more apt to thinking about Halloween. So, I ask:) I wonder, do you mean
    when we had the story 'Shudder?'
TERRY: Oh, yeah, yeah! 'Shudder.'

Terry's experience was so viscerally felt that he remembered the interruption, not the story. A kind of shock happened when he fell out of
the storyworld and landed in the classroom. The cognitive leap across
language and places, and the resulting shock and disappointment,

were so powerfully felt that the interruption became more memorable than the story.

Jack remembered his disappointment about losing his place in the storyworld three years ago. When he told me about this, he showed as much passion as Kyla and Shasu, who talked about much more recent interruptions.

ME: So are there things that can interrupt your imagination?
JACK: Yeah, like when someone starts tapping you and stuff and bugging me. Then I start forgetting what I was imagining.
ME: Does that happen to you sometime?
JACK: Yeah like in Grade 1, Mrs K was reading a story and she didn't show us the pictures because she wanted us to imagine, and this kid kept bugging me.
ME: Oh! So, what story was interrupted? Do you remember?
JACK: No, I don't really remember.
ME: You just remember that you were bugged?
JACK: I didn't like it. But. And then I forgot what the story was about.
ME: You were interested before that?
JACK: Yeah!

Interruptions destroyed the deeply held imaginative engagement with the storyworld. Children were emphatic that imaginating can't happen when the classroom world demands attention. Using meta-imaginative and listening abilities, they prevented intrusions and breeches of the boundary.

ME: So what breaks your imagination?
LAYLA: When people start to make noises, like rock on their chairs or start talking and stuff like that ... then I can't ... I can't remember where ... where I left off.
ME: And what do you have to do when you're listening and you want to go back to the story then?
LAYLA: Ummmm, I'll just forget them, take off my ears, put them in my pocket, and then I can get back to the story! (Layla pretends to unscrew her ears, she tugs them off and puts them in her pockets, patting them shut. We both laugh.)
ME: Okay, so, it's almost like you skipped part of the story when that happens?
LAYLA: Yeah. Like when you're having a dream. You're sleeping and you wake up in the middle of a great dream. And I can hardly even go back.

When Layla said she 'took off her ears,' perhaps she was being playful. But her point is serious. She had a sharp awareness of herself as a participant in two places that require different ways of listening. If she listened from within the storyworld place and imagined with her classroom ears, she wouldn't hear the story. To stay inside the story demanded story-ears. Layla went on to compare the experience with dreaming. When a noise from outside the dream intrudes on a sleeper, the dream is usually irrevocably lost. In the same way, if the classroom intrudes, return to the story is a long journey with an uncertain destination. Returning to storyworld life demands listeners' determined ability to tuck away the place from which they listen. Her point was also made by Daron earlier. He said he listened 'with his nerves' while imagining. He listened in a specific story-way while inside the storyworld.

Children's wish to stay inside the storyworld was dramatically evidenced when the recess bell rang. In other circumstances, all other activities were terminated by this sound. Before it rang, children's eyes flicked regularly upwards, and when it rang they were ready and poised to rush out. If Linda restrained them, their annoyance about a thwarted desire to leave was expressed plainly in snorts, sighs, and facial expressions of frowning and irritation. However, when the recess bell rang during a storytelling, like it did during 'Rumpelstiltskin' and 'Theseus and the Minotaur,' children did not move to leave.[15] A few children glanced at the clock, but they held listening positions, suppressing a strong habitual response. Aware of the fragile border that secured the present experience and, later, their valued memory of it, they held the boundary as well as they could. I can't be sure whether they did this for themselves or for each other, but in either case, this is a significant and highly unusual action.

In this way, imagining with a story is not like talking with a story. Story-talk was permeable to 'interruptions.' Children freely and gladly allowed others' amendments, questions, and diversions from stories they were telling. But in the middle circle, where children lodge in deep imaginative engagement with their storyworlds, imagining with the story, interruptions have the power to breech the experience. It could be punctured by a light touch or whisper, and students knew this. Thus, during a storytelling they actively prevented interruptions; they exercised self-control and common social understandings to limit them. Children changed their usual practices.

Linda wrote about this in her journal:

Wednesday, September 11.
Storytelling this week? An almost audible silence during 'Eponiandes.'
Tych seemed genuinely embarrassed to interrupt it when he dropped his
water bottle. He didn't seem fearful of a reprimand; rather, he seemed to
appreciate, himself, that the noise had somehow assaulted the spell of the
story. Quietly, he moved his bottle out of reach. I notice during other lessons that the water bottles offer a welcome distraction for the kids. They
suck on them, pour little drops into the lids and drink from them as if
they were miniature tea cups, roll them along their desks, drop them to
the floor. Sometimes I feel like I'm teaching in a bowling alley.

Children valued the experience so highly that they modified behav-
iours for the sake of storyworld experiences, their own and others'.
Linda notes Tych's consideration. Looking back, we also see how Leon
gently set down his water bottle in the midst of a story; Kyla decided
to sit somewhere else; and Jack knew his friends well enough to shut
them out of his listening. Anyone who works with children realizes the
significance of such sensitivity and determination. These acts demonstrate how strongly interested children are in the experience of imaginating with a story. They exercised a commonly shared restraint. They
also applied self-discipline, shutting out interruptions from within the
mind. Alt talks about this:

ME: So when you're listening to a story, like when Ms. Stender is telling you
    about the bear ... what kind of things will make you stop or interrupt your
    imagining the story?
ALT: What would make me ... oh, it would be like your mind goes somewhere
    else and it thinks about something else. I think ... like, not listening.
ME: Huh. So ...?
ALT: Yeah. Yeah (spoken softly).
ME: So ... sort of drifting in your head?
ALT: Yeah.
ME: Can other people interrupt your imagination too?
ALT: Yeah. It's kind of like if you're imagining something and your friend
    comes and then he talks to you and then ... absolutely it goes away and you
    can't remember it again. And then about five or six minutes it comes back.
ME: Oh yeah! It's like that, it's true. So, like in a story, how can you get back to
    it again?

ALT: So to listen again?

ME: Yeah.

ALT: Actually, if somebody was bothering me I would ignore them and just hear the story.

ME: So you have a pretty strong mind!?

ALT: Yup!

Alt began by thinking about his listening as also interruptable by his own thoughts. If he let his 'mind go somewhere else' or 'think about something else' he would lose the story. In this awareness, Alt deliberately held onto the story by redirecting his mind. He purposefully pushed the intrusion of a classmate and friend to the periphery of his attention in order to 'hear the story.' Thus, listeners assume some control over their desire to engage fully with the story. As Pender said earlier, listeners know how to 'concentrate real hard.' Children's desire to stay in the story leads them to develop abilities to shut out disruptions. Such self-monitoring and purposeful thought is a significant element in learning.

Students developed protocols and understandings that held the boundary around the story-listening place. Linda did too. She arranged seating to minimize possible disruptions. She would sometimes suggest that a student move. She scanned the class, checking for potential trouble spots. This was so obvious that when I asked Kyla what she 'recommend teachers do when they tell stories,' she answered:

Have expression, make sure people pay attention, make sure people are listening. Look around the classroom before you start.

Linda was attentive to her listeners from within the storyworld place. She minimized verbal interruptions by using her eyes to warn a child to be quiet. When she had to warn a child, she usually used words from 'inside' the story, rather than interrupting it. This was illustrated during her telling of 'Sody Salaratus.'

Thursday, November 14.

Linda is telling the story. She is at the moment where the bear who lives under the bridge has just leapt out and stood in front of the squirrel, who is the last living member of the household to cross the bridge. The bear roars lustily, 'I ATE THE OLD WOMAN AND NOW I'M GONNA EAT YOU TOO!' With the dinner of the girl, boy, old man and his cane, and then the old woman, children have been motioning and gulping down each of the bear's dinners with Linda, and with increasing gusto.

During the story, Marcus, Leon, and Taza joined in with enthusiasm – so much that they were distracted from the story into their own interaction. Linda, never pausing in the story, touches Leon on the shoulder. Then, in the big voice of the bear she looks Taza straight in the eyes and says, 'AND I'LL EAT YOU TOO.' Taza understands perfectly and retreats back into the story-space. He stops playing with friends.

Linda worked to stay inside the story-place. She used eye contact to say, 'Stop that!' and answered questioning gestures or expressions by putting the answers to anticipated questions directly into the story's text. When Linda noticed a child's confusion about a word, without breaking the rhythm of the story she would supply its meaning. As Tajo explains in the following account, this kept children with the story. For example, in the story of 'Rumpelstiltskin,' Linda said, 'the girl went into the pantry' and then, seeing Tajo's questioning eyes and upward-moving arm, she promptly added, 'a little room where they kept all their food.' Tajo was unaware of her neat, seamless insertions of definitions into the text of the story.

ME: What sorts of things make your imagination stop?
TAJO: Stop? When, if it's a hard word. Then that makes it stop. So that's when I put my hand up and then she tells us and then I can keep on going.
ME: Oh! Yeah, that can be a big one. Are there other things that can make it hard for you to listen?
TAJO: Okay, if someone interrupted it, my imagination will still be going, I can still imagine it, but if everyone is talking then my imagination will go away.

Over the course of five months, children learned when and how they could interrupt a story. Questions were answered *after* the story. They knew that when the story finished, they would enjoy the freedom they needed to respond with exclamations and questions. That freedom was evident in the chanting, singing, stomping play that happened at the close of 'Abiyoyo.' Such unified, spontaneous, noisy rebellion only happened after storytelling. They had the story-listener's right.

In the same way that Linda could talk from inside the story, children could. For instance, Jack's 'snort' of laughter, the children's participation in Abiyoyo's song, stomping with the giant and making taunting noises, eating up the Sody Salaratus people with gusto, all came from within the story. These did not disturb the story. Rather, such participation intensified our experience.

Before I leave this section, it is important to acknowledge that sometimes a storytelling might not fully draw in a student. Perhaps the story didn't interest the child, or tiredness or a personal concern kept the listener out. Still, in all my observations, such children still participated in the effort to not disrupt their fellows. We saw that earlier in Leon's listening to 'The Three Golden Hairs.' Linda offered privacy to those who used the storytelling time to think about other things, to engage with the story in peripheral ways, or simply to rest.

ME: What about somebody sitting outside the group? You could have a child
who is disruptive or not listening. Like Leon, for instance. He has a tendency
to sit back, playing with his shoes, drilling holes in things, you know. What
is the effect of the non-listener in a story telling?
LINDA: Well, if it's a good story, then hopefully he will come in … [but] a good
story can tolerate Leon. Like, he can be a part of an audience. I think you can
have somebody there doing their bit, don't you?
ME: Yeah …
LINDA: I worry that I'm not catching somebody. Like, the thing that bothers
me about Leon is that, 'Aw, he's not listening. I need to tell this differently.
Or I need to … to … I need to do something more.

Leon sometimes did not seem to listen. Yet without fail he knew what had happened in the story. He could outline the specifics and had comments to make. While he might not have been 'inside' the circle imagining every time, he did think along with it. Linda could see the difference. She responded to the small signs that suggested a child had not fallen into the deeper listening place, and worked at ways to bring them there. But she also gave them freedom. Storytelling was a time in which they could sit close and 'do their bit.' She let them think their own thoughts and enjoy a time during which not much else was demanded of them. Linda granted them privacy and freedom inside the border of storytelling. She trusted children to self-direct their experience and applications. In this subtle way she did not interrupt the story for others, while gently encouraging story-entry abilities for others.

Linda did other things to prevent interruption. She always closed the door, for the sudden noise of a child laughing or stomping in the hallway, a slammed locker door, the chatter and clatter of a class on rotation, or the janitor working in the hall could suddenly tug a listener loose. The shut door muffled the noises but did not prevent other intrusions. Children burst in, a parent came with a forgotten lunch, other teachers knocked to ask for masking tape. Sometimes a group came from another class to get a set of history books or to make a sports team announcement.

I think the most powerful interruption of all was the PA intercom. Its sudden blare would nearly physically wrench us out of place. It had that quality at almost any time of the schoolday, although in my experience it was most intensely felt during a storytelling. Pender described its effect on his listening:

'I'm just like, I'm just like ...' He trailed off and demonstrated what he meant with his posture: eyes wide and startled; he sits frozen in mid motion. 'I can't keep ... keep on [doing what I was doing] when it's going on.'

Interruptions damage children's storyworld experiences. If teachers want to encourage deep imaginative experiences and develop children's facility with it, then it is critical to keep mind its absolute intolerance of disruption.

It is quite surprising, given what we know about the importance of sustained engagement in almost any learning activity, that 'interruption' is so common in schools. This is not only true about storytelling. Think of how we teach reading and use literature in the classroom. Teachers regularly teach book-stories in small sections. Reading periods are conducted in arbitrary time blocks of as small as seven to ten minutes or as long as fifteen to twenty minutes. Children are told to pick up a storybook 'for a few minutes' while waiting for others to finish a math or geography assignment. All of these directions are premised on an assumption about story engagement: it can be easily, even quickly, resumed after interruption.

Certainly, reading a story differs from telling one in significant ways. Importantly, with a book it is possible to review previous pages and settle back in. Readers can independently pick up where they left off. This is not true of storytelling. Reading facilitates review and recall of the story, making interruption less damaging than in storytelling. There are also differences in the relationship between a teller and listeners and that between readers and text. Meaning made of words on the page is done in a different time and in different ways than is meaning constructed from listening to spoken words. All this illustrates work like Walter Ong's (1977, 1982), in which he describes abilities and participation with text in contrast with those held with oral forms. We might add 'interruptability' to the list of comparisons and contrasts.[16]

However, in both reading and listening to a story, imaginators are inside a storyworld beyond the place where they hear or read. Children's insistence that the storyworld has fragile boundaries and that interruptions threaten its existence calls our attention to the ways we do both activities. Children make clear that interruptions are not innocuous: they deeply affect imaginating with a story, and it is quite possible that they also affect the quality of engagement with a read story.

Permit me to digress a little: it is likely that this point extends to more activities than listening to or reading a story. The children's strongly made point raises a worrisome question about what we are learning about listening in a culture that normalizes interruption. Capacities for sustained engagement are much threatened by accepted telephone intrusions mid-conversation, television stories delivered in spaces between advertisements, and hyperlinking out of computer-delivered text, to name just a few examples. This point must be addressed in school culture. If we wish to nourish the ability for sustained engagement, and especially for deep imaginative experiences like those held in the centre circle of storytelling pedagogy, unnecessary disruptions of the experience must be prevented.

Getting the Details Right

When children wrote or talked about events of the classroom world, like fishing in the Fraser River or an accident on the bridge, they worked to get the details 'right.' They established who they were with and when and where the event happened. They worried about the correct pronunciation and spelling of names like 'Kelowna.' They challenged and corrected themselves and each other when they remembered the details of things that happened and things they did.

This contrasted sharply with children's writing or talking about purely imagined storyworlds. Details were freely constructed and not subject to challenge. In the following examples, children describe their Abiyoyos. They filled in their pictures of the giant on the basis of just two details from Linda: he was 'bigger than a mountain' and his 'feet could make lakes.' From those two starting points the giant sprang to full life in each child's storyworld. The following responses from children were answers to my question, 'So, what did that giant look like?'

ZARA: He is grumpy and has fluffy hair like this (she gestures wildly around her head) and his shirt is up to here and his belly is sticking out ... and, uhm, shoes, big old shoes like the India type, you know, like this? (She is gesturing and shaping the top of her shoes into a curving point.)

ME: Oh! Shoes that curl up?

ZARA: Yeah!

~

TERRY: They said that his face is like ... uhm ... he never takes a bath and his hair is all gross and his legs are all hairy, arms are all hairy.

ME: What is he wearing?

TERRY: Nothing. (We both laugh.)

~

MARCUS: He has a jaguar's face and really big hands.

ME: Huh! Does he have clothes?

MARCUS: (pause) I think he has a shirt on with holes. Lots of holes ... And hair on his teeth and gums.

~

JACK: When she didn't show us it, I thought he was just a big ugly giant.

ME: Yeah! What does he look like?

JACK: He has got horns and he drools green drool.

ME: Anything else?

JACK: He's got huge feet and huge horns and when he sleeps he snores so much that he wakes up the whole town.

Aren't these marvelous and extraordinary pictures? They are richly detailed and joyfully creative. Each detailed description adds delight on delight in the imagining listener.

To be sure, all the children's descriptions of the giant were consistent with the details Linda gave about his size character, and actions. The outline of story events was common across the variations. But the details of appearance and movement were as varied as the students in the room. Descriptions were elaborate, evocative, and all different; but they were given with confidence. Although we heard the same story and saw the same book, children knew I could not and would not contradict them.

I saw another example of this when the children drew parts of the story 'Theseus and the Minotaur.' The drawings were absolutely dissimilar. Clothing, colours, sizes, details in the landscape, the character of the Minotaur, and other parts of the story varied greatly. Yet their teacher expressed appreciation of and praise for each variation. Each picture was 'right.'

Storyworld experiences are not verified by the same criterion as classroom events. This difference was tacitly understood and practised. Classroom-world methods for verifying or confirming details demand corroboration of detail. For instance, if I described Linda's classroom one way and another researcher described it another way, the difference would call for a rigorous accounting. However, varying accounts of what listeners saw during the same storytelling required no explanation, nor did it threaten the giant's veracity. These accounts had a story-way of making sense and establishing the fact of the story experience.

This is an important point to make during a time of great attention to evaluation practices that depend on getting the information right. In chapter 5 we referred to the language of story as 'symbolic.' We referred to the story's demand for a high degree of personal interaction and substitution. A story entails using different semantic rules to get information or an understanding out of the communication. We approach a story with different expectations about what we should 'get out of it.' The emphasis today on evaluating comprehension by responses that reiterate details in story texts risks compromising children's abilities to think with stories. Howard Gardner warns:

> Young children ... are becoming literate in the *literal* sense; that is, they are mastering the rules of reading and writing, even as they are learning their addition and multiplication tables. What is missing are not the decoding skills, but two other facets: the capacity to read for understanding and the desire to read at all. (1991: 186)

Learning to read includes learning to read stories, being able to get inside them, experience them, and make them your own. For this reason, Linda chose folk, myth, and fairy stories, learning laboratories of experience that were developed over generations. They are flexible to listeners who come from dissimilar times, places, ages, and interests. Folk stories perfectly explain aspects of human experience. Its listener establishes the story's authenticity not by the designation of words, but rather with its strong resonance of experience. Imaginators in the deep centre of listening participate in an ever-dynamic, collective, and personal expression of familiar circumstances.

So, we could say that Abiyoyo's storyworld mimics the situation of children who have troublesome fathers or struggle for social acceptance. It is about leaving home, fighting mighty enemies, climbing mountains, and the profound power of music to soothe. Engaging with these stories offers a practice-ground world. Children face giants who are teachers, parents, a neighbourhood menace, and the like. The ally of a good father, or parent, is (magic) power to face threats felt from outside home walls. Ultimately, however, the father's protection is inadequate, and the boy must use his own power and gifts to live fully. When he sings, the giant is banished. This story demonstrates a common human dilemma along with its solution. Understanding it in this way also explains the sense of triumph children communicated when they came out of their storyworld engagement. Children make, use, and play with characters and landscapes in an effort to explore 'real' issues. They emerge later with understandings, insights, and solutions.

The psychological power of originally oral folk stories is described by writers such as Bruno Bettleheim, Robert Bly, Robert Coles, and Clarissa Pinkola Estés, the authors of the accounts edited by Alison Cox and Albert David (2003), and others.[17] Maria Tatar writes:

> The study of fairy tales tells us something about the way in which the mind draws on the double movement of language between literal meaning and figurative expression to fashion stories that dramatize psychological realities. (1987: 82)

But if storytellers and teachers take this to mean that stories like 'Abiyoyo,' 'Rumpelstiltskin,' and 'Sody Salaratus' simply furnish psychological truths, they miss the most important aspect of the experience. Children emphatically declared the story to be about the giant, father's tricks, and a wonderful ending. This mattered. They loved and remembered the story precisely because the giant wore Arabic slippers, drooled, or was naked and hairy. Fully two months later, Jack remembered the story and giggled to think of his giant snoring so loudly that he woke up the town. The relished significance of the story was the delight of experience. The story's meaning develops significance over time. Life-learning done in a storyworld demands the same kind of germination over time as 'real-life' experiences demand. Storyworld events need to be stored in memory, ready until needed for counsel or illustration.

Scholarly traditions that routinely explain the story's power as psychological diminish and degrade the bright light of knowing in children's eyes: it was fun and satisfying to be there. It was a memorable and important experience. The too usual, prompt shift of focus from children's imaginative experience to its 'meaning' has missed a truth that demands renewed attention and emphasis. As Perry Nodelman writes:

> To assume that [stories'] significance is the meaning they give to ordinary reality is to miss the point of their extraordinary characteristics. We do not enjoy fantasies because of their psychological or moral meaning. (1996: 175–6)

Storyworld experiences satisfy an ache that wells up over the dry days, months, and years of schooling. Inside the deep well of imagination, loosed to create and explore new landscapes, children find what they need. Cultivating playfulness, imagining with a story, nourishes abilities to re-create. Participants practise and try out relationships and situations. They develop aesthetic senses. They satisfy or renew curiousity about people, emotions, and the quality of power. They develop empathy. They explore nuances of relationships that elude their touch and talk in the other life. Freed from the limiting logic, rigid detail, and time constraints of the classroom world, children try out ideas, images, and dilemmas. They do this in the safety of the story's world.

Storytelling brought children where they wanted to be: inside a story. The experience was substantial and affecting. It lodged deeply in memory and was later recalled in detail, with sensual specifics. A sense of mystery and elusiveness was part of the experience, and participation couldn't be forced. Although children did everything possible to make it happen, they had to wait for the small slip from pictures into the presence, imagining with a story, of Wonder.

Wonder

Alone and in the company of others listening to a story, the imaginator is in the midst of Wonder. I capitalize the first letter of the word on purpose to emphasize the extraordinary quality of experience and effects of imaginating. When I write 'Wonder' in this sense, I do not mean: 'I wonder whether the bell will ring.' Neither do I mean something like: 'Isn't that drawing wonderful?' I mean a breathtaking sort of experience, one that is rather magical or holy, one in which something incredible happens. In deep imaginative engagement, where children imagined alone with their stories, they found Wonder.

Wonder had some regular features. As the listeners and tellers described it, their experiences of a storytelling and tumbling out together afterwards developed a sense of harmony or love for one another. They experienced a profound sense of refreshment from the storytelling experience: hearts and minds were replenished and invigorated. It also included a heady new sensation of expansiveness. Children dreamed possibilities for themselves, for how the world might be and what they might do in it. Finally, the experience had an unmistakable magical or spiritual quality. Children talked with a sense of awe about a reality that was located beyond classroom walls, beyond touch.

In a book about storytelling as pedagogy and an argument for its inclusion in school, I find myself struggling a little to insist on this treasured, savoured aspect of being inside the storyworld. It is of such elusive quality. Although it is unequivocally experienced and deeply affecting, it won't be touched or seen. At the same time, the teller and her listeners insist we consider the vitality of imagining with a story. The sense of Wonder imbues all of it. In the following discussion, I take up each of those features of Wonder: love, replenishment, expansiveness, and awe.

When I asked Linda why she told stories, she gave many reasons: oral language abilities, helping children work with each other, reading and writing skills, studies in literature, and the pleasure of its gift. Among all her reasons for storytelling, there was one she repeated often:

ME: So, why do you tell stories?
LINDA: I'm ... I ... just, it has so much to do with love. It has to do with how you're feeling about people.
ME: Over and over you come back to that.
LINDA: Yeah.

Linda told stories to her students because she loved them. She was also sure that storytelling helped them love each other. It was necessary. How surprising it is to consider how little writing and research we can find on this foundational-to-learning element in school, perhaps because the word is so fraught with other aspects and applications. It can't be legislated or tested. It is hard to teach. Yet, the necessity of affection is inarguable. In a place where people live and work closely together, they have to like each other. Children need to feel valued and accepted. Such a framework frees students to learn in safety. True, 'love' has many intangible qualities, but it is fully tangible in experience. Six weeks into my study in Linda's classroom, I wrote this description in my reflective journal:

Tuesday, October 15.

Children's talk, our learning together, and our thickening of story-life is fanning us into a kind of unified luminescence. The room hums with glad life. Voices, friends sharing scraps of gladness about being together. Children have brought photos, forms to sign, homework. One child has brought Linda a small gift. Tajo is standing on the seat of his desk and is silently dancing. It's humanity's song, an ode to the joy of being together. This room is full of people who have their own unchallenged places in this bit of the world. They've been through adventures together. I know it's early to say this … but I feel like all the sharing of stories has so much to do with how I experience this.

I have taught long enough to know that much of this, the life we have together in the classroom, is a matter of a kind of grace, or luck. Every class is different, but so much of it is similar. There are children who come to school rested, happy, and ready. Others come to school soaked with the pain of the morning. They come wounded with events and reminders of failure, feeling ugly. They live with smouldering anger born of disappointments and an overflow of rejection. There are children who come to school and simply don't feel well. They haven't slept; they haven't eaten. Some leave a kitchen where the first alcoholic drink has been poured. Some come cloaked with the scent of extinguished cigarettes and missed bathing routines. Some children come from homes crowded with people competing for bathroom and kitchen space, madly rushing off in many directions.

I certainly don't know the particulars of children's home lives here. I do know that children typically come from diverse, often difficult starting points to meet in a classroom. I can't help but feel like our stories, children's stories and Linda's storytelling, have a lot to do with how we all are together. We're comfortable, loved; happy to be here.

Storytelling fostered a strong connection between listeners and tellers. Sprawled together on the floor, they were shoulder to shoulder. They fought giants together, held tender baby birds in their hands, failed and won quests, mourned and danced triumphantly. Alone but mysteriously together, listeners forged a sense of kinship as they went into storyworlds from the same starting point and surfaced together afterwards. As Linda said:

During storytelling I feel a much warmer connection with the children when they're gathered around me on the floor. We're all closer to one another.

Shared and repeated storytelling experiences built affectionate and accepting relationships among those who went into the circle of deep imaginative engagement together. They were joined together during a significant experience.

The story of Bekkah, in the last chapter, showed that a sense of camaraderie and ease can't be assumed. It demands time, sustained effort, and trust. Linda's storytelling pedagogy of story-talk and storyworld-making did much to make this happen. Something important happened when she led them into their own storyworlds to face giants and ravenous bears under bridges. She helped them to boldly, audaciously pluck three golden hairs from the devil's back and to banish a giant destroyer. When they came out from these experiences, together, they felt joined by adventure and thrilled by their outings. They reached immediately for each other. Affection grew through these adventures. This nourished a sense of 'we' in the room. Linda named it love.

The second feature of storytelling, replenishment, happened in 'the pause.' Pulling out of the clamour of the classroom to sink into a story-world, offered a refreshing retreat. As Linda said:

> You feel taken away, you know. You feel very detached from aches and pains ... I think they feel very safe during storytelling. They don't feel competitive. And it's one time they don't have to produce.

A classroom is an extraordinarily busy place. If the students shared my sense of it, they felt the constant demand of company, the pressure of waiting tasks and tasks underway, senses of expectation about behaviour and performance, ever-changing subjects of study, and shifting modes of activity. Woven through all of this was the sound and motion of all of us living together in a small place.

Storytelling gave a significant pause within which we rested. In the following journal entry, Linda puzzled about the restful effect of story-telling. She wrote:

> Thursday, September 26.
> When I was in school I got so tired of all that social engagement ... group work. I used to long for a class in which I could sit back and listen and absorb knowledge from a brilliant, trusted, inspired lecturer ... I wonder if storytelling in the classroom offers the same relief. As storytellers we know that we are demanding much of our listeners: physically, emotionally, and intellectually. But it's not so obvious or concrete. You don't have

to take out pencil and paper and find the right coloured duo- tang or wait
to take your turn in group discussion. It's a rest. Storytelling's a rest.

At the same time, storytelling sparked a heady sense of expansiveness. All the rules and constraints of logic, mortality, and time were
banished. The classroom borders broke open, and new worlds opened
wide for the imaginators. Listeners explored possibilities of landscape,
action, and relationships. They defied their own limitations and faced
the improbable. Rivers, mountains, battle fields, haunted castles, and
the Minotaur's maze came into view. Imaginator's storyworlds introduced other children, monsters, goddesses, silent corpses, and cunning
women. Life there included tingling senses of possibility for themselves, encounters, experiences, and understandings that couldn't oc-
cur in classroom life.

I can hardly imagine a learning posture more important than this.
All problem-solving abilities, from physics and math to social studies
and environmental science, depend on such senses of possibility.
Learning depends on believing there is a possibility of solution or response. We can understand this literally. When we learn about political
conflict zones or consider the nature of global climate change, students
need to reach beyond what they know from a small Canadian neighbourhood. They need to imagine possibilities and believe in them. It
can also be understood metaphorically. When a child meets a tyranni-
cal boss or a situation where a 'baby bird' has been robbed of shelter,
they need a bank of possibilities. Learning and solving problems demand an ability to imagine, loosen the restrictions, challenge a logic
that apparently binds the world.

That sense of expansiveness, of possibilities blown open, was experienced personally as Wonder. Children lived unfettered inside the storyworld. They became what they longed to be, or what they understood
themselves to be. They could try on different ways of 'being' for fitted-
ness and fun. Children were heroic, desperate, invincible, terrible, and
wonderful. They grew 'bigger,' they found identities and ways of
being that elude classroom life. This was exhilarating.

Children talked about this with delight. They came out of their
storyworlds empowered and were ready to vanquish the world's
dragons.

JACK: You imagine and in your brain, your brain makes you think. Your brain
gets bigger. Bigger.

ME: Oh! I like how you said that. It is like that, isn't it?

JACK: As big as a giant. You can hold a giant in your head.

(His eyes are shining and he is grinning, grinning with deep gladness at me.)

~

BEKKAH: So (when I can't sleep) my dad draws pictures of sunsets on my back. And he'll be, 'Okay, get this nice beautiful picture in your head of trees and you're lying on a beach, you're just looking out at the waves, and it's just about sun … Now, the sun is just about gone down.' And I'm just lying there and then he goes, 'Now paint black with your paintbrush over it!'

ME: Night time! So that's imagination?

BEKKAH: Pictures in your mind that you feel. Wouldn't it be neat if scientists actually know how that happened?

ME: It is surprising. Feel your head how little it is (we both feel our heads with our hands). It's little! But inside is a whole beach and a sunset and a sky and clouds!

BEKKAH: How can you fit all that in?

ME: I don't know.

BEKKAH: Shelves and shelves! Help! I've run out of room. Uh-uh! (She shakes her head vigorously to mean 'NO! I HAVE NOT!')

~

LAYLA: It's all just a big picture inside. Like, it's not like this small. (she puts her hands around her head.)

ME: Bigger than your head?

LAYLA: Yeah!

ME: But it's not outside of it?

LAYLA: It's in here!! I wonder how the brain does that!

Finally, the Wonder unleashed in the deep centre, where listeners imaginate the storyworld into being, has a spiritual quality. Kate alludes to this.

ME: So, think about a story and think about yourself listening. So … like when Ms Stender talks to you, something happens inside your head?

KATE: I feel a little person, a little woman in there. Like … I can't explain it. (Her voice trails away. She does not seem confused to me, only unable to explain what she experiences.)

ME: (I am uncertain but curious about her meaning: does she mean that she imagines a 'picture' of a little woman, or is the 'little woman' the director of pictures in her mind? I respond, hoping I am ambiguous enough not to prejudice her answer.) Like a kind of picture in your head?

KATE: It's imagination.

ME: What is that?

KATE: A thing, she's in your mind, it's like … uhh. I don't know what I would say.

ME: So, you call that person, the little woman, imagination?

KATE: Uh huh, but it's something you feel while listening and … yeah.

Kate's explanation of her experience was startling. In the interview it seemed to me that she was determined to explain exactly what happened 'inside her head' while she participated in a storytelling. She wanted to get it right. She was in earnest when she spoke of the 'little woman' in her head. But she also struggled or felt awkward in explaining her personal sense of experience, aware that her idea is an uncommon one. It is not expressed outside storyworlds.

Kate experienced her storytelling participation as led by an 'otherworld' being. Her sense of 'a little person in there … a little woman' is no whimsy; she expressed astonishing sensitivity and knowledge about her experience inside the storyworld. She felt the presence of Wonder. Kate sensed that 'someone' was present in her mind during her story-engagement. She was not the only one to mention a sense of a presence or a force other than herself within her imaginative experience. As Violet said once to me, the story 'walked around' inside her head on its own. Children talked about the loss of volition when they went from pictures into presence. At a certain point, imaginators no longer 'made' the *storyworld*. The story was blown into a living presence by something beyond participants' control.

Kate's explanation leads me to think of the long relationship between spirituality and storytelling. It is no accident that every religion is rooted in and maintained by a story. Buddhism, Christianity, Hinduism, or Islam: all these religions inspire understanding, participation, and commitment through the listener's experiences inside a storyworld. Imaginating with the story, adherents or visitors come to know something unavailable else where.

We have come to the end of this chapter. Perhaps the passion of the storytelling-teachers I described at its beginning has become more explicable. Mostly, I hope I've convinced my readers of the high value of imaginating with a story. It develops skills that range from listening and imaginative capacity to community development and flexible thinking. The classroom walls fell away and the world under study expanded boundlessly as children learned to think in story-ways. They challenged rigid constraints of time and detail, challenged oppression and fear. Inside the circle, with a storyworld in mind, children restored senses of magic, mystery, and the possibilities of their experiences. They developed abilities, understandings, and ideas only nourished in the centre of storytelling pedagogy.

10 Thinking with Stories

The Circle Between

In the last chapter we encountered the deep, inviolable hush of children imagining their ways through storyworlds beyond the classroom walls. Two chapters ago, we were in the midst of the lively classroom, filled with the sounds of children remembering and recounting, chanting and joking together. Now we settle into the middle circle of storytelling participation. We will discover that participants have another kind of learning relationship with the story, the teller, and other listeners. Specific kinds of abilities and knowledge are developed in this circle. When we finish learning about what is happening in this circle of stories, telling and listening, we will be ready to think about the full pedagogy of storytelling. Three circles of participation make one integrity of teaching and learning activities that nourish abilities, relationships, and understandings particular to the telling of a story.

. In the middle circle, participants think with a story. Let me begin with a small example of Linda Stender's using a storytelling to direct children's thinking.

Wednesday, September 11.
The class is getting ready to go to the library. The room is in mild commotion. Children are finding the right duo-tangs and making sure they have a pencil and enough paper. Most children are talking, some more loudly than Linda thinks is necessary. A couple of children are play-fighting. Gradually they line up along the back of the classroom. Well, sort of ...

Linda says, 'We need to be quiet on our way to the library. I remember last year, one time, we all had to go into the grade 7 classroom and every one of us had to apologize to the Grade 7s for interrupting their learning. We were so noisy we made it too hard for them to work. So we went in there and every single one of us had to say sorry to the Grade 7s.' She smiles, just a little, then invites the class to leave for the library. Zara leads the subdued class out into the hallway.

Children listened attentively to Linda's small bit of story. When they considered its implications, they all came to a similar conclusion and quietly made their way down the hallway. Linda's storytelling made children imagine an event and think about its connection to what they were just about to do. They were thinking with a story.

Storytelling: 'Well, That's Different'

In the last chapter we witnessed the extraordinary pleasure of imaginating with a story. That was the experience that hooked teachers like Linda and me into including storytelling as a classroom teaching practice. Linda also sought out opportunities to imaginate her way through stories in the company of listeners beyond her classroom. Every month she attended the 'Cric? Crac!' gathering of listeners and tellers from the Vancouver Society of Storytelling (VSOS).[1] She went there for her own enjoyment and revitalization.

The following transcript comes from our Monday morning interview after an evening's storytelling event. As I began interviewing Linda about her uses of storytelling to teach, we remembered the enjoyable evening we had. After talking about the previous evening, we paused and got to the business of the interview. I asked her about using storytelling to teach.

Monday, September 2.
LINDA: Just to be ... in the milieu of stories. That is pretty exciting! (We both pause)
ME: Okay, back to here, now. So, what does it mean to be teaching with storytelling as part of your goal for learning to happen in the classroom?
LINDA: Well, that's different.
ME: Why do you say, 'That's different?'
LINDA: Well, I think first of all there is such a thing as a continuum of learning. There is a progress in learning. The kids start someplace, and you hope that they move along. So there's that idea. So at some level you always have to be thinking about their thinking. And their moving. They're getting challenged a little.
ME: Into complexity?

LINDA: Yeah. And what is expected in terms of response. I think that when you're a storytelling teacher, you have to have some kind of response that's measurable.

ME: From the kids to you?

LINDA: Kids respond to the story. To the story. I think you can also have the kinds of stories they're listening to and they just stay there. And there's nothing that has to happen to them. But I think that because they're told in relation to a school system that evaluates and that there has to be assignments that follow stories or that connect to stories. Just because of how the system works.

ME: You're thinking about how storytelling works in a classroom?

LINDA: Yeah. But isn't that also about being a storyteller, storytelling teacher? Because at the same time you're paying attention to stories that are going to work in terms of the learning outcomes that you need to make happen.

ME: So, then, do I hear you saying that as a teacher-storyteller your storytelling is shaped by considering where the learning happens?

LINDA: Exactly. In relation to the curriculum. I have a responsibility. Like … at 'Cric? Crac!' I have a responsibility to give pleasure or to share something of beauty. But here, in the classroom, there needs to be a response to that gift, or you have to … uhm, make sure. It's your responsibility to see that the children are clear about what they've been given.

ME: So, it's like creating a bigger or another kind of purpose?

LINDA: Uh huh.

ME: So you tell towards a goal. Connecting the storytelling to reading, writing, social studies.

LINDA: Yes. To all those basics, the skills that children need to work on in school.

ME: That's interesting.

LINDA: Uh huh. Yeah.

ME: That storytelling, a storyteller in teaching is directed by something else than the impulse that directs the storyteller person – like you at 'Cric? Crac!'

LINDA: Yeah. There has to be a balance. The balance is important. Between storytelling and assignments …

ME: Yes?

LINDA: When there is a story, they don't seem to mind doing them. I don't think kids mind doing assignments connected to stories that they've heard. It's really not seen as work, as an assignment. And there needs to be an assignment! There has to be some accountability, to the listener, others things than … I guess just listening.

Linda's classroom storytelling was directed by different expectations than her participation at 'Cric? Crac!' She was guided by a strong sense of responsibility for children's education. She began by learning about her students' starting points, and then went on to challenge and help children 'move along' in their learning. 'At some level' during her storytelling, she was 'always … thinking about their thinking.' She used storytelling to direct and lead children's thinking and schoolwork towards 'outcomes' that could show that children had learned something over the course of the year. This was part of her professional 'accountability.' Such goals and practices made her experience and practice of teaching with storytelling feel 'different' from her experience and practice at an evening's gathering of adult listeners and storytellers. As we go on to observe and consider how children think with stories, we need to remember Linda's words: 'Well, that's different.' Telling stories in the classroom is not quite the same thing as having the delight of a storyworld opened in an evening of storytelling. It is a deliberate use of storytelling for calculated outcomes.

An overview of the literature will show that this 'different' storytelling is the most common sort in schools. Nearly all published work about storytelling in school is dedicated to showing how it can most effectively meet challenges across curricula. By the end of this chapter I will confirm this with even more good evidence for storytelling as a powerfully flexible instructional tool. But in light of the last two chapters, this instrumental understanding of storytelling should be met with caution and hedged with constraints. Our understanding needs to widen to include two other storytelling participations.

Much of what I've read about storytelling and teaching encourages the idea that storytelling is (only) a great tool. Educators think of it as a technique, not realizing that it is a distinct praxis with its own complex of practices, knowledge, and meaning-making language. I'm reminded of Paolo Freire's comment about dialogue in education:

> We should understand liberating dialogue not as a technique, a *mere* technique, which we can use to help us get some results. We also cannot, must not, understand dialogue as a kind of tactic we use to make students our friends. This would make dialogue a technique for manipulation instead of illumination.
>
> Dialogue is a moment where humans meet to reflect on their reality as they make and remake it. (1987: 98).[2]

It is possible to substitute 'storytelling' for 'liberating dialogue' in his text. Storytelling is no '*mere* technique' or 'kind of tactic.' It is a not a 'technique for manipulation instead of illumination.' Three participations, taken together, nourish and develop capacities that include social facility, imaginative ability, and meaning-making skills that include vocabulary and story-language. As we go on to learn about Linda and the children who think-with-stories, remember that they do this within a larger frame: between talking and imagining with a story. The 'difference' Linda talks about will lead us to think about the specific abilities and understandings that are nourished by storytelling in the middle circle. At the same time, we need to be cautioned against instrumentalizing storytelling relationships.

In the other two circles of telling and listening to stories, there was an immediacy to the activity. By that, I mean that Linda's teaching purposes were accomplished within the time of talking and telling stories together. Although strong purposes also direct Linda's teaching with the other storytelling participations, she was far more explicit when she led them to think with stories. She expressly made connections between the storytelling and other topics of study or work – the storytelling was one part of an articulated lesson. Thus, the storytelling was part of something more than itself. Thinking with stories entailed reading, writing, drawing, and talking about the story. Sometimes this happened in the midst of a telling, sometimes before or after it, sometimes many days afterwards. Then Linda had the children 'do' something with the storytelling they remembered. When it happened, the storytelling was usually set in the midst of a lesson. She began by asking students to take out their notebooks and pencils and reviewed earlier or related work, then introduced the topic of study.

In these and other ways, she prepared children to think with and about the storytelling in specific ways. Afterwards she led students to make applications or engage learning activities nourished by and even dependent on their storytelling experience. For example, she used storytelling to contextualize history. When children were learning about Remembrance Day, she told the story of Anne Frank. The story helped illuminate the situation of the Jews in the Second World War. Afterwards children looked at maps, discussed the Nazi movement, chose books related to the war, and so on. Sometimes she used thinking with stories to make a math problem accessible. She told a story about buried treasure and how two people, far apart, used graphs to explain where it was. The story piqued interest and plunged students into making graphs. In another instance, storytelling helped children think about social studies applications and connections. The children told each other stories of 'house-blessing.' They did so after they watched a film about houses around the world. They learned about different materials and geographical considerations that determined the look of the house, and went on to think about what it means to have a 'home.'

Linda also used storytelling to help children develop reading and writing abilities. In this case, a story experience came first. Then, counting on the vivid, felt engagement of being in the storyworld, Linda directed children to go back in their memories. The experience strongly nourished children's reading and writing work.

In this chapter, I've selected just three main ways Linda used a storytelling to help children think and learn. First, she used storytelling to help children think about concepts: storytelling grounded and illustrated ideas that were otherwise too abstract. Second, thinking about storytelling encouraged children who were learning to read. Third, it facilitated the teaching of writing. In the sections below I show how storytelling richly affected children's learning. Finally, I discuss a main, overarching reason that storytelling is used to teach: it is memorable and 'sticky.' This will raise some ambivalence and sharp questions about our uses of stories to get children thinking in school.

'The Flying Head': Storytelling to Understand a Concept

Children did not need Linda or anyone else to tell them to think with stories. They did this on their own. In the midst of storytelling or afterwards, inside the memory of a storyworld experience, they mulled over a story and came to their own conclusions. Over the course of my time in the classroom, I began to more fully appreciate the thoughtful relationships children had with the storytellings. They regularly made applications and drew out the story's implications for themselves. For instance, Shasu retold the story of 'The Field' in our interview. When she was finished, I asked:

ME: Ah! Did you like that story?
SHASU: Yeah.
ME: I liked it too. What do you think it's about?
SHASU: Taking care of people, help people.
ME: Even though it's about birds?
SHASU: Yeah.

Linda had not given 'a lesson' about the story or directed a conversation encouraging the drawing of conclusions. Shasu's own interaction with the story brought her to this idea. When I asked Tajo what he thought about the same story, he said, 'If that story wouldn't have come, I would've learnt to fight. Now I don't want to so much.' Violet made an entirely different application. She suggested the story told her to 'think your own thing, not what other people tell you.'

Whenever I asked children what they thought about a story, they responded promptly. They showed that a wide range of related understandings could be drawn from one story. As we discussed much earlier, story-language creates a flexible mental framework that encourages a thoroughly personal way of thinking with it. The rich variations expressed by Shasu, Tajo, and Violet testify to a story's capacity to carry a wide range of nuances and aspects of meaning.

In the following example of storytelling used to think about a concept, Linda asked the children to think about what it means to be 'heroic.' On the first day of the unit, she told the story 'The Flying Head.' A few days later she asked the children to think about what 'a hero is.' She began the discussion by having the children retell the story aloud together, taking turns. She asked Daron to begin. He introduced and described the monstrous head that flew about and ate people. The next teller went on to tell about the terrified villagers who had to flee their homes and hide in the forest. Teller followed teller, recalling how the Flying Head came back to terrorize, kill, and devour.

Linda kept the pace of retelling brisk. She would point to a new teller, stop him or her after a few lines, and invite another child to pick up the story. Here we begin at the point where the story is coming to its climactic moment. A village woman decides to put an end to the death and terror that have paralysed her people. Bekkah picks it up:

Thursday, November 28.

BEKKAH: After [the Flying Head] left all the people were freed from outside to go into their homes. One lady, she had a child, and she said somebody should stand up to him and put an end to this. So she roasted a rock in the fire. It takes a long time to get it red hot. Then she pretends to eat it with sauce but passed it behind her back.

(Bekkah scrambles to her feet and stands to demonstrate. She offers the class her profile, passes the rock past her open mouth, then smacks her lips and rubs her stomach, pretending to have eaten it.)

Mmmmm, smack, smack … what good meat this is, she says. And [the Flying Head] thought it was meat and ate up the red-hot rocks in the sauce.

(She sits down. The story is almost finished. She stops. There's a pause.)

LINDA: Azun?

AZUN: (Azun was startled when Linda called his name.) What happened then? He died.

LINDA: What power did she have, as a hero?

AZUN: Her brain.

PENDER: The monster is not very smart. He don't do smart stuff.

TYCH: That lady taught the people a lesson, to stand up for themselves.

KREENA: She kept the village from hiding all the time and being scared.

AZUN: And if that girl didn't do that, that thing, there would hardly be anyone left in the valley.

JACK: One part some people left out. The monster only kept coming at night. He had matted hair, if you tried to pull a comb through you wouldn't be able to.[3]

SHASU: There wasn't any sauce in the story. Just red-hot rocks.

AZUN. A bomb. A suicide bomber just killed eleven people. (Azun has just remembered something from the news. The class is suddenly very, very still.)

LINDA: Well, that connects with this story, doesn't it? Pockets of people all over the world are living in fear, valleys of fear, and in war. Is there something about what Tych said that we could use to think about it?

KREENA: If ... it's like a school that has a big bully that no teacher knows about, and a new person comes who doesn't know either, and she stands up to him.

PENDER: Yeah, stands up to him. She tricked him because that lady got hold, control of herself and she made a good plan.

Kyla: Do they know who did it? Was it one of the tourists?

AZUN: (Shakes his head no.)

BEKKAH: It's kind of like when something's wrong you have to just think it through, thinking all about it. Like, if she died, it's better her dying than the whole village.

JACK: She must've been smart. How can a person make a plan like that happen so fast?

AZUN: Something happens to me and I can't do anything. I always think about what to do another day.

DARON: I disagree with who done that bomb. I don't agree with it. What they should do, do it in the country they have war with.

I'm quite sure that having given the story a period to 'settle' into children's thinking helped the discussion. Linda's purposeful introduction followed by group recall of the story facilitated depth of thought, as was evident. Children's comments raised challenging questions and pointed to complicated moral issues.

To some degree this discussion was similar to the conversations I recorded during class meetings. Diverse applications, connections, and personal interactions interplay throughout. However, a much tighter drawstring is drawn around the kinds of experiences and stories shared in the discussion of 'The Flying Head.' That conversation was firmly anchored in the storyworld life and held by children's thinking there. Children made meanings and drew applications from the story, considering what it means to 'be heroic.'

Pender suggested that the stupidity of the monster diminished the woman's status as a hero, implying that an adversary must be wily if a conquest is to be a heroic one. Tych contended that the woman's heroism was an act of 'standing up for herself.' Thus, a hero is a person of independent character. Azun, who was well informed about current issues and events in the Middle-East, connected a recent Palestinian suicide bomber with the woman's act.

From my experience in the classroom and listening to Azun carefully in this conversation, my sense was that he connected the bomber with the woman, not the monstrous Flying Head. Both the woman and bomber acted on behalf of an endangered community. The woman, with hot stones, and the bomber, with dynamite, took up roles that demanded trickery, and they both used their own lives as collateral. It is possible I'm wrong, of course. However, both Bekkah and Daron returned to the same question later: is the bomber a hero or monster?

Kreena observed that the woman saved the villagers from 'hiding all the time and being scared.' This seems especially significant when I consider that she fled the Taliban regime with her mother and siblings. In her next comment she went on to think about playground bullies at her own school. She thought of a bully, the ignorant teachers, helpless students, and one brave newcomer. In this way she connected several life events with the story to help her understand 'heroic': a hero is someone who stands up to a bully without support. Kreena shows a complex thinking process, a network of related ideas bringing her to important understandings.

Jack's first comment reminded everyone that the monster only 'came at night,' an unkempt horror that belonged to darkness. He might be thinking about the nature of nightmares, or of the way night cloaks the movement of monsters. Perhaps he's thinking of the courage to face 'the night.' Later, he admired the woman's quick thinking and planning. That was a heroic quality: rather than being afraid in the dark, her undaunted, bright mind came up with a way to defeat the monster. Azun ruefully remarked that he often thought of what to do about trouble the next day – too late.

Bekkah posed the old, hard question of whether it is better that one person should die than many. Her comment is linked to Azun's. Daron picked it up. He said, rather firmly, that dangerous acts should affect only those immediately concerned. Daron extended the story and Azun's comments to think about the hero as part of a community. Is a suicide bomber heroic? I suspect, by his comments and demeanour, that he did not consider such acts of endangerment and destruction heroic. By his definition, a hero doesn't hurt the innocent.

The conversation might be understood as an example of how 'a story teaches a lesson.' But this would be simplistic. Children's thoughtful interactions with the story and with each other revealed layer after layer of difficult aspects of what we might mean by 'heroic.' The conversation demonstrated considerable insight concerning human behaviour and ethics. Children challenged one another to develop the idea of 'hero.' An evolving, dynamic, and mutually informing relationship for learning was loosed by a shared storyworld experience in this short discussion. This was a valuable stream of learning that culminated in practical applications: being a hero is standing up for yourself; heroism is not impulsive, it entails clear thinking and planning; heroes have a self-sacrificial aspect, they stand up for others against all and deadly odds. Children also tugged out issues that resist resolution: opposing points of view and circumstance are each rooted in values and ethical frameworks that do not easily mesh. In this conversation 'a hero' is a complicated, situated, social, and personal idea.

Frankly, during that conversation in the classroom and later, as I thought about it again, I was regretful. I wished the conversation had gone further and deeper. I wished that the class had come to some conclusions, even a single shared conclusion. But when I reflected on my desire, I realized that I was mistaken. The good development of an idea demands exactly these kind of small incremental shifts: a series of opportunities and nudges to reconsider, amend, and develop an idea. Without the pressure for a conclusion, which necessarily will not be accepted by all participants, children learned to think more widely. Under the spacious umbrella of storytelling, they shared and risked: they put their ideas to the test of the story and each other. This placed such a divisive issue as a suicide bombing within a context where it *could* be considered together.

Such conversation teaches that knowledge is dynamic, it grows and evolves. Once in a while it blossoms into a new realization or application. A good story waits, germinating into readiness for such moments. The conversation also illustrated the collective nature of knowledge-growing. Learning about heroism built on, and benefited from, everyone's ideas and experiences. Children participated without didacticism or anticipation of the intractable wall of an 'answer.' They were encouraged to develop the idea, and the storytelling gave a common ground.

How, then, does such an activity done with a storytelling differ from one based on a piece of reading? To some extent the two would be similar. The class could have done a shared reading of this story and had a conversation that was comparable. There is, however, one significant difference: storytelling is a medium of presence. Words and ideas in the air have a tenuousness and dynamic nature, and the same could be said about the understandings they lead to. The circle of present faces insists on learning as a socially shared pursuit. Because they are bound to open their thinking to each other's experiences, the search for an answer can't lean on print or end in a book. Storytelling is a medium that says knowing is done in company and is stored in hearts and minds. The usual authority of text is absent; there is no print refuge, substitute, or weapon. The medium of presence nourishes and emphasizes this understanding.[4]

Significant ideas about social values, ideals, and behaviors are developed in discussions like this, spurred by a story. Ultimately, such discussions and stories affect the quality of survival and harmony for people who live with each other. Linda and the children showed that the shelter of the story offered a flexible, safe, and neutral ground for thinking about a difficult and even contentious idea. Finding the answer together is a part of an ongoing quest to understand our experience in all its variations. Another storytelling, another conversation, another experience will further develop the idea.

Storytelling for Reading: Getting 'Addicted to the Book'

I'm talking with Linda:

ME: Where do you use storytelling more?
LINDA: Well, language arts, obviously. And social studies some. Other times ... well ...

ME: Like around different events?
LINDA: Oh yeah. Like the Terry Fox Run. That sort of launches the hero stuff in my language arts unit.

Linda most frequently used storytelling to teach reading. It encouraged reading, developed abilities to decode words, expanded vocabularies, and nourished fluency. For example, when the class started their unit on 'fables,' Linda told a few fables. Afterwards she set out a collection of books that were available for language arts silent reading time. By my observations the books were in hot circulation. As she said about the relationship between her storytelling from Aesop's fables and children's independent reading afterwards:

> What a perfect way of preparing a child for reading: have them hear the story. They always go to the books. Look at them with Aesop! They are volunteering to read those stories. They're choosing them for silent reading.

In a class where the majority of children spoke English as a second language, Linda realized 'not every child can get a story' from a book. For children who struggled to decode text, her *telling* stories gave them the experience they needed to pick up books. It provided the vocabulary and meaningful context for their reading work afterwards. Storytelling powerfully motivated children's reading. Even the most reluctant reader, like Leon, and struggling readers, like Terry, were motivated to pick up books to read because of their storytelling experiences.

LINDA: Often we teachers tend to introduce something, a book or something, by saying, 'Well, read this.' But it's probably the last thing they should do. Doesn't work. But, storytelling! It certainly gets them to text very quickly. It's the pleasure and the knowing it. They'll pick up the text. They'll write. They'll draw. They'll express themselves in all different ways. They'll do drama.
ME: Motivating?
LINDA: Yeah. Hands down.
ME: They might not want to learn to read but they do want the story because they know what it's like?
LINDA: Some might like the little puzzle of putting the vowels together. That's intriguing for just a little while. For other kids who can't read, it's such a struggle that they don't get beyond the mechanics. Stories allow them. Storytelling.

If children enjoyed a storytelling, they knew they would like the book. Once, I was puzzled to notice a thick and rather unattractive book being passed from one child to an other. It was a thick book of about six hundred pages. Its worn cover featured an indistinct illustration. Curious, I asked Terry what he was reading.

Tuesday, September 10.
TERRY: It's Rumplestiltskin! I sat … I sat beside Leon and Leon read it. He read Rumplestiltskin and then he gave it to me and then I read it and then we said, let's read Rumplestiltskin again!

Linda had told the story of Rumplestiltskin the day before. She'd left the book on the counter with other, related books. After every storytelling, she made sure her students could count on the story and other books being available. They were propped up on the classroom's back ledge. Children lined up for them and fought about whose turn it was to have them. Linda checked these out at her local public library. After three weeks they would go back. In her many years of teaching, no book had gone missing

After her storytelling, the *The World's Best Fairy Tales: A Reader's Digest Anthology* became a popular commodity. The children enjoyed her storytelling and wanted to get back into the storyworld; the printed text made it possible to recapture the experience. The unexpected popularity of a book like the one Leon and Terry shared was significant: two of the weaker and more reluctant readers in the room were enthusiastic about reading. It was also surprising because children *did* judge and select books by their covers. In the following conversation, I was walking back from the library with two students and asked them about the books they selected:

DANIELLE: It's hard to pick a book. Like last time. Like you can't tell. Like the cover of one book was about a boy in the girls' bathroom but that was a tiny part in the book. I can't even remember it. And last year there was another one called the mystery of the snake but there wasn't even a snake hardly in the story.
VIOLET: It's cheating!

The girls were indignant and disappointed to find their expectations unmet. Readers wanted to know what they were getting into when they got a book. The cover was one way of knowing that the effort of reading would be worthwhile. For students in grade 4 or 5, with years of struggle behind them, encouragement for the long, slow work of decoding is badly needed. For children who work to read in a second language or have non-fluent reading abilities, Linda's storytelling promised re-entry into a storyworld they liked. It provided the context they needed to read unfamiliar words. Children knew their efforts would be satisfied.

Tuesday, October 15.

ME: Did you get the book [*The Devil and the Three Golden Hairs*] because she told you the story?

JACK: Yeah, and [to] try to see if it's kind of the same or different. It's different, but it's a grandmother. This one, he, he doesn't go to bed. He, um, … puts his head on the grandmother and the grandmother rubs his forehead and then she tells the little boy all those same answers that she has to get out three gold hairs. She turns the boy into an ant so that he can hide.

Jack went straight to the book after the storytelling. He found what he wanted and went through the book, cross-checking what he remembered against the text in his hands. This helped him learn to read words. He talked about this in our interview later.

ME: So, why do you think Ms Stender tells you these stories? Why does she use stories to teach you? What are you learning?

JACK: Learn how to tell stories and some words that you don't know. And to use your imagination.

ME: Yeah! Wow. Those are three big things.

JACK: And to learn how to use your brain.

ME: Yeah. So, how do you think a story helps you learn words you don't know?

JACK: Uhmm … Uh, like getting to know in hearing words. And then the sentence that words are in and you just look at the rest of the sentence and you can find out what the words mean.

Jack's limited reading skills and vocabulary prevented him from reading easily. He remembered the storytelling to fill in words or parts of the text he couldn't figure out. He carefully compared Linda's telling with his reading and found the variations interesting. I was impressed by his commitment to getting the story in text. He made a great effort to learn more words. Here, storytelling for reading was extraordinarily motivating.

Jack's account suggests that his mindful interaction with the story probably happened after the storytelling. However, when he says that storytelling helped him 'learn how to use [his] brain' and 'learn words you don't know,' he showed that during the storytelling he did puzzle over words and filed them away in his memory for later checking. He was thinking with the story.

Layla also said that storytelling made children want to read:

ME: Okay. Here's a hard question! You're a student and Ms Stender's a teacher. And she wants you to learn: she tells you stories!

LAYLA: It's kind of fun.

ME: So, what are you learning when she does storytelling?

LAYLA: Well, to listen. Don't fiddle around or you won't get a good mark when you fill in a sheet. (She is talking about pages they filled out during their unit about heroes. After a storytelling, like Theseus, children filled out a chart to help them think about the qualities of a hero and the pattern of the story.)

ME: How does a story help you to listen?

LAYLA: Well, they get really interesting. Easy to listen.

ME: What else? What else does a story teach? Is there more, you think?

LAYLA: To read. If you tell us a story I think … Uhmm … like after she finished telling a story, then I saw a person reading the book of it. Yeah? Like read the words of the same story. They keep reading that so they learn how to read other words and stuff. They get addicted to that book. They heard the story and now they can keep having it.

Imagining the story into life created a deep longing for 'more.' Layla called the craving for the storyworld experience an 'addiction' satisfied by the book. As Layla, Jack, and others suggested, this was not just typical of storytelling. When children liked a story told or read, they returned to it as often as they could. Kate said that she had read *The Woman in the Wall* 'about thirty times.' Kreena read *Matilda* and *The Secret Garden* 'lots of times.' Tajo read *The Mouse and the Motorcycle* 'a million times.'

This was the same kind of impulse that led to children's love for book series. Violet had read most of the *Boxcar Children* series. As she said, 'My mom told me about them and now I like them as much as her.' Tych had all the *Series of Unfortunate Events* books published to date and had read each several times. Pender regularly read the *Goosebump* series. Books featuring the Olsen twins, Mary-Kate and Ashley, made their way around the room. There were other sorts of 'series' that involved video games. For instance, Daron read about and collected Yu-Gi-Oh! cards and paraphernalia. In these ways, children revisited favourite stories and books over and over again.[5]

Although notions of 'novelty' and 'new' guide many educator's ideas about a story's values, children suggest that repeated engagements develop understandings and intensify engagement. Children were wary of the 'new.' They were suspicious that an untried book or story might be disappointing. They wanted assurance that their time and effort in reading would be rewarded, and rewarding. Familiarity with the storyworld invited children to go back. This has several implications for teaching. First, we know that re-reading develops reading fluency. Repeated reading of a story text enhances students' mastery of vocabulary sight words through repetitive engagements.[6] Second, as Jack suggested, children's subsequent visits to the book seemed to develop increasingly thoughtful and deliberate learning interactions with the text. Because he knew and loved the story, he studied its vocabulary and considered differences between versions. Such activity facilitates strong language arts learning. Gladly and with strong interest, children re-engaged with a favourite story, going back into the same storyworld again and again. This also increases the potential for thinking about the story's meanings and life applications. As we saw in the discussion of 'The Flying Head,' a growing depth and breadth of understandings can be drawn from a story. A good story is not quickly exhausted.

Storytelling invited children into books they otherwise might not have picked up. Storyworld imaginators' experiences motivated interest in reading. For some children, storytelling provided the incentive to take up the long struggle with words they didn't know. All the children went on to read with enthusiasm in the wake of a storytelling. After Linda told the story 'Theseus and the Minotaur,' books with stories from the *The Iliad*, *The Odyssey*, and collections of Greek myths circulated during silent reading time. After she told some fables, Fontaine's and Aesop's collections were quarrelled over and eagerly pulled from the shelves. Children read books like *Abiyoyo*, *The Devil and the Three Golden Hairs*, and others. When Linda told the stories of Anne Frank and Terry Fox, children lined up for the books about them.

Their enthusiasm for reading books related to storytelling was unanimous. This is so extraordinary that some readers might find it to believe; however, my visits to schools and classrooms across Canada and now in Michigan support my claim. Such unanimity of enthusiasm for language arts activity is uncommon. However, storytelling teachers will confirm what I write: storytelling stimulates astonishingly strong interest in reading. By first imaginating the storyworld into life, children became 'addicted to books.' Remembering their experience, they eagerly grasped a means to go back and revisit the story. Storytelling richly benefited children learning to read.

Storytelling for Writing: 'Writing the Heart Way'

In my interview with Natisha, she suggested that storytelling motivated writing as powerfully as it affected reading.

NATISHA: Stories can be like teaching. If they have a good imagination about what the story is about, they go up to the teacher and tell them, 'Can we write about what we saw?' And they have lots of writing about it. Ten or twenty pages.

Linda knew this. About half of her storytellings were followed up by writing assignments connected to the story. Most often, Linda asked them to rewrite the story. This usually happened the day afterwards, and sometimes several days later. Students could 'retell' all of it, or just the parts that interested them, by writing it. They began relatively promptly and wrote with silent intensity. As I'll show shortly, they also wrote with uncommon skill and at greater length after a storytelling. The results confirmed what Betty Rosen (1988) found in similar practice:[7]

I want to illustrate the range in styles of the writing that resulted from my telling of the Tantalus story … As invariably happens after a storytelling, the ability of my pupils leapt out and stared me in the face. I am amazed every time, even though I know it's going to happen. (p. 77)

They got down to the job of writing very readily, with none of the signs of reluctance or doubt: not a single 'But I don't know what to write about, miss.' They knew all right. (79)

This could be said in Linda's class too. Her storytelling was a successful strategy for developing children's writing ability. Linda wrote that because of storytelling,

they have such stimulation. I notice their written work is way better. I think that if I tell a story and ask them to retell [write], it is better than when I have them read a story and write about it. Right in the first draft you see it. I think it is 'going to that other place' where they don't have other interferences. Maybe, it's because they need to use ... (She pauses and doesn't finish the sentence.)

They have only the oral. You're not showing the pictures ... they're in the creation of the story. It's that, having it come in words, and that words are not going to stay there. And you're immediately creating the story. It's in a picture, a visual way, or some other way, a heart way.

Linda struggled to explain how and why storytelling positively affected children's writing work. The labour of writing was invigorated by a live engagement with the storyworld. Imaginating the story left a vivid memory, one that did not depend on 'words [that] are not going to stay.' Words simply nudged a storyworld into life. Children drew from felt, real experience. Linda knew that after storytelling, they wrote with interest and for sustained periods of time. Yet, as readers will see shortly, children did use Linda's words. Their writings showed increased complexity with increased levels of vocabulary and complexity of syntax.

Following are three pairs of writing samples that show the contrast between two kinds of assignment outcomes. The first is a piece of writing done after Linda asked children to write about a heroic, famous person they liked. Each child chose his or her own subject. They were to write a description and/or something interesting the character did. They could include a drawing if they liked. For this assignment children were given a full class period for preparation. They thought about and chose a topic, talked about their choices with a partner, and used paper to brainstorm and make story webs. A day or two later, the children wrote their samples during one forty-minute class period.[8]

The second sample of writing from each child was a response to hearing the story of 'Theseus and the Minotaur.'[9] This writing was done the day after the storytelling. As with the first sample, students had about forty minutes. They were asked to write any part of the story that interested them. During the writing time Linda spelled on the board any words children asked for. The children edited and rewrote both of their samples in another class period. When I copied them I did not amend spellings or writing conventions. Readers should note that the samples were written about seven weeks apart. This accounts for some of the evident development of writing ability.

Writing Sample 1 from Taza
Tuesday, October 8.
Once there was a cricket player named Shahid Afridi. He was angry because last time when he was playing he never got to make any points because he always makes hundred point and stuff and then he shot it so hard it went out of the ground and hit a house window and break it.

Writing Sample 2 from Taza
Tuesday, November 26.
Once all of the people from the town gathered together for going to the palace all the teenager names were in the box or the can or container. The picked 13 names and they were almost going to pick 14th name and Theseus came and said pick me, don't pick no one else I will go and his dad said son please don't and he said you could stand right here and wait for me and I will come back with a white sail and I will try my best. If I come back with a black sail then I won't be in it. So he travel's with his boat till he get's to Creete so he meet's aridne. So she said that the minitour is ver strong and powerful you got to be careful with him so he goes and a guard went pass the door its dark and freeky so he take and step and another quietly and he close to the fire and hide's and looke's at the minitour the minitour is getting sleepy, sleepy, sleepy and goes running to the minitour but he make a sound and minitour wake up and makes a loud sound and fight. He pushes Theseus right on the fire Theseus jumps ovr the fire and runs and gets minitours horn and cut's it and goes back out and he marry's with Aridadne and goes back with a black sail and forget to put a white sail and his father saw a black sail and jump's and dies.

Taza wrote about the Minotaur for the full time of 40 minutes. This was extraordinary: during all other kinds of writing assignments, it was rare for him to write for longer than two or three consecutive minutes. Writing fatigued and frustrated him, but this time he wrote with a confident energy that had eluded him when writing his first sample. The other difference, more visible to readers, is the great increase in number of written words: from 55 words in his first sample to 256 written words in the second, or nearly five times as many words. The sample also shows that he considered writing conventions. Clearly, he had recently learned about the use of apostrophes; his 'errors' are promising signs of this learning.

Taza's story about Theseus is complex, fully formed, and eloquent. He created an affecting composition in which he communicates his own emotional responses to the story. His writing is a successful effort to capture the senses of the story through vocabulary, phrasing, and pacing. The dialogue between the father and son is stirring: 'Please son, don't.' (Lest readers think the story is a mere retelling, they should know that Taza's dialogues are of his own making.) He incorporated rhythm in his writing: 'He take [one] step and another quietly.' Another good example of rhythm is: 'Sleepy, sleepy, sleepy.' As he approaches the end, there is a blast of action as the story races to its conclusion. Notice all the verbs that tumble after each other: '"wake," "fight," "push," "jump," "get's horn," "cuts it," "goes back," "marries," "goes," "forgets," "jumps" and dies.' The pacing of his story-writing is masterly. Interestingly, in Taza's story, Theseus has a bride and companion after his father dies. This is no accident; it mitigates the otherwise too bitter ending. He retold the story to his own liking so that it comes to a conclusion in which the tragedy is softened by a marriage. Also, interestingly, Linda did not describe Theseus and his friends as 'teenagers;' in Taza's storyworld, they were.

Like Taza, Alt speaks English as a second language. For his first assignment he chose to write about the famous king Gilgamesh, whom he had recently read of in a book. He spent a little more than 15 minutes drawing the king before he wrote about him.

Writing Sample 1 from Alt
Tuesday, October 8.
This [depicted in his drawing] is a king. He's the king of Uruk. He has to do his quest to find the secret of immortality. He need the secret of immortality to het his friend Enkidu. First he has to fight the beasts to get to the other side. The end.

Writing Sample 2 from Alt
Tuesday, November 26.
In a hot day a king named Aegeus in Athens. Every two years they have to sacrifice fourteen people to kill the ferocious ugly, hideous Minotaur under Mino's castle in Crete. The day has come it was time to send fourteen to go to Crete to kill the Minotaur. They had to pick names to kill the Minotaur. One after another until it was thirteen. Aegeus's son Theseus came up and said in a clear voice, 'I will be the fourteenth person to kill the hideous Minotaur.

Don't son. I don't want you to die. You might not be picked nest. Aegeus said. Don't go said all the boys and girls. Aegeus and Theseus argued a lot. Aegeus finally said, 'Well if your gonna go, you'll always be my son. If you survive you'll see a white sail and a with it the black sail.

Fourteen people went on the black sail and wetn to Crete. Fourteen of them went in the cage and waited. A princess named Ariadne saw Theseus and fell in loved with him and Theseus fell in love with her. Ariadne said take this silken thread and tie it on the linten[10] and the thread will guid you to the Minotaur. Do this at night. Theseus agreed at night Theseus walked step by step so that the guards wouldn't hear theeus. As he got to the door he threw the thread at the lintel and the tread tied itself. When it was morning theseus was the first person to go inside. You won't make it said one of the gueards laughing. Theseus stepped inside. The door slammed quick like a book has fallen from a char. The thread gied him to the Minotaur. Some fire at the top of the maze. There it was. The Minotaur. Theseus came closer and closer to the Minotaur. Theseus took out his sword and curt his horn off. Theseus grabbed the horn and ran to the Minotaur, the Minotaur got up in rage to kill Theseus. Theseus grab the Minotaur other horn and stabbed it by the back. The Minotaur ran to Theseus by Theseus threw the horn at the Minotaur and died. Theseus ran outside. Ariadne said, Let's go to see my dad. As they got there Theseus asked if he could marrie Ariadnes. Ariadnes' dad said no. Okay said Theseus. They went to Athens and Aegeus saw the sail and it was black!! Aegeus standed at the top of the castle and jumped off. He drown and died. He made suicide. The end.

Alt's work demonstrates how storytelling powerfully motivated his writing work. He wrote 47 words in the first sample and 425 in the second – more than 9 times as many words. As educators know, the sheer volume of writing significantly develops writing fluency. For a grade 4 child, recently from the Philippines, and an English language learner, this is an outstanding piece of writing. Aside from the spectacular rise in the number of words written, Alt showed several other high-level writing abilities. For a story written in about 40 minutes, this one is lengthy and has integrity as well as an aesthetic sense. At the end, in one dark fell swoop Theseus loses two fathers. Alt redesigned the storytelling to yield this powerful conclusion. His chosen vocabulary items are also higher level. The simile he wrote is startlingly powerful and original: 'The door slammed quick like a book has fallen from a chair.' This was his own creative effort to evoke what he heard inside the storyworld. The dialogues are powerfully evocative and skilfully spare, and the story is dramatically paced – Alt tells the story in a way that recreates the tension he felt when he listened.

These two writing examples were not exceptional. In the writing samples I examined, those in response to a storytelling usually surpassed all other story or expositional writing work. Let me take a moment to mention the exceptions. These were the creative writing projects of a few children. Violet, Layla, Tych, Bekkah, and a few others wrote sustained and well-developed narratives for a writing project assignment. Tych's, for example, was a 9-page story, illustrated and well thought out. Of about 650 words, it showed the kind of complexity and sustained narration more typical of the sorts of retellings/writings we read above. Layla's work ran to about 1120 words. She had taken hers home to finish. However, these story-writing projects were accomplished over at least four or five class periods. The daily word count was less than that done in the wake of a storytelling. The variety of vocabulary used and complexity of sentence structure were at lower levels than was common in the writings done after storytelling.

Children's retellings in writing are powerful evidence of storytelling's effectiveness in motivating and developing writing abilities. Vocabulary levels were higher, sentence structures more complex, the content more developed, and more literary devices were incorporated. The texts were rich with apt vocabulary choices and complex constructions of phrases, dialogue, and sentences. They also showed more elusive qualities of the writing craft, such as tone, drama, tension, and rhythm. The stories children wrote were fully formed, evocative of the event, and emotionally revealing of the character's plight. And in every case, children took up the task with similarly sustained interest.

It might be argued that children simply retold the story that Linda told, and that this task lacked opportunity for creativity. However, both Rosen's (1988) work, in which she recorded samples of telling and a great variety of responses, and my collection of the work done by the children in Linda's classroom belie such an idea. Because storyworlds are so expansive, children chose their vantage points. Natasha made much of the love story, Taza of the father-and-son relationship, and Alt focused mostly on the fight. Children chose their emphases, shaped the story to suit their time frames and writing abilities, and chose the details of events they wanted to emphasize. Some added to Linda's stories, and all of them subtracted events, images, and whatever else they didn't want to or think to write about. This was especially clear in Azun's retelling: he amended the story to harmonize with his idea of how things should be. He wrote about powerful boys and rewrote the death of the father to suit his concepts of correctness and justice. Azun also wrote his own title for his story.

Writing Sample 2 from Azun
Tuesday, November 26.

Minotaur Horn Nightmare for Theseus

Every four years boys and girls would go in a very scary labyrinth to slay the Minotaur. He would eat your body and leave the skeleton of your body. They would draft bullys names out cause they were pretty tough. Theseus, was the biggest bully in the country. The princess really liked him. So, she gave him a silky thread to tie the Minotaur up.

He got in the maze. He took one step in the maze. He fell into a dark tunnel. He walked and saw a little fire. There the minotaur was waiting. Then Princess Ariadne got in and fell into the trap too and the boy was gone. The girl saw the light too. She saw Theseus the biggest bully was behind him he was going to tie him until the Minotaur saw Ariadne and killed her. Bully Theseus was going to kill the Minotaur, but the Minotaur fought back. The Minotaur hit Theseus the bully with his horns especially sharp horns. But Theseus got up and tied the thread to the minotaurs neck and killed him. He went to the palace. His father was KILLED. The minotaur's brother and sister did it.

The vocabulary usage and his recounting of the plot are, like the others, in remarkable contrast with his other writing (below). He used words like 'slay,' 'labyrinth,' and 'silky thread.' The story has a logical, clear flow, and the images are sharp. A sentence like 'The Minotaur hit Theseus the bully with his horns especially sharp horns' shows a wonderful sense of rhythm, drama, and affect. It seems to me that the Minotaur has drawn Azun's admiration. In the end, Azun gave the Minotaur the justice he felt was its due. But the Minotaur's relatives avenge the half-bull's murder, and this rewritten ending is clever in many ways. Rather than being rejected for marriage, Azun has Ariadne killed by the Minotaur. He also amended the 'suicide' of the father to prevent the disgrace he felt was attached to it. In Azun's version the father was 'KILLED,' written in capital letters: Theseus is freed from the horror of guilt for his own thoughtlessness.

To offer a comparison, I include below Azun's writing sample done for a school district – wide assessment of language arts abilities. The children spent three classes on this assignment. In the first they chose a topic, talked about it with partners, and had a lesson about writing. In the second period they brainstorming on paper to get details of content, outlining their stories of 'A Summer Adventure.' In the third class period, Linda got the children started as soon as possible. Her class was ready to do their best. And 'no talking!'

Writing Sample, Azun
Thursday, September 19.

Summer Adventure
My granma was going to New Zealand and Fiji. She asked me 'if I wanted to go' and I said 'Yes.' But my cousin wanted to go too. So me, my granma and my cousin went. We had a cat at the place we stayed, which was New Zealand. Then we went too Fiji which I liked the most. We had two weddings and they were two days. In fiji we play lots of soccer and it was fun. In fiji some houses have cold showe and some have not shower. Fiji Kids have lots of fights. In fiji I went to lots of fun places like to peoples' house for parties. We saw a lizard and it went on my granma's older brother. Three was a chick and it died. Someone died in Fiji. Most of our party was outside. My cousin got a broken nose. In Fiji we have an alarm clock as a chicken

Azun worked hard and with some enthusiasm. I was sitting beside him while he wrote for 35 minutes. He was determined to do well on this test and was pleased with how long his story was getting. Often he gestured for me to read what he was writing and see that he had started a new page.[11] He wrote with as much energy and effort as when he wrote about the Minotaur. He was attentive to narrative flow, but did not write a conclusion. Azun wrote 40 more words in his story of the Minotaur than in his 'Summer Adventure' piece. His Fiji account was clearly recounted and coherent by subject. He showed a good range of details, of both action and images; was careful to make 'complete sentences' and spell correctly; and communicated the important details of his adventure in a good narrative sequence. But his 'Summer Adventure' is written more like a list than a story. He does not communicate the experience: recreating an experience for a reader demands more than recounting events. By contrast, that high-level expectation is met in 'Minotaur Horn Nightmare for Theseus,' in which he fully conjures the experience by means of aesthetic devices.

Azun's and the other boys' stories about Theseus and the Minotaur above show that after a storytelling, 'retelling' helped them to learn about writing a story. Inspired by an authentic storyworld experience, they were able to go to its aesthetic heart; they wrote powerfully and well. Thus storytelling effectively taught story-writing. All three texts showed strong plot movement, good word choices, and narrative integrity. Writers used complex devices like foreshadowing, irony, comparison, and characterization. Their writing also showed a depth of response to the perplexing questions about life raised by the story. In spite of Theseus' grand victory and adventure, the story concludes in disappointment. The hero comes home without his prize: the woman he loved. His thoughtlessness causes his beloved father's suicidal leap. The story is about the age-old tension between children's need to leave home and parents' desire to keep children safe. These are complex, tough issues.

Thinking with a story, children learned to write stories but also to consider human experience. Using stories that are made vivid by hard questions about life made writing activity meaningful. Helping children inside that experience with a storytelling made writing possible. When, earlier, they imaginated with the story, they entered its 'real life.' This was why Linda chose to tell folk tales; as she said earlier:

> they pose moral and ethical questions, response to which help shape our values. They teach lessons about human behavior that are common ... [and] can be enjoyed and understood at different levels. They're ideal for the inclusive model of education that we practice today.

When Natisha considered how memorable told stories were, she described them as 'sticky.' In the following transcript, she begins by answering my question about why imagination is important.

NATISHA: Imagination is important because you'll know what the story's about. You'll have a picture in your head all the time and you'll still remember it and you'll say to your friend, 'Hey, remember the story ...?' Then they'll still have an imagination of it. It sticks more than words.

Yet, the story *was* in words. When children were thinking with the storytelling to write it, they remembered the words that conjured up the images, places, and events of the storyworld in their minds. Listeners depended on what they heard and saw of Linda in order to imaginate their way into the story's living place in their deep imagination. The intense engagement of imagining during a storytelling made language memorable. When they picked up their pens and pencils, children reached back for the words that powerfully brought the story to life in their memory. Even when they were lost with Theseus in the labyrinth, they appreciated the pungency of good words to make the story live. Their writing showed that the words of a storytelling *did* stick, and forcefully. Thickened by context, the words were given voice and meaning by the storyteller's expression. Children's use of words like 'ferocious,' 'labyrinth,' 'lintel,' 'silken,' and 'container' and phrases like 'got up in rage' are evidence of their attention to vocabulary and their growing ability to use new words.

Remarkably, children all made sure that they finished their stories within the allotted class period. Their experience of a beginning, middle, and end drove them to 'get it all down.'[12] If we remember Daron's experience with Spider-man, we can appreciate the task of shaping the storyworld into something that fits on paper and within one class period. Linda's storytelling gave them the words and story shape they needed. It offered a ready but flexible framework for their writing that they could emphasize and reshape as they needed. Thinking from inside the story afterwards, they wrote well.

'It Sticks More than Words'

Natisha brings this chapter to my final point: storytelling is 'sticky.' Recalling a story is usually easier than remembering lists, information, instructions, or explanations. The mere mention of a story heard, even much later, instantly summons the experience to listeners' minds. Simultaneously it casts a net for its associations. This is a highly valued aspect of storytelling used to teach and learn.

I remember a moment in math class when Linda reminded children that the graph design was guided by the kind of information organized. Pointing at the problem they were studying, she asked, 'Is this about lemon cookies or treasure?' 'Lemon Cookies' was a story she told earlier about baking for the queen and the kinds of cookies readied. Its graph was for types and quantities of cookies. The second story was about a hidden treasure and the use of graphs to plot its location. In an instant two stories yielded a complex of understandings. Storytellings can be tapped from a long temporal distance to vividly remind and quickly contextualize or inform a discussion. Weeks and months later, stories retained such potency.

Countless books talk about this sticky quality of the story with an odd hint of romance. They suggest that before the time of books and computers, people used storytelling to remember what they needed:

important facts, events, and rituals were embedded in stories because they were easier to remember that way. Stories and storytelling were once clever means of keeping track of needed information when there wasn't a better way. The implication is, we have progressed, and there is a better way. This idea of progress, of 'a better way,' is simply nonsense. Writing takes care of some communication needs, talking takes care of others, and storytelling is needed for still other kinds of understandings and relationships. Storytelling is not a cultural plan for preservation. It is an act of remembering to serve a present need.

Yet storytelling does relate to memory in a very different way than text does. Being able to tell demands the ability to remember. And the detail with which children remembered storytellings suggests that there might be a stronger recall of storytellings than of books read. The vocabulary chosen in the three boys' writings testifies to this.

During my interviews, I asked children to remember as many stories as they could. Since I interviewed them over the course of 4 months, they each had a different number of stories available to recall. But all the children promptly remembered several. Bekkah topped the list:

ME: I wonder how many stories you can remember that [Linda's] told to you or read to you. You start off and I'll help you ...
BEKKAH: Does it have to be in order?
ME: No!
BEKKAH: Thank God! (We both laugh heartily.)
ME: Any order, the order is in how you remember it.
BEKKAH: 'The Field.' 'Three Theseus's.' All three of Theseus ... (pauses lengthily)
ME: There's this one about a giant behind the mountain ...
BEKKAH: 'Abayoyo!' Uhm. 'The Boy Who Learned How to Shudder.' 'George's Marvelous Medicine.' 'The Rat'... I wasn't there for some of it. And 'Li Chi Slays the Serpent.' ... Uhm. 'The Head.'

When I asked Daron to remember as many stories as he could, he said:

DARON: 'Finn Mac'Cool,' 'Abiyoyo,' and 'Three Golden Hairs' and the 'Devil and the Three Golden Hairs' ... uhh ... (pausing)
ME: There's one ... about the war ...
DARON: 'The Field!' Oh. 'The Boy Who Learned How to Shudder.' That was a good one.

At the time of Bekkah's interview, almost four months had passed since Linda told 'Abiyoyo.' Thirteen full weeks of school time have interposed, as well as such events as Halloween, Christmas, and holidays. There were noon hours, things that happened inside and outside the classroom. So much happened between the telling of the story and her recollection. The story of 'Abiyoyo' was just a 20-minute incident, accounting for about 0.001 per cent, or less, of transpired class time. Yet, like the other children, Bekkah remembered the story promptly. She could retell it in substantial detail. Significantly, Bekkah was not unusual in this: all of the children I interviewed easily named several of the eleven folk stories Linda told.

In my notebook I had a complete list of all the 'stories,' the bigger ones told by Linda; there were about 24. All of them had created the characteristic hush of listening. I had included on my list the stories Linda told in the midst of her teaching to illustrate, contextualize, or make a point memorable. For example, she told the story of Teddy Roosevelt to explain the origin of teddy bears. The story began with his hunting and ended with the singing of 'The Teddy Bear's Picnic.' On Remembrance Day Linda told the story of Anne Frank and concluded by showing Anne Frank's diary and another book with pictures of the tiny apartment in which the girl lived for several years. When the class was discussing urban change and the situation of the many homeless persons who were using the old abandoned Woodwards department story, she told a story of her Christmas shopping there, many years earlier. She told the stories of Rick Hansen and Terry Fox on two separate occasions and in considerable detail. There were other stories, like a fatal accident on the New Westminster bridge involving a school parent or a hostage-taking in Ivory Coast.[13] In some of these, the storytelling lasted more than ten minutes and children uniformly sat in stillness. But none of these stories were named by the children.[14]

At the same time, I'm sure the children remembered the stories. If I had asked, 'Do you remember that story about when Ms Stender went to Woodwards?' or 'Do you remember the story about Terry Fox?' they would have remembered it. In fact, they'll probably remember some of these stories for a long time, and better than most of the other learning activities they did that year.

Still, their unanimous omission is significant. They didn't think of these storytellings that were thoroughly imbedded in a lesson as 'stories.' The children's omission supports Linda's sense of 'difference.'

Her use of stories to meet her curricular outcomes was not really 'storytelling' in the larger sense she had of it. The firm connection to the classroom kept the story from displacing that space with imagined storyworlds. And the immediate reach back into teaching at the story's conclusion affected how children interacted with the story afterwards.

When Linda told stories to help children imaginate, the event was clearly differentiated from other kinds of storytelling. As we have seen, children changed the way they sat. The storytelling was longer and was introduced and concluded in a specific way. Children were allowed, even urged, to slide deep into their own storyworlds. Afterwards they recalled an activity in which time slowed and details were personal. There was much freedom in how they thought about and used the story afterwards. Such experiences were the standards for 'a story.' Everything else that had a story in it wasn't similar enough. This affected how other stories, like those of Terry Fox or Anne Frank, lodged in memory.

Natisha's point about the 'stickiness' of a story is significant to education. All of teaching and learning concerns the development of memories. New ones are made over the course of study; older ones are in constant development. During a learning activity, teachers depend on learners' abilities to reach into memory and search for the necessary furnishings, connections, and associations needed to make thinking possible. Aterwards, the memory must be somehow moored, made available to the next need. That is why education includes so much review and practice. Teachers make lessons visual, oral, and experiential in order to anchor them in memory, and help students use such mnemonics as visual aids, graphs, songs, and stories.

In my very simplified description of the inextricable relationship between learning and memory, note that imagination and memory are also inseparable. Imagination makes it possible to call or recall something to mindfulness when it is not present. To think about heroes, homelessness, graphing, or anything at all demands the ability to conjure it in mind. When we need to think about something, we search our memories to bring it to a kind of life. Sometimes we find it; other times the 'thing' eludes every effort and won't be recovered. There are two theories about this inability to recall: memories can be lost or worn away by time or trauma; or, alternatively, all memories are stored, as they might be on a computer hard drive, and we just lose our ability to retrieve them. In either case, in school we want to keep certain things in memory ready and available.

Of all the devices for remembering, stories are outstanding ones.[15] Not only are they easier to remember than lists of things, but they surface with a significant set of ready links. Like the lemon cookies and treasure, they come to mind with relative completeness.

A story lodges in memory differently than other kinds of activities, material, or information.[16] This aspect is directly related to the qualities of story language I wrote about briefly in chapter 5. Its language of symbol is flexible to the diversity of listeners. A story memory also has a kind of wholeness to it, a beginning, a middle part, and an ending. If any of these parts is missing in memory, the gap nags at one's mind. Remembering a story includes a personal sense of having been there: imaginators took a position inside the storyworld. An emotional thread runs through the memory; values and a sense of identity are associated with a story, as we saw with 'The Flying Head' as well as with 'Theseus and the Minotaur.'

We do not remember a story in the same way we remember, say, the order of the planets and their names. Generally, we can remember the stream of a story and its parts more easily than we can the roster of planets, the table of elements, or the stages of photosynthesis.

For this reason teachers think of using a story to help learners recall hard-to-remember information. With that in mind, Linda attended a workshop led by Billy Teare, a storyteller, writer, and teacher.[17] Teare is acclaimed for his successful uses of storytelling to help learners remember information about a subject being studied. Linda wanted to develop her storytelling abilities so she could help children do the same. She wrote about her workshop and thoughts later in her reflective journal.

Tuesday, November 5.
Saturday morning I attended Billy Teare's workshop in search of ideas restory as a way of enhancing learning. He offered interesting evidence to show that children's recall of information improves when [that information] has been presented in the context of a story. He used the example of young children learning the names of the planets and their location in relation to the sun. On the spot, it seemed, he made up some absurd story featuring planets' names, and it worked!

He explained, too, how he used story to teach facts such as the periodic table in chemistry and historic dates. Basically, he argues that a story is a connection, that the story connects one side of the brain to another. The right brain responds with visual images to the information the left brain receives, which then reinforces learning. Billy Teare displayed his own prowess by describing the content of a 150-page *People Magazine* that he claimed he spent about an hour studying. A few workshop participants held the magazine and asked, 'Billy, what's on page 44?' His recall was correct 100 per cent of the time. He could remember what was on every page.

This 'trick' might be familiar to some of my readers. Perhaps you know the game in which you bring in a tray of 20 assorted goods. The contest is to see how many you can remember. The most successful strategy is to make a quick story that includes all the items.

But in spite of her professed interest and workshop attendance, Linda didn't try this technique later in the classroom. When children had to learn the body's main bones or the parts of speech, she did not make up a story to help teach them. I found this puzzling. At first, I wondered if she simply couldn't think of a good story. But her creativity and ease with storytelling did not support such an idea. I then thought that perhaps my presence inhibited her. But she told lots of stories and was daring enough to play her ukelele 'badly' in front of me![18] So, why wouldn't she use this means to help children remember a hard list?

I concluded that such storytelling jarred with her deeper understandings about storytelling. Teare's technique demands that participants mix classroom and storyworld lives, that the experience of imagining with a story become thinking with a story. Story-language, which uses words symbolically and is flexible to each listener's life, is confused with the language of explanation. In a storyworld like 'Abiyoyo' participants freely supplied the details of the story. When children thought about 'The Field' or 'The Flying Head' they came to a variety of conclusions that were not experienced as contradictory by the group. The content of stories is human experience, and story-language is used to hold and share what we have all learned about living through our experiences. Stories are about us, who we are.[19] Whether the story was a joke or folk tale, it was always about 'us.' Whether silly or serious, fantastic or earnest, story-language explains what our lives are like.

In contrast, a story like Teare's mnemonic for learning the planets demands a static and absolute use of details. The precise point of the planet-story lies in the order and details, remembered exactly as they were told in the story. A list of planets is not about us, who we are and what our lives are like. Even if its playful 'absurdity' makes it look and feel like a story at first, it's not a 'real' story. It is just a good parlour trick, sometimes necessary and valuable, but a trick nevertheless.

Thinking with stories happened 'between' two other circles. It was supported by and dependent on participations on either side of it. On the one side, the vigorous life of talking with stories built learning relationships and the vocabulary and connections learners needed to think together. On the other side, storytelling in deep imaginative engagement exercised and developed strong abilities to make up things. Children learned how to imaginate, a skill critical to thinking and learning.

Children's thinking with stories yielded extraordinarily rich learning outcomes. They eagerly looked for books to read, they wrote with uncommon fluency, and they thought about their lives in the world. Using the story as a safe thinking place, they considered tough ethical questions and political conundrums. Thinking with a story thus is a vital key to unlocking language arts instruction and developing critical literacy abilities.

11 A Pedagogy of Storytelling

'What's Going on Here?'

On 15 November I wrote in my reflective journal:
There was a knock on the door [of the classroom]. A parent opened it and looked into the classroom. She had come to bring a lunch. Children were in the midst of a math lesson about graphing statistics. Pairs of children had clipboards, markers, poster papers, and a mission to ask everyone in the class a demographic question. Some were lying on the floor drawing graphs. Others sat in or on top of desks checking their 'respondents list.' Some children were nearly shouting questions at each other. To the parent at the door it was very hard to see that anything was 'happening.' It looked like chaos.

The woman's inquiring face clearly asked: 'What's going on here?' Linda, who planned and knew what was 'going on,' flushed when she saw her classroom through other eyes. Her 'plan' was invisible to the observer.

I think storytelling across the days and weeks is something like this. In the beginning, I wondered, 'What's going on?' The chaos of conversations, the limp sprawl of curious intensity, and story fragments flying, guiding lessons. How did all of this fit together? Did it?

I am coming to the end of my description of how all the storytellings 'fit together.' Skinny stories like Kate's fishing and Tych's football player; children thinking about being heroic under the shadow of the 'Flying Head,' and the time everyone stomped down from Abiyoyo's mountain. These are separate storytelling events that connect deeply. They depend on each other to form a coherent course of abilities and understandings. Children's participations, which looked so dissimilar on the outside, were tautly joined. The lively exchanges during a class meeting, the pauses in the midst of a lesson for thinking together or writing and reading, and the hush around the spinning chair are unified by a pedagogy of storytelling. Talking, thinking, and imaginating together form an interdependent, complementary set of activities.

Three Circles

In the first circle, children talked with stories. Conversations, teeming with bits of story, jokes, and remembering, made a language-learning place in Linda Stender's room. The children flourished, learning about each other and themselves. Social boundaries shifted and identities grew. Talking with stories helped children grow into a learning community. They also learned about the use and nature of stories between people. They realized that stories are socially constructed and mediated, and concern experience in a situation. Every story needs another one; identity and knowledge are a process. In this circle, children and their teacher developed the language abilities they needed to talk together, acquired understanding about each other, and crafted the relationships they needed for storytelling and learning together.

In the second circle, children were thinking with stories. The stories were practice grounds for gaining the wisdom brought by experience. Stories were laboratories in which children could safely learn about hard things such as war, and terror, or simply the importance of laughter. Thinking with a story was the means to grasp abstract concepts or thorny issues. Ideas and their applications were worked out and realized by means of the storytelling experience participants shared. In this circle of storytelling, the teacher also found a powerful and authentic means to teach reading and writing. Children, thinking back into their storyworld experiences, advanced their writing abilities and vigorously pursued reading interests. Reading work towards fluency and vocabulary development was sharply stimulated. Children picked up books and wrote out of an experience that was not only motivating, but enabling.

In the previous chapter, as we considered thinking with stories, we saw how children showed the extent to which the experience of living in a storyworld affected their work in the classroom world. The experience of 'The Flying Head,' 'The Field,' 'The Three Golden Hairs,' 'Abiyoyo,' 'Sody Salaratus,' 'Theseus and the Minotaur,' and the other stories critically spurred students' reading, writing, and literacy skills. The special brilliance of storyworld memories lit children's way to further and other learning.

In the third circle, deep inside the bounded and extended pause created by a storytelling, children fell into their storyworlds. The promise of a highly desirable experience motivated children's determined efforts to imaginate their ways into a waiting world. On the threshold of their storyworlds, children developed abilities to imaginate. This ability to 'make pictures' is, as we have noted, critical to all subject learning. Across the schoolday students need to imagine contexts, frameworks, applications, and contents that are not present in the room. Inside the third circle, children learned how to do this. They learned to visualize and interiorize subjects of study. They also exercised social controls and developed the ability to pay attention to a subject of interest. Hungering for every new word and turning of the story, listeners enlarged their vocabularies. They gained appreciation for the power of the right word. They also grew more adept in using such potent linguistic devices as metaphor, irony, and imagery.

Linda used folk stories for much of her storytelling. These provided common motifs and experiences set in story form. In them, children actively engaged with the complexity and perplexity of human experience. They learned about loneliness, death, joy, terror, hilarity, responsibility and foolishness, the perplexities of family life, and the struggle to grow up. The felt reality of the storyworld experience offered vivid memories and the means of later tapping those memories to understand experience, issues, and ideas: memory served listeners' need for meaning for a long time afterwards. In this circle, children learned what a story is and what it can do for learning about life.

In these three ways of being together with a story, children enhanced their knowledge and learned abilities that were taught by storytelling.

Usual and Unusual

Many of the ideas found in this book are not new. My organization of events may be new, but the content is not. Many of my readers will have heard and told stories in school: it happens in every classroom in the world. Children talk about what happened at home, tell about movies they have seen, talk about a trip they made or about the fight on the playground during recess. Classroom discussions and class gatherings around literature include storytelling. Teachers pause to tell stories about their own experiences, explain a news item, summarize a book, or give an example of what they mean. In fact, wherever people get together, they tell stories.

Thus, nearly all teachers encourage talking with stories in their class-rooms. They know that empathy, tolerance, and friendships are nu-tured by the sharing of stories, which helps students to enjoy simply being and learning together. This social ease makes the long haul of as-signments, instruction, studies, and activity possible. And nearly all teachers include some storytelling to help children think about a topic or learn something. They use examples and metaphors, explain why something is the way it is, or sometimes tell the story of a scientist's or author's life to add relevance and a human connection to a subject of study. These are ordinary sorts of teaching activities that, if children are to learn, depend on their mindful interaction with a story. Such good practices make good teaching, but do not make their practitio-ners storytelling teachers.

Of course, I encourage teachers to do all these things, regularly. The activities of story-talk and thinking with a story are effective and en-joyable techniques. But they should be understood as *techniques*: as very good tools and methods. The life force of the pedagogy of story-telling is not fully realized until children imaginate their ways into storyworld life in the midst of the classroom. Unless the teacher searches for the stories children need, and meets the expectations of a child who wants badly to imagine her way into a waiting story-world, the full pedagogy of storytelling is not realized. In short, the teacher must be a storyteller.

This kind of storytelling is not usual; in or out of school, it is rare. In hundreds of visits to classrooms, I have met only a handful of teach-ers who do this. Not many educators know how to break a story free from paper and hold it comfortably in memory. Most teachers don't have any models to help them know what this looks like or how it feels. They've received no encouragement to try it. They've not ex-perienced a storytelling event or festival and probably don't know about the numerous but small community groups and tiny handful of organizations for storytelling. It wasn't included in their teacher training, or if it was, it wasn't demonstrated or strongly urged. So, without help or experience it's hardly likely that a teacher would take up storytelling.

We might ask if this is necessary, anyway. Does the deep imaginative experience really have to come from story*telling*? A good story in a book offers a similar experience. The reader emerges at the end of the story also saturated with its affect and full of a vividly remembered storyworld time that feels nearly the same. And we could take this one step further: reading a book out loud might further narrow the gap between telling and reading.

I grant that the experiences of telling a story and reading out loud are comparable – but they are not the same. Even if a teacher reads out loud often and expressively, even though the reader and listener both emerge affected by the storyworld experience, telling and reading aloud are importantly different. Storytelling participation is shaped into specific meanings and significance by the living interactions forged between the listener and a circumstance. The story, other listeners, the teller and place all affect the experience and thus the meanings that can be drawn from it. So, yes, it must be story*telling*. If the pedagogy of storytelling is to be unleashed, a teacher needs to take the risk of remembering, love the weight of waiting listeners, and relish the learning life inside a storyworld brought into being by the words of a teller. Here the language of story is restored to its primary medium.

The pedagogy of storytelling entails its medium of presence. The medium is the sounds of words, the faces and gestures of one another, and the warm contact of each other's bodies in physical place. Over the last three chapters we have considered the many learning and teaching aspects of this medium. Not the least of these concerns what meanings and significance listeners constructed within 'a story.' As the discussion about 'The Flying Head' showed, the understandings listeners arrive at in each other's company demanded a widening context and flexibility or openness of thinking. Additionally, sharing a story in the presence of one another is a social activity, a shared learning event of 'we-ness.'

Storytelling was just one of several ways in which a story was experienced in Linda's room. Children read alone and together; read aloud and silently; and read chosen and assigned books. From my time in the classroom, I know they enjoyed each kind of engagement with a story for what it was. However, they preferred storytelling, even to having a text read aloud.

The class had a regular reading-aloud session. On most days of the week, at the end of the day, the class from across the hall joined Linda's children, and the two teachers took turns reading a storybook for twenty minutes.[1] Linda's students manifestly looked forward to this time and greatly enjoyed it.

During my interviews I asked children to compare stories told without a book with those that used a book. Children sharply distinguished between a story read out loud and one that was told.

ME: So, if you could pick between [Linda] telling you a story, or reading a story, what would you pick?
KYLA: Telling.
ME: How come?
KYLA: Uhmmmm, I just like it when she tells, [more] than when she tells us with reading. I feel like I'm in the story. Cause she points to you. She is with you. And it's different. Different than when she is reading a book. A book gots words. It's about words.

Attention to words got in the way of the story; the pages got in the way of listening. Children liked best to be with a story freed of the signage on paper.

ME: Which one did you like better?
DARON: Her telling it (emphatically).
ME: So quite a bit better?
DARON: Yeah.
ME: What do you like about that, when she's telling without books?
DARON: Because then, well, just when you hold a book up to your face you can't really hear it. Like … if you have no book it's easier to tell it. And like, she doesn't, like … like, if you had a book you would kind of look at the words and then quick up. But she has no book so she just looks straight at us (smiles).

Daron said he could 'hear' better when Linda didn't have a 'book up to [her] face.' But, by my observations, when she read the book simply lay on her lap, low in her hands. It was never in front of her face. It created no visible obstruction even for children who sat on the floor nearest to her. To my listening ear, she spoke clearly and her volume was nearly the same as when she told a story from memory. Although she was plainly reading, she looked up often, and her face and voice were expressively responsive to the text she read. Thus, it surprised me how much children felt a book interposed itself between the story and themselves during reading aloud. Pender's comment is especially dramatic:

PENDER: Oh! It sounds better when somebody's telling it to you. They don't have to flap the book around and stuff like that. It sounds better anyway time. Yeah.

In a subtle way the text filtered or screened the story experience. It located the story in a book, not in a teller's mind and mouth, and this shift blunted the story's message. The printed text stepped between the teller and listener, affecting their the relationship. A book interposed itself between the story and the listener, between the story and imagination.

KATE: Well, telling a story you don't have a book with pictures or like a chapter book with writing on it. Uhm. Telling a story is … is like you don't have anything but you are just telling it from your mind. You hold it. You tell it. It feels kind of better to have just telling.

When I asked the children about their preference, they were unanimous: they all liked the teacher telling the story 'best.' Bekkah, the most voracious reader in the class, clamoured more for storytelling than any other child. Significantly, storytelling did not replace reading for her. It was simply something else that she liked. Those children who did not like to read also valued storytelling. When I asked Leon, the most reluctant participant in classroom life, he said promptly, 'Her telling. It is way better.'

Without text in hand, Linda told her children stories 'by heart.' This created an immediacy about the story and the experience of being in it. Storytelling led to an imaginative experience or a quality specific to itself. It seemed to unleash a greater intensity of experience and pleasure for the whole class. Heartened by each other's presence during a storytelling, they shared the effort to 'get into' the story. They imagined their way into storyworlds where the world was wide and full of beckoning possibilities. They played and learned in a world that resonated with the reality of each child's experience.

Storytelling also entailed a specific story-relationship between the teller and listener. That's why getting a storyteller to come and visit is not enough. Because of the intimate and knowledgeable relationship between Linda and her listeners, she knew the stories and words her children needed. Because children knew Linda, they quickly settled under her eye and plunged into the story. And because they would later use their storyworld memories for thinking and learning together, teacher and children needed to go as one company of travellers.

Theory, Don Quixote, and a New Story

In these pages I have no intention of diminishing the need for or value and pleasure of stories in books, reading-aloud time, shared classroom reading, or silent reading, in the classroom. The significant place of reading and reading activity in school is indisputable. In my own life, reading is a regular life-giving practice, deeply treasured. However, I am urgently calling our attention to storytelling as a vital pedagogy for abilities and knowledges specific to the circle of telling and listening together. As we have seen, storytelling richly benefits the teaching of reading and writing and nourishes critical literacy and thinking.

It is surprising, if not shocking, to realize that in spite of what is known about the critical function of children's social and oral language experiences, we do not pick up such an ideal curriculum as storytelling. A growing pile of 'scientifically based evidence' shows that children's home language interactions are the strongest possible variable in reading success. Shirley Brice-Heath's *Ways with Words* (1999) laid the ground for our understanding that children's home and social experiences with language profoundly affect their reading ability. Victoria Purcell Gates' *Other People's Words* (1995) confirmed this relationship. Betty Hart and Todd Riseley's rigorous study of the language practices in 42 homes has led educators to conclude that there is an almost determining relationship between social-cultural language experiences outside of school and children's successful reading outcomes. Higher levels of oral language experience lead to successful reading abilities. This suggests that classroom experience must include a rich range of spoken words if we want all children to be successful. Teachers need to incorporate a greater variation of language functions, now almost exclusively centred on instruction, direction, and information-giving. Educators need to offer the means for expanding the levels of talking and listening experiences. If this doesn't happen, some children are headed for 'catastrophe.'[2]

As research shows, research that now includes Linda's classroom, there are compelling reasons to incorporate storytelling pedagogy in schools. But I am writing this book in the face of an educational trend that is all but hostile to storytelling. An increasing emphasis on decoding abilities and information-reading is threatening what I consider an inalienable right: to tell and hear our stories. In this era of 'standards-based instruction,' story-talk and storytelling are squeezed into the small pockets of leftover classroom time. Language arts instruction currently emphasizes phonics skills, writing conventions, information-hunting, and related abilities. Reading fluency has come to mean speed, not thoughtfulness. Teaching strategies are shaped by such scientific methods as pattern recognition, repetition and replication, and sorting and graphing information. Talking about and mulling over a story resist the specificity demanded by the current language of goals and outcomes. Story talk and thinking, storyworld experiences are not easily captured on assessment forms. Current language arts pedagogy is less inclusive of the qualitative aspects of learning to read: sharing experiences, thinking about life, and wondering about possibilities.

I think we are in deep trouble. To use Pender's unflattering description, today's educators 'flap the book around': books of standards, assessments, evaluations, and charts. These threaten the ordinary but vitally important learning relationships between people who share a room. Although I endorse accountable teaching and high standards for success, I am worried about classrooms in which relationships, personal stories, and the sense of wonder and curiosity are considered tangential. Some of the undoubted benefits of teaching as driven by current emphases are outweighed by the associated loss of 'balanced instruction.'

The children in Linda's class and in other teachers' classes have offered a compelling rationale for storytelling in the classroom. But storytelling teachers are still difficult to find. In school culture they are considered a bit quixotic or quaint. Storytellers tilt at the great windmills of paper and books, computers and keyboards, reference materials and resource centres, for storytelling is a practice that harks back to a time of campfires, a time of no paper. Storytellers are also considered remarkable or notable. Students and teachers at Linda's school certainly thought so. On the playground I sometimes a child say who her teacher was: 'Linda Stender.' 'Oh, the storytelling teacher,' was the unfailing reply. When Linda's colleagues asked me about my work, I told them I was studying storytelling in school: they immediately understood why I was in Linda Stender's classroom. 'Of course,' they said, 'she's a real storyteller, isn't she!' Her work was unusual, an anomaly, but not a model to emulate. At the same time, I heard respect and admiration in any reference to her effective teaching work.

Part of the reason there are so few storytelling teachers is because it is not easy to learn about storytelling or get support. It is perhaps even more difficult now than when Linda began. Other storytelling teachers are widely scattered across school districts. They usually work without mentors and don't have colleagues from whom they can learn. Teachers have to make storytelling space for themselves and their students without professional support. When Linda became convinced that storytelling must transform her educational practice, she had to find her own way to incorporate it and work out ways to account for and assess her practice. She looked for books, went to workshops, and found other storytellers. This was a lot of work. Fortunately, she was dedicated.

Most storytelling teachers know there is an inherent conflict in using storytelling in the classroom. As we discussed in chapter 2, there is an uncomfortable tension between the reasons teachers give other educators for storytelling and the reasons they experience, urging them to storytell. Because the culture of the classroom demands a very specific way of learning participation and teaching rationale, storytelling teachers find themselves bending the flexible, yielding language and forms of stories to fit another pedagogy. Earlier I quoted Ruth Sawyer:

> I am decrying ... the telling of stories to impart information or to train in any specified direction. The sooner this unhampering [is] accomplished the more positive and direct will be the approach to our goal, which I take to be creative.
>
>   ... It has been with a kind of horror that I watched eager and intelligent young minds being thumb-screwed under the belief that storytelling could not stand alone as an art, that its reason for existence depended on some extraneous motive. (1962: 32)

Using storytelling as one of several tools in a kit, a way to obtain certain outcomes, is not storytelling pedagogy. Teachers certainly may tap the powerful and flexible language of stories for many curricular needs; and they will surely find their work nourished by the learning relationships implicit in storytelling. But, as a method, it is merely a tool. It can do many things; it crosses disciplines and tremendously varied needs. It can yield the outcomes teachers need. However, where it is persistently instrumentalized, participants are barred from story-world experiences. Imagination, wonder, and motivation are stunted by narrow and constantly forced applications. Children may be unlearning authentic storytelling. School culture has steadily appropriated storytelling as a tool to acculturalize the stories, listeners, and tellers in the classroom. Cut off from its full methodology of abilities, knowledges, and learning life relationships, its educative integrity and full potential are blunted. Storytelling must be considered a methodology, not just a method. It is an integrity of practices.

Storytelling teachers may (not surprisingly) be reluctant to admit it, but their primary reason for storytelling is not to help children learn to read, figure out a problem, remember history, develop language arts abilities, or improve artwork. These are some of the other outcomes.

They storytell to satisfy the human longing for talking together, thinking together about life, and imagining possibilities with a story. This is an aesthetic yearning. When a storytelling teacher opens the circle of talking and listening with a story, she does so because of the quality of experience and learning that happens there. That is what makes storytellers and story-listeners radically change their way of teaching. In this book I have given good reasons for storytelling in school. In the current educational climate I have briefly outlined, it is especially necessary to consider the vital pedagogy and learning that happens during a storytelling.

For well over a decade, storytellers and teachers have sought to articulate the reason for storytelling. We have looked for a rationale or theory consistent with the phenomenon that transforms teaching. Michael Rosen comments:

> As yet no major work has appeared which presents a coherent educational theory of narrative. Even more significant, perhaps, we have no full accounts of narrative in the classroom by teachers who believe in it as a pillar of the curriculum and who have translated that belief into practice. (1988: 164)

More than a decade later R. Craig Roney similarly challenged researchers, storytellers, and educators, writing that

> too little research exists [and even] far fewer studies [examine] the effect of storytelling on the cognitive and affective aspects of a children's growth towards literacy. (2001: 116)

I've read and studied too long to believe my 'coherent educational theory of narrative' is definitive. As a storyteller I know that every story needs another story. As a researcher I know that each new understanding raises new questions and needs more answers. However, I have certainly demonstrated how storytelling richly nourishes literacy and language abilities for the children in Linda's room.

Storytelling gets at the heart of education, our reason for schools. We want to help our children find what they need to make their way through the world. They need the power and abilities to break down walls that restrict learning. They need compassion and courage to bring their journey's companions into a just community. They need fearless curiosity to explore ever-changing circumstances while pressing joyfully forward. Children need the hope or magical sense of a world imbued with possibilities. Storytelling teaches these things. The teacher who tells stories plants story-seeds that will yield sustenance and wisdom for the long roads ahead.

Children need this, for surely they will meet with sorrow, beauty, anguish, and sometimes Wonder on their ways through the world. Teachers, caregivers, and storytellers must help our children get ready to meet the world and to come out singing and stomping and ready to meet giants. And afterwards?: tell us a new story.

12 New Storytelling Teachers

Perhaps you are a teacher and you would like to open up storyworlds in your classroom. The accounts of what happened during and after storytelling in Linda Stender's room made you determined to include the full pedagogy of storytelling in your classroom, made you want the benefits we have discussed. But you have never told a long-ish story to a group of waiting listeners. You may feel puzzled about how to begin and a bit anxious about trying it. In this chapter, I offer some encouragement and guidance.

Those who have read to this point have already had some guidance: Linda has modelled good storytelling practices. Additionally, at the back of his book, there is a list of resources for new storytellers. Readers can also turn to the Internet and discover storytelling organizations, groups of tellers and listeners, festivals and workshops that support learning about storytelling. Most important, new tellers should know that the goal is within easy reach. Storytelling is the lightest of arts. No special tricks, materials, or conditions are necessary to practise it. A teller has two simple needs: the company of listeners and a good story in mind. For teachers, these needs are almost automatically met: the listeners are in place and the stories are suggested by the circumstance. Storytelling teachers have a ready learning place. Just as swimming is learned in the water, not on the dock, storytelling is learned inside the circles of telling and listening. Jump in! Perhaps, new storytellers also need a bit of courage. Western culture is so accustomed to stories being in folded within books and other textual support that it has become difficult to speak without scripts, notes, or outlines.

Preparing to storytell has four main parts: listening for storytelling; finding a story; learning the story; and finally, telling the story. I will take up each of these in turn.

Listening for Storytelling

If you are new to storytelling, it is important to find a place where stories are being told. The Internet is your best guide to finding them. There are festivals, workshops, and other gatherings that help new storytellers learn about possibilities for telling and the work of listening. Most larger cities and towns have a storytelling group that gathers regularly. They warmly welcome new listeners. Try a few different venues, like a gathering, a workshop, or a special event.

Put yourself in the company of others, imaginating with a story. This will teach you about being a listener among listeners and about interruptions, effective strategies, and the importance of being able to hear and see the teller. Listening experiences are the best way to learn what is needed to 'get into' a story and imaginate more easily. You'll also discover the varied ways in which audiences can participate.

New tellers will discover that storytellers are as different from each other as any other group of persons. A story can be told in so many ways. Some tellers use special voices, some use just their ordinary talking voice. Some tellers use lots of gestures and expressions and some hardly use any at all. Some storytellers use puppets, costumes, and other aids while many others simply get up in their street clothes and tell a fantastic tale. There is so much difference among tellers that you should be delighted and encouraged. Every person has her or his way of being a storyteller. In fact, the best storytellers are perfectly themselves: flamboyant, a bit shy, chatty, laconic, and so on. They tell the story without artifice. A storyteller who is authentic frees the story to move easily from the teller's mind to be imagined in the listener's. This is good news for all of us. Be yourself when you tell your story, your best story-self.

Storytelling is a listening act. A teller listens to her listeners; Linda illustrated this well. Listeners let their teller know where the story lags or where it needs more explanation. A storyteller learns about the story in the midst of storytelling. Listeners reveal funny spots in a story that the storyteller did not even realize were there, or will suggest that a pause needs to be longer to increase tension and drama. In the midst of telling, it will become apparent that a gesture is more eloquent than a word. Storytellers often find they need to 're-paint' a picture, explain a word, warn a straying child, increase their volume, or use less or more eye contact. Over time, they learn to understand the myriad of listeners' expressions, postures, attention and inattentiveness, as these guide them. And this takes practice. And this is why it is important to start soon and start small.

Finding a Story

A storyteller needs a story. That sounds simple; but if you are like most storytellers, you're bound to discover that finding the story is not easy. It demands diligent effort. Listen, read, and look for stories all the time. It is a lot like shopping for something to wear when you're uncertain of what it is you're looking for until you meet it on a rack.

Most tellers today find their stories in books. Anthologies, picture books, story collections are waiting on the shelves. There are also many good books by teacher-tellers that include stories that 'tell well.' Read folk tale collections, fairy tales, legends, short stories, and joke books. Classroom storytellers also find and choose a story because of a certain subject being studied, a certain celebratory season of the year, or the press of some current event. Once in a while, a story falls on the teller's lap like manna from a heaven. There are some storytellers who write their own stories. Athough there is much available, I think it is fair to say that all storytellers work hard to find the story they need.

The story you want is the one that snags your interest and imagination. It seems somehow significant, has substance and freshness. From the first encounter, the teller feels like the story needs to be shared. The story might be ridiculous, perplexing, awfully sad, or have an ending that is too good to be true. In all cases the first impulse is, 'Oh! What a good story. I like it.' This is an important part of choosing a story. The storyteller must like the story, a lot. Be careful not to select a story solely to teach a lesson. If your first thought was about the lesson, it is probably not the story to tell. It is more likely a lesson for a think-about than sink-into story. A strongly didactic purpose tends to get in the way of imagining. Trust wise listeners to enter and find what they need in a good story.

This is a bit of a tricky aspect. Of course the storyteller is purposeful in choosing a story. For their joy, laughter, sense of triumph, or poignancy, teacher-storytellers choose stories that illuminate life. But when the story is released for the listeners' storyworld making, children must be freed to imagine their way in and come out with the learning that was pertinent. Remember that children in Linda's class tugged out a variety of different but significant lessons from one story,

'The Field.' Children will find what they need in their deep imaginative places without you, just with the story.

A good story snags imagination with its visual qualities. The reader-teller almost immediately imagines parts of it. It provokes curiosity. Images, motions, the colours and sounds of the story jostle in the reader-teller's mind. It feels like a storyworld the teller would like to enter.

For the first storytellings, choose stories that are short enough to remember. They need to be concise and have strong story-patterns. New storytellers are not advised to choose a story like 'Theseus and the Minatour' for a first storytelling. Linda did not choose it for her early storytelling either, for two good reasons. First, the beginning of the school year was too busy for her to keep such a big story in her mind. Second, her students were learning to listen. A storytelling teacher needs to realize that, in the beginning, students also have to learn how to listen to and participate during a storytelling. As the teller grows increasingly confident and is ready to tell longer, more complex stories, listeners will have developed corresponding abilities to settle into listening and imaginate their way into storyworlds. They will develop the same protocols as Linda's children, quieting themselves, paying attention, and working for the opportunity to get into their storyworlds.

New tellers are well advised to begin with small fables and jokes that are easy to remember, or to choose a story that is already well known. For example, 'Rumpelstiltskin' was one of Linda's early choices. It may be an old, familiar story, but it was so well received that children didn't pay attention to the recess bell. Two children enjoyed this old story so much that they later picked up a book rather than reviewing their hockey cards. Today many storytellers find it rewarding to choose one of the good stories exhausted and even distorted by Disney. It is exciting to discover the power of a story that has been told and retold for centuries. If you do this, find the older versions or more accurate historical accounts and track down several rewritings of the tale. If you've never done this before, you will find yourself delighted, shocked, and energized. Tell it your own way. Your children will enjoy plunging easily into a familiar storyworld and will relish finding new vistas, making changes, and meeting new people there.

Folk tales are tellers' favoured stories. They make excellent starting blocks and storyteller's fare for at least two good reasons. First, originally oral stories were developed to be easily remembered. They are concise in shape and have patterns of images, events, and words. The mnemonics are already in the story. Second, and importantly, these stories are about significant human experiences. Over generations of telling, they were developed to focus on the dilemmas, issues, experiences, and quirks of human nature that are significant to us. Many folk tales include listener participation. In stories like 'Abiyoyo' or 'Sody Salaradus' the teller can share some of the storytelling work with the listeners.

One important caution: if then you decide to take a story from a culture that is not familiar to you, learn about where the story came from. Read other stories from the same cultural milieu. Find out some of the history and origins of the story and its tellers. Learn about the land and language of the story. Try very hard to find someone for whom the story is familiar, and talk to him or her about it. Although stories can teach us much about other lives, times, and places, using them to 'teach children about different cultures' may risk violating the integrity and sanctity of the story. And there are stories that are truly inviolable; they have sacred qualities that often escape the understanding of strangers.

Learning the Story

You have chosen your story. If you are like most storytellers, you found your story fastened to a page; now you need to extract it from the book. Find the courage to tell the story. That is why it is important to begin with stories small enough to remember. It is also important to give yourself enough time to get into the story and 'live' through it several times before you tell it. Remember that Linda, who was an experienced storyteller of many years and had a large repertoire, told only two or three times a month. If you tell a story just once a month, at the most, for your first year, that's enough. You'll gradually do it more often.

A common question for a storyteller is, 'How do you remember all that?' Think of it this way: most of us can easily remember something important that happened to us. Linda knew her stories in the same way a person remembers an important experience, simply recalling what happened and how it happened. It is our life-long dependence on paper, scripts, notes, and outlines that suggests a story is hard to remember. Here I can only urge new tellers to go ahead: try it. My experiences and those of others suggest that remembering a story is easier than remembering a grocery list. A story is sticky.

In what follows, I give the 'steps' for learning a story that work well for me. These do not make a rule: each teller finds his or her own way.

After finding a good story for telling, carefully read and reread the story. Read it like a storyteller: do not skim over the words. Read all of them, seeing and tasting them. Read the story again, out loud. All this reading helps you learn word choice possibilities and experience the sound of the story, its flow, pace of events, and rhythms. When you think you can remember the names of characters and everything that happened, put the paper away (immediately!).

Tell the story out loud to yourself. I do this when I am busy with something that does not demand thinking, like washing dishes or driving down a highway or just before I go to sleep. In this second part of learning the story, you free yourself from the noose of the page and lodge the story in your own imagination and language.

You do *not* need to memorize the words of the story. At the same time, we can't forget that words have power. We saw and heard that in Linda's storytelling. This is a difficult point for new tellers as well as old ones. I suggest keeping a few good phrases and a few of the especially lovely words. Remember how words like 'lintel' and 'skittered' were caught by Linda's listeners. Keep a few words, but do not be trapped or halted by the search for the 'right words.' It is good to remember what Kyla said: 'A *book* gots words.' The teller has a story. The most important thing is to have an authentic 'remembering' voice in the telling. Tell the story from your heart and out of your pleasure in the story. Words come afterwards.

Telling the Story

Linda's routines illustrate good storytelling practices. She always began by telling the children that they were going to have a storytelling. She changed the way they were sitting. This helped children prepare to listen and participate in a different way. She ensured that every child could see her whole face and hear her voice. This made the connection between teller, story, and listener strong.

Linda told her stories mostly from her teacher's 'spinning chair.' Although she was seated, she was vitally alert, poised, and active. I was often impressed by how the chair's flexibility was useful to her telling. She could turn, move back wards and forwards in it. She could adjust the height. However, every storyteller finds the most comfortable position from which to tell. The storyteller can stand, lean on a table, use a special stool, move around, or be still. The storyteller can arrange the space into a circle of listeners; have children on mats, in rows, on chairs, on pillows, or in desks. In my experience it matters that you change the way children sit, to free them from desks and evoke the sense of company.

Looking over the class, Linda would check for potential 'trouble spots.' She prevented every kind of interruption as much as she could. She shut the door and usually did storytelling during a time of day that was less prone to interruptions. Knowing how distressing and harmful these are to storyworld experience, all storytellers must take care to guard against them. Turn off a noisy fan, hang a sign on your door, and plead with your administration for a 'no-PA' time.

Just before starting the story, Linda gave a little reason for telling it. Her explanations were not substantial enough to construct a hurdle before the story, just a little connecting point between herself, the story, and the reason for its being there. This links the story, listener, and teller. Then she began promptly.

Linda took her time in telling; you should too. Don't hurry. Your listeners depend on every word. They need to hear each piece of the story, make it, and set it in its place. They are making pictures, arranging and rearranging images and characters. Don't rush. And don't forget that the small bits of silence, the pauses, are perhaps the most eloquent of all. Use them at important moments.

Perhaps the most frightening aspect of storytelling is the possibility that you will forget. Don't worry about that. Leave your book or your notes available but on the other side of the room, too far away to reach for them. If you forget, you can do one of two things. Just keep going and change the so-called original story. No one in the classroom is holding a script; you are the story. But if you can't do that, pause, get up, pick up your papers, find your place and read what you need. Put down the papers and go on telling. Do not apologize or even explain: this interrupts the story. If you really think it's necessary, you can tell your class what happened afterwards.

When you are finished telling the story, give it a few minutes: be a storyteller and not a teacher for a few moments more. Keep the space free enough for listeners to come clambering back into the classroom, still drenched with their storyworld time. Children will be a bit tired. Don't expect them to have deep conversations and stunning insights or even to respond to your questions with much interest at that time. They might or they might not. Remember that Linda did activities and retellings *the next day*. In fact, you can take longer than that if necessary.

If you've never done this kind of storytelling in your classroom before, you'll find that a great blast of fresh air has blown through your room. It reaches well beyond the circle of telling and listening, invigorating all the other things you do with students. It promises to nourish all those activities immediately related to thinking with a story: reading and writing; learning about characterization, symbol, irony, and metaphor; and thinking about tough issues and ideas. As an educator, you will feel satisfied, even thrilled to note the growth in students' vocabularies, language abilities, and learning relationships. Linda's class has demonstrated this potential.

But she and other storytellers tell stories for more than that reason. In the deep hush cast by storyworld-making, another syllabus was loosed. The subjects are possibility, courage, companionship, and humanity. By means of imagination, listeners go beyond what can be seen, heard, or touched. Unlimited by the classroom, they learn about the wide, wide world. Experimenting with life in the storyworld, they learn empathy for others and gain insight about themselves. The gift of a story told and shared in the presence of each other may become the hope, wisdom, and laughter needed over the course of a lifetime. May my readers receive and give this gift.

APPENDIX A
Dates of Interviews with Children

I began interviews in October, when children had become familiar with me. All caregivers signed permission. Children could decline by simply talking to Linda, their caregivers, another teacher or me. All the children's names are pseudonyms. In the classroom, Linda let me explain what would happen. I demonstrated the tape recorder's role. Interviews were conducted in another room with the door open. All children were posed exactly the same questions, but the order sometimes changed. The shortest interviews were about 35 minutes (Leon and Natisha) and the longest were nearly 90 minutes (Bekkah and Lyla). Children seemed very pleased about coming for the interviews. They were unfailingly thoughtful, wise, and friendly. These sessions were a gift to me, to all of us learning about children's experiences of listening to stories.

1.	1 October 2002	Kyla		13.	28 November	Layla
2.	3 October	Buzz		14.	2 December	Daron
3.	7 October	Kreena		15.	5 December	Shasu
4.	10 October	Leon		16.	10 December	Taja
5.	16 October	Zara		17.	14 January 2003	Azun
6.	22 October	Taza		18.	16 January	Bekkah
7.	29 October	Terry		19.	21 January	Kate
8.	31 October	Natisha		20.	23 January	Pender
9.	5 November	Tych		21.	23 January	Alt
10.	12 November	Jack		22.	24 January	Moe[1]
11.	14 November	Mila		23.	28 January	Danielle
12.	26 November	Violet		24.	28 January	Marcus

---

1. A new student. I did not include his interview in the data. However, he was included for social reasons.

APPENDIX B
The Classroom

Fig. B-1. The three windows on the left belong to Linda's Grade 4/5 classroom.

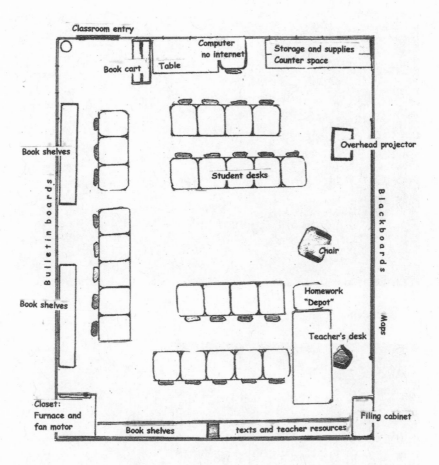

Fig. B-2. A diagram of how the desks, school equipment, and materials in the room were arranged. As this diagram indicates, space to move about is limited.

Seating arrangements were changed roughly every month. Linda had the Grade 5s sit with each other. They took up one of the three blocks of desks.

When Linda called the children for a storytelling, they sat in the centre space of the room, in front of the chair. During the class meeting, the chair – a 'spinning chair' – was taken from behind Linda's desk. The computer was not used once during my time in the classroom.

Fig. B-3. A view of Linda's desk from the back of the classroom.

Fig. B-4. This view is from the back of the classroom, looking towards the front. The centre space is where Linda told stories.

APPENDIX C
Class Meeting

All the children had this agenda glued into their class meeting duo-tang notebooks. Class meetings followed the order of subjects indicated and children chose to make presentations and talk about them in a variety of ways.

Class Meeting

We will have class meeting every _____, _____, and _____.

1. **Chairperson.**
   a. Runs the classroom meeting
   b. Waits for quiet
   c. When the presenter is finished, asks the class for applause and then asks for comments, questions or suggestions
   d. Tries to keep the meeting running on time
   e. Makes sure everybody has a chance to speak
   f. Asks for compliments, final thoughts or suggestions at the end of the meeting from the entire class

2. **World News**
   a. Find an interesting article from the newspaper (Sun, Province, or local New Westminster), clip it out and glue it into class meeting book.
   b. Read over your article. Ask someone at home to read it with you.
   c. Write a summary (4 to 6 sentences) about the article in your class meeting book.
   d. In your summary tell us:
      - What the article is about?
      - Where did the event take place?
      - When did the event take place?
      - What do you think – opinions, impressions?

3. **Personal News**
   a. In your class meeting book, write some news about your personal or family life. You may want to write about:
      - An upcoming event
      - Things you did or are going to do on the weekend
      - Something you are excited about
      - Something you enjoy doing
      - Special collections or hobbies
      - Things you like

---

4. **Sports**

    a.   Find an article in the newspaper about a recent sports event or get the information from the television or from the radio

    b.   Tell about a game you or someone you know played

    c.   Write a summary about the event, telling:

                – Who was involved?

                – What the sport activity is?

                – The final score?

                – Any highlights?

5. **School News**

    a.   Share some interesting information about what is happening or going to happen at school.

    b.   Share some information about something that is happening or has happened in the neighborhood.

6. **Book Talk**

    a.   Name the title of the book

    b.   Name the author and illustrator

    c.   Tell if the story is fiction (made-up story) or non-fiction (true events).

    d.   Choose an interesting passage to read to the class. It would be a good idea to bookmark the page before the class meeting begins.

    e.   Tell why you chose that passage

    f.   Tell **why** or **why not** you would recommend this book to others.

7. **Weather**

    a.   Is responsible for finding the weather conditions in the newspaper, TV, or radio

    b.   Finds the **sunrise, sunset, hours of daylight, temperature**

    c.   Record this information in your class meeting book

8. **Fantastic Fact**

    a.   Shares something interesting and fantastic with the class

    b.   Writes it in the class meeting book

    c.   You might want to look through non-fiction books or the Guiness Book of Records or the Internet.

9. **Joke of the Day**

    a.   Brings up to three jokes or riddles for the class. The jokes need to be written or glued into your class meeting book.

10. **Arts Report**

    a.   Bring something to school to share with the class. You may choose to share:

                – something about your religion or heritage

                – something you have made

                – something you got on a trip or someone got for you

APPENDIX D
Languages Spoken by Children

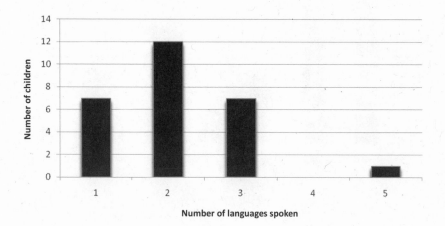

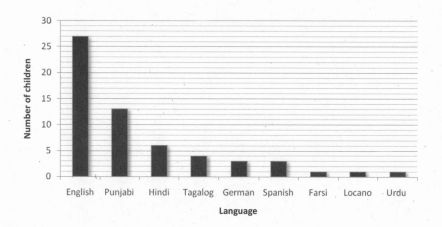

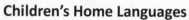

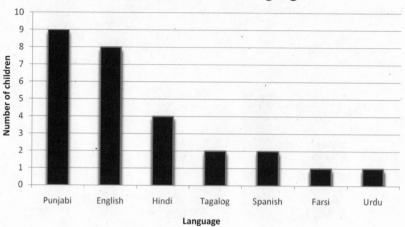

APPENDIX E
Stories Told in the Classroom

Children Retell the Story of a Film

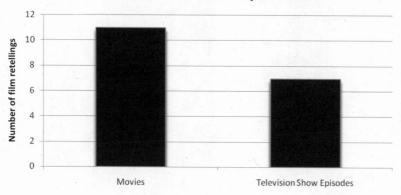

Children Retell the Story of a Book

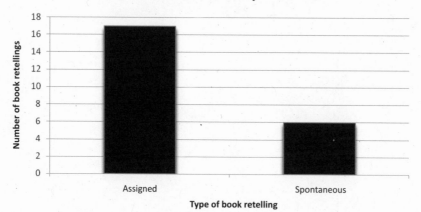

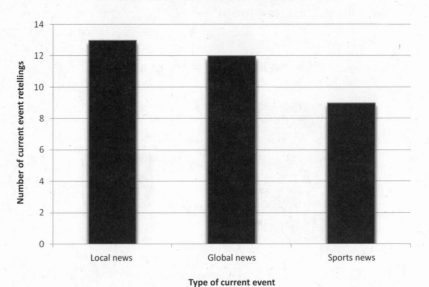

Stories Told during Class Meetings

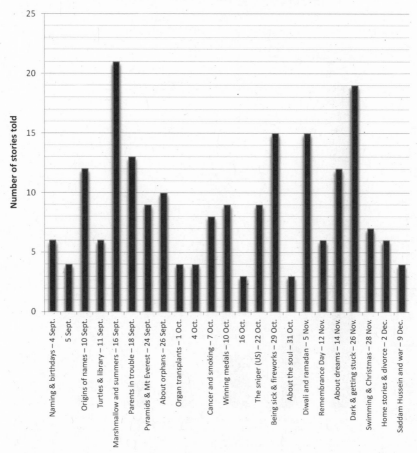

Topic and date

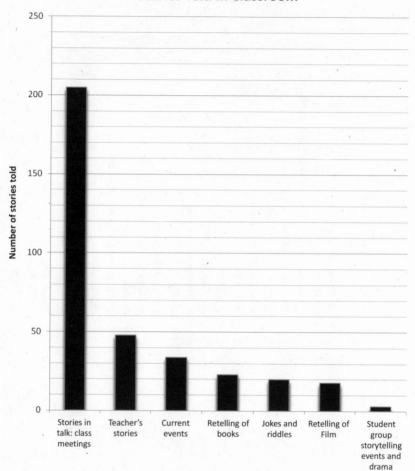

Teacher's Stories

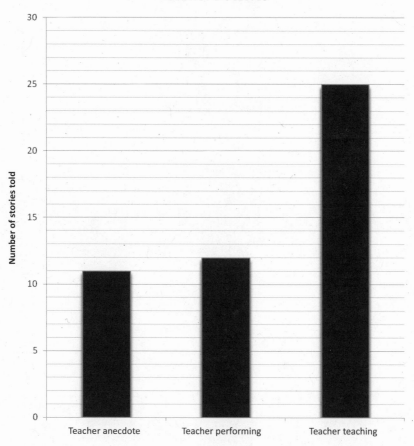

Notes

1 Growing into Storytelling

1 The literacy project was based Paolo Freire's: *Pedagogy of the Oppressed*. His work leads to reading and writing that meaningfully emerge from learners' experiences, interests, and needs. The project literacy, was directed by Karanke Marah. Currently, adult literacy classes are still regularly held across northeastern Sierra Leone (Koinandugu district). Today several organizations, including Mr Marah's, conduct adult literacy teaching.

2 Yagbe Tarawale and Siri Suwari were the women's storytellers. Mamorie Marah, the chief's son and storyteller, told stories with the authority of a teacher and judge or formal arbitrator. They are from Badala, Sierra Leone, where I lived from 1981 to 1985. Since that time, the village has grown considerably and become an important market town. However, a ten-year civil war (1991–2001) dramatically changed life in Badala. All three of these storytellers were killed. When I visited in 2001, I learned that in Badala more than six hundred lives were brutally ended, and every house was destroyed.

3 All then members of the Toronto School of Storytelling and currently members of Storytellers of Canada, which formed later. I am a co-founding member of the latter.

2 Linda Stender: The Storytelling Teacher

1 Laura Simms is a storyteller, writer, and teacher of storytellers and is based in New York. Linda Stender was inspired to take up storytelling in a workshop she took with Simms. See http://www.laurasimms.com/.

2 Dunc Shields is a Vancouver storyteller, writer, and retired fisherman. Paul Yee is a West Coast writer whose work concerns Chinese immigrant

experience in Canada and includes *Tales from Gold Mountain* (1989), *Roses Sing on Snow* (1991), and *Ghost Train* (1996).

3 See Further Resources for a selected list of relevant works.

4 In Canada four universities offer courses in which students can learn about storytelling: Cape Breton University in Nova Scotia, Memorial University in Newfoundland, Trent University in Ontario, and the University of Alberta. Only the University of Alberta locates 'Storytelling' near education, in Library Sciences. Of the sixty-five higher education institutions listed by the Storytelling in Higher Education Special Interest Group of the National Storytelling Network (USA), ten universities offer coursework for education in schools. Note that just two of these are housed in a teacher education program. See http://shesig.pbwiki.com/.

4 Landscape and Soundscape

1 A few other works that emphasize the relationship between place and storytelling are Cruikshank (1990, 1998), Basso (1996), and Lopez (1988).

2 Jerome Bruner's *The Culture of Education* (1996) offers further insights and a deeper, thicker description of what this means for Canadian and American schools.

3 All children's names are pseudonyms.

4 Phone interview with author, 14 2003. The Department of Funding and Allocation in the British Columbia Ministry of Education collated the figure of twenty-one hundred from school district reports. Glen Seredynski notes that this does not represent the number of classes held in portable buildings. Some are leased for daycare, some function as storage facilities, some provide for maintenance needs, and others are being warehoused for future needs. Still, optimistic arithmetic suggests that as many as thirty-two thousand children go to school in similar circumstances.

5 Marshall McLuhan's famous dictum 'the medium is the message' is further discussed in Jack Goody's *The Interface between the Written and the Oral* (1993), Walter Ong's *Orality and Literacy* (1982), and Sylvia Scribner and Michael Cole's *The Psychology of Literacy* (1981). Many other works demonstrate the multitude of ways in which oral communication significantly diverges from written communication in form, content, and function.

6 See Anthony Pelligrini et al.'s study of children's playground games and adjustment to school (2002: 1010).

7 See Howard Gardner (1991: 149–55).

5 What's Storytelling

1 Other writers and scholars describe storytelling as the use of a specific kind of language. Jerome Bruner (1996) talks about 'narrative thinking' instead of 'logical-scientific thinking.' Kieran Egan (1997) distinguishes story language as 'mythic.' Charles Taylor (1987: 215–91) describes the difference as one between associative and designative language. Barry Lopez (1988) writes about story-language as speaking for our 'inner landscape' rather than the shared 'outer landscape.' For Northrop Frye (1963), stories are the language of imagination.
2 This is the principle of reading response theory.
3 See Karen Nelson's *Narratives from the Crib* (1989) for an example of earliest childhood talk that uses stories to think about experience. Maureen Kendrick's *Play, Literacy, and Culture* (2003) is a close study of a child who is storying in her play, learning about her life.

6 Talking, Thinking, and Imagining with a Story

1 Grimm's Tale 029, the Grimm's collection, 'The Devil's Three Gold Hairs.' The story is variously titled in folk tale collections, on the Web, and in several children's picture books and storybook collections: 'The Devil with the Three Golden Hairs,' 'Three Golden Hairs,' or 'The Giant and Three Golden Hairs.' It has also been made into a movie directed by Enzo Peri (1977).

8 Talking with Stories

1 Vivian Paley's writings are rarely included in lists of readings about 'storytelling.' Her work is more commonly referenced as 'play curricula.' Time for free play and storytelling is possible in a kindergarten room, but is not found in grade 4–5 classrooms. In Paley's more recent book, *A Child's Work: The Importance of Fantasy Play* (2004), she also describes how the focus on content knowledge and reading skills crowds out room for important play-talk still available in a few kindergarten rooms. Vivian Paley's work extends over and draws from her 37 years of teaching.
2 The work of Lev Vygotsky (1962) showed the vitality and significance of the space between talkers and listeners. It is the 'zone' in which learning happens. Teaching practices have been developed on the basis of his seminal work; see Lee and Smagorinsky (2000) and Wertsch (1985). Betty Hart and Todd Risely's work (1995, 2003) has shown a correlation between children's language use at home and their reading abilities at school. The

spoken interactions children experience – content and function – affect their learning to read. The idea that socially interactive talk matters very much in learning is understood by language theorists and teaching practitioners.

3 Researchers sent questionnaires to 2,933 British Columbian women under the age of 75. The survey suggested that girls who smoke in adolescence have a 70 per cent risk of breast cancer. The report is also posted on the website of the Canadian Association for the Advancement of Women and Sport and Physical Activity, http://www.caaws.ca/Whats New/2002/oct/smokers.

4 'Sody Saleratus' is a traditionally oral story. It's been used to make picture books, like those authored by George Pilling and Aubrey Davis. It is found in several collections of good stories for storytellers; see Margaret Read MacDonald's *Twenty Tellable Tales* (1986) or Richard Chase's *Grandfather Tales* (2003). The second part of the name is spelled variously: 'Sallyratus,' 'Sallyrytus,' 'Sallyritus,' or 'Sallaradus'; and sometimes the first part, 'Sody,' is omitted. 'Sody Saleratus' is the grandmother's word for baking soda!

5 The 'Beltway Snipers' were arrested in Washington, DC, on 24 October, 2002. They were John Allen Muhammad and Lee Boyd Malvo, who posed as Muhammad's son. In a three-week shooting spree they killed 10 people and injured others. Linda's children, in spite of the maps and instructions, struggled to differentiate Washington state and Washington, DC. They worried about the proximity of the snipers because our school, in British Columbia, was close to the border with Washington state.

6 Finnegan includes riddles in her description of traditionally oral narratives with 'conversational genres' (1996, p. 151). As Green writes 'the riddle is one of the oldest and most culturally widespread of folklore genres' (1992, p. 134). Folklore scholars (Abrahams and Dundes 1973: 129–43), oral language scholars (e.g., Ong, 1982: 43–5), and those who study oral genre all list the riddle as a distinctive interaction between tellers and listeners that belongs in oral narrative tradition. It is part of a genre of verbal interactions in which participants play at outwitting, each other.

7 Riddles and jokes can be considered part of a dialectic Mikhail Bakhtin describes as the language of laughter. In *The Dialogic Imagination* (1981: 68–83) he looks at parody and jokes used to manage positions, languages, and power differences. In *Rabelais and His World* (1984) he describes the important role of the carnival in medieval times. Participants, usually sharply divided by barriers of status, economics, profession and other social markers, jostled as equals, facilitated by laughter-language.

8 Scholars and collectors frequently lump these together. See Yolen's *Favorite Folktales From Around the World* (1988) or Abrahams and Dundes' (1972)

chapter on 'riddles' that carries examples of wit-testing questions as well as the sorts of jokes I recount in these pages.

9 This again indicates how we can think of the school as exerting hegemonic power.

10 Children's use of jokes and ritual insults challenge power structures and open them to the 'corrective of laughter' (Bakhtin, 1981: 59). Riddles and jokes express what Bakhtin called social life's 'ritual roots of laughter' (1981: 57–8). He describes 'parodic' or joking language that provokes laugher as important to challenging assumptions of the 'straightforward genres, languages, styles, voices.' As mentioned above, Bakhtin calls these forms our 'laughing words' (p. 59). He goes on to show that laughter violates social power strictures. Thus, riddles and jokes are formal constructions developed in storytelling tradition to open spaces for restrained voices.

11 Such disruptive but socially bonding and playful kinds of talk were recorded and discussed by Shirley Brice Heath as 'talking junk' (1999: 174–9). Anne Haas Dyson in her classroom study calls this 'verbal gaming' (e.g., 1997: 214).

9 Imaginating

1 'The Field' is a story about two armies fighting over a stony field on which one tree stands. In the course of the fight a mother bird is killed. A soldier sees this and, at great risk to himself, stops fighting and carries away the nest with the surviving baby birds in his helmet. The Iroquois folk legend can be found at http://pyramidmesa.netfirms.com/iroquois2.html. It is also included in many available collections of First Nations traditionally oral stories.

2 Reading through Maria Tatar's collection in her *The Annotated Classic Fairy Tales* (2002) bears out the diverse and persistent 'retellings' of folk tales in western Germanic tradition.

3 In fact, school as a cultural institution does not value storytelling as a way of thinking, talking, and learning. Jerome Bruner in *The Culture of Education* (1996), writes, 'There appear to be two broad ways in which human beings organize and manage their knowledge of the world, indeed structure even their immediate experience: one seems more specialized for treating of physical 'things,' the other for treating of people and their plights. These are conventionally known as *logical-scientific* thinking and *narrative* thinking' (39). He goes on describe the treatment of more narrative arts as more 'decorative' and inexplicably treated as a 'natural ability' (40). His work

offers a explanation of how school privileges other discourses and relationships over storytelling.

4 From Pete Seeger's book of the same title. Those who have read this book
will notice that Linda has developed her own version of this story.

5 She told me this in a conversation after school. Oddly enough, the children's
enthusiasm about sitting on the floor conflicts with their own comments
about how uncomfortable and dirty the floor is (Zara, 22 October). Significantly, as Zara described her experience, the 'uncomfortableness' is mitigated
by the pleasure of close company and later forgotten during story-listening.

6 Sheila Dailey (1994), in her introduction to her edited collection *Tales as
Tools* (1994). Storytellers write about their work on p. vii.

7 Quoted in Mooney and Holt's *Storyteller's Guide* (1996: 149). Flora Joy is a
well-known storyteller, writer, and teacher of storytelling. Professor emeri-
tus of Storytelling at Eastern Tennessee State University, she founded their
Storytelling Master's Degree Program in Storytelling. She also set up the
National Storytelling Youth Olympics.

8 Shasu also used the term 'imaginating' when she probably meant imagining. Layla coined the word to describe the effort of 'making pictures.' The
coined word aptly captures the effort involved in making images, and is
wonderfully specific. I gratefully take it up – but point out that I have
changed her meaning. This will become clearer below: making up the pictures prepares the way into the deep imaginative experience of being inside
a storyworld. When I talk about 'what's happening' there, I say children are
imaginating. Currently there is no word to distinguish such an interaction
with a story from the work of 'making pictures' or deliberately imagining
boxers or queens.

9 I remind the reader that many of the children were not fluent in English.
I have taken care to accurately transcribe children's comments. While I did
not indicate pronunciations in my transcriptions, I do record all their
words. Taza's words are written as he spoke them. They suggest both his
effort to explain something very difficult to explain, as well as his effort to
speak English. I was impressed by his feat of crossing languages to articulate complicated ideas. In fact, when he says 'their minds' it is likely that he
means 'the author's.' Such a response was as complex as it was thoughtful.

10 I am thinking here of animated film, cartoons like Sponge Bob SquarePants,
or *Toy Story* characters who change expressions and postures, yet, whose
form remains remarkably unchanged.

11 When I tried this question on adults who were less familiar with storytelling there were two kinds of answers. One was that they needed a visual
aid, an illustration or object. The second response was bafflement.

12 For example: Silko's *Ceremony* (1986) gives the movement of time that spins from myth into presence and memory. This is a very fine example and explanation of how time moves purposefully yet fluidly inside the story-world. Another, entirely different kind of resource for my thinking is Bakhtin's essay titled 'Forms of Time and Chronotope in the Novel' (1981: 84–258).

13 I remind the reader that I use '…' to indicate silence, hesitation, pausing in speech. These 'pauses' are as significant as the spoken words in their commentary.

14 Not infrequently, children said 'reading' when they meant story *telling*.

15 5 September and 26 November.

16 Ong (1982) writes about the 'psychodynamics of orality' in his discussion of how the historical shift from oral interaction to print interaction over the course of several centuries has reshaped consciousness. I suggest an idea of 'interruption,' as broadly hinted at in his thinking about the static nature of text, might be developed as another characteristic. (See also his earlier work *Interfaces of the Word* [1977]).

17 Tatar and writers who work in psychology and narrative read stories as psychological analogies. A developing field in psychology and narrative inquiry views them as emotional or psychological landscapes. See, for instance, Saris (1995) or Coles (1989). This literature has considerable popular influence on storytelling for meaning and emotional healing. Two widely popular examples are Bly (1990) and Estes (1992). Bettleheim's *Uses of Enchantment*, one of the more influential works in this field, has been discredited by Pollak's 1997 biography.

10 Thinking with Stories

1 See http://www.vancouverstorytelling.org/ for the VSOS's schedule of storytelling events and activities. The regular Sunday evening storytelling is called 'Cric? Crac!' This is the opening invitation traditionally used by Creole storytellers in Haiti. The teller invites, 'Cric?' The audience responds with enthusiasm, 'Crac!' If the enthusiasm isn't strong enough, the teller will reiterate.

2 Paulo Freire in Ivan Shor, *A Pedagogy for liberation* (1987: 98).

3 Jack is here quoting the exact words of the storytelling. This description seems to have been called up with his recall of the image.

4 I don't make the argument here. See the following works that explain the authoritative and inflexible nature of text as it contrasts with spoken communication: Eric Havelock's *The Muse Learns to Write* (1986); David

Henige's 'The Disease of Writing' (1980); Jack Goody's *The Interface between the Written and the Oral* (1993); Walter Ong's *Orality and Literacy* (1982), especially the chapter titled 'The Psychodynamics of Orality'; and Silvia Scribner and Michael Cole's *The Psychology of Literacy* (1981). It's important to realize that the variation in the medium determines the aptness and application of it use. School's prioritizing of text over talk diminishes vital understandings and abilities related to the medium of presence.

5 See *The Woman in the Wall* (Kindl 1997); *The Mouse and the Motorcycle* (Cleary 1998); *Matilda* (Dahl 1988); *The Secret Garden* (Burnett 1988 [1909]); *The Box Car Children* series (G. Warner 1989); *A Series of Unfortunate Events* (Snicket 1999–2007); *Goosebump* series (Stine 1992–2008) *Mary-Kate and Ashley in ACTION.*

6 Rereading develops fluency. However, children still need a variety of genres and topics and increasing levels of difficulty in vocabulary and structure. 'A million times' would be too many to be helpful for reading skills!

7 Rosen's work provides evidence that storytelling experiences to increased student master of vocabulary, sentence structure, sense of pacing, and successful creation of such literary devices as tone, humour, and irony. She also showed that her uses of storytelling to teach writing were astonishingly effective over the longer term. Over the course of five years the percentage of boys who passed their O-levels went from 6 per cent to 29 per cent of graduates. Storytelling created an opportunity for children to practice writing that nourished rich learning.

8 Some readers might ask why I chose this particular writing sample. The main reason is that it was the only set of non-storytelling pieces of writing for which I had a full class set. As well, this assignment was somewhat similar to the storytelling writing assignment that follows: each had a preparatory session, a writing session, and an session for editing. Finally, the time frames were similar.

9 In this Greek myth a young man faces a monstrous creature, part man and part bull, that was kept in a labyrinth belonging to King Minos on the island of Crete. Linda told the story using what she knew of the myth-legend. There are many retellings of this complex story.

10 'Lintel,' the beam over the doorway. Alt has remembered this uncommon vocabulary item.

11 I want to assure readers who know about such testing that I did not comment on Azun's work or direct him in any way. I kept my observations non-intrusive while silently indicating my support and encouragement.

12 This observation can be related to Kermode's *The Sense of an Ending* (1967) and Linde's *Life Stories* (1993).

13 Specifically: Teddy Bear, 4 October; Anne Frank, 12 November; Woodwards Christmas shopping, 28 November; Rick Hansen, 16 September; Terry Fox, 7 October; lemon cookies, 10 September; accident on the bridge, 26 November; hostage-taking, 26 September.

14 I regret that I didn't ask children about these stories during the interview. There were ways in which I might have tested their memory of these stories. I could have asked, 'Do you remember about a girl who was stuck in her house during World War II, or do you know the story about why Rick Hansen is in a wheelchair?' However, I still consider the 'omissions' to be relevant to the data; and the interviews were already about as long as they could be without fatiguing respondents.

15 Kieran Egan's *Teaching as Storytelling* (1990) is fully premised on this understanding.

16 This is related to the difference that is story-language, which I briefly discussed in chapter 5. The following writers especially helped me learn about this aspect: Keith Basso (1996); Walter Benjamin, (1968); Jerome Bruner (1987, 1990); Kieran Egan (1997); Northrop Frye (1963); Sean Kane (1994); Frank Kermode (1967); Barry Lopez (1988); Paul Ricoeur (1992); and Charles Taylor (1987).

17 Billy Teare is an Irish storyteller. He is internationally known by story-listeners, who also appreciate his juggling, music, and highly interactive presence. His workshops concerning memory, learning, and storytelling are popular, well reviewed, and adopted for practice.

18 Her description, not mine.

19 See especially Northrop Frye, *The Educated Imagination* (1963).

11 A Pedagogy of Storytelling

1 Two of the books were Roald Dahl's *George's Marvelous Medicine* (1997) and Phillip Pullman's *I Was a Rat* (1999).

2 Betty Hart and Todd Risley, 'The Early Catastrophe' (2002); see also Hart and Risely (1995).

Works Cited

Abrahams, Roger D., and Alan Dundes. 1972. 'Riddles.' In *Folklore and Folklife: An Introduction*, ed. R.M. Dorson. Chicago: University of Chicago Press.

Applebee, Arthur N. 1996. *Curriculum as Conversation*. Chicago: University of Chicago Press.

Bakhtin, Mikhail Mikhailovich. 1981. *The Dialogic Imagination: Four Essays by M.M. Bakhtin*. Trans. M. Holquist and C. Emerson. Austin: University of Texas Press.

– 1981. Forms of Time and Chronotope in the Novel. In *The Dialogic Imagination: Four essays by M.M. Bakhtin*. Austin: University of Texas Press.

– 1984. *Rabelais and His World*. Bloomington: Indiana University Press.

Barton, Bob. 1986. Tell Me Another: Storytelling and Reading at Home. Markham, ON.: Pembroke.

– 1992. *Stories to Tell*. Markham, ON: Pembroke.

– 2000. *Telling Stories Your Way: Storytelling and Reading Aloud in the Classroom*. Markham, ON: Pembroke.

Barton, Bob, and David Booth. 1990. *Stories in the Classroom: Storytelling, Reading Aloud and Role-playing with Children*. Portsmouth, NH: Heinemann.

Basso, Kieth H. 1996. *Wisdom Sits in Places: Landscape and Language among the Western Apache*. Albuquerque: University of New Mexico Press.

Benjamin, Walter. 1968. Chapter entitled 'The Storyteller: Reflections on the Works of Nikolai Leskov.' In Benjamin, *Illuminations: Essay and Reflections*. New York: Schocken Books.

Bettleheim, Bruno. 1977. *The Uses of Enchantment*. New York: Vintage.

Bly, Robert. 1987. *Actual Minds, Possible Words*. Cambridge, MA: Harvard University Press.

– 1990. *Acts of Meaning*. Cambridge, MA: Harvard University Press

– 1990. *Iron John: A Book about Men*. Reading, MA: Addison-Wesley.

– 1996. *The Culture of Education*. Cambridge, MA: Harvard University Press.

Burnett, Frances Hodgson. 1988. *The Secret Garden*. New York: Tom Doherty Associates.

Chase, Richard. 2003. *Grandfather Tales*. Boston: Houghton Mifflin.

Cleary, Beverly. 1998. *The Mouse and the Motorcycle*. New York: HarperCollins.

Coles, Robert. 1989. *The Call of Stories: Teaching and the Moral Imagination*. Boston: Houghton Mifflin.

Cox, Allison, and David H. Albert, eds. 2003. *The Healing Heart ~ Families: Storytelling to Encourage Caring and Healthy Families*. Gabriola Island, BC: New Society.

– 2003. *The Healing Heart ~ Communities: Storytelling to Build Strong and Healthy Communities*. Gabriola Island, BC: New Society.

Cruikshank, Julie. 1990. *Life Lived Like a Story*. Lincoln: University of Nebraska Press.

– 1998. *The Social Life of Stories: Narrative and Knowledge in the Yukon Territory*. Lincoln: University of Nebraska Press.

Dahl, Roald. 1988. *Matilda*. New York: Puffin Books.

– 1997. *George's Marvelous Medicine*. New York: Puffin.

Dailey, Sheila. 1985. *Storytelling: A Creative Teaching Strategy*. Mount Pleasant, MI: Storytime Productions.

Daniels, Harvey. 1994. *Literature Circles: Voice and Choice in the Student-Centered Classroom*. Portland, ME: Stenhouse.

Dorson, Richard M., ed. 1972. *Folklore and Folklife: An Introduction*. Chicago: University of Chicago Press.

Dyson, Anne Haas. 1997. *Writing Superheroes: Contemporary Childhood, Popular Culture and Classroom Literacy*. New York: Teachers College Press.

Egan, Kieran. 1990. *Teaching as Storytelling: An Alternative Approach to Teaching and Curriculum in the Elementary School*. London, ON: Althouse.

– 1992. *Imagination in Teaching and Learning: The Middle School Years*. Chicago: University of Chicago Press.

– 1997. *The Educated Mind: How Cognitive Tools Shape Our Understanding*. Chicago: University of Chicago Press.

Estés, Clarissa Pinkola. 1992. *Women Who Run with the Wolves*. New York: Ballantine.

Fargeon, Eleanor. 2000 [1937]. *Elsie Piddock Skips in Her Sleep*. Cambridge, MA: Candlewick.

Finnegan, Ruth. 1996. Oral Traditions and the Verbal Arts: A Guide to Research Practices. In *ASA Research Methods*, ed. A. Good. New York: Routledge.

Freire, Pauolo. 2000 [1970]. *Pedagogy of the Oppressed*. Trans. Myra. New York: Continuum International.

Frye, Northrop. 1963. *The Educated Imagination: Massey Lectures*. Toronto: Canadian Broadcasting Corporation.

Gardiner, Howard. 1991. *The Unschooled Mind: How Children Think and How Schools Should Teach*. New York: Basic.

Goody, Jack. 1993. *The Interface between the Written and the Oral*. Cambridge: Cambridge University Press.

Green, Thomas. 1992. 'Riddle.' In *Folklore, Cultural Performances, and Popular Entertainments*, ed. R. Bauman. New York: Oxford University Press.

Greene, Ellin. 1996. *Storytelling Art and Technique*. 3rd ed. New Providence, NJ: R.R. Bowker.

Grimm, Wilhelm Carl, Jacob Ludwig, and Nonny Hogrogian. 1983. *The Devil with the Three Golden Hairs*. New York: Random House.

Hart, M. Betty, and Todd R. Risely. 1995. *Meaningful Differences in the Everyday Experience of Young American Children*. Baltimore: Paul H. Brookes.

– 2003. 'The Early Catastrophe: The 30 Million Word Gap by Age 3.' *American Educator* (Spring).

Havelock, Eric. 1986. *The Muse Learns to Write: Reflections on Orality and Literacy from Antiquity to the Present*. Binghamton, NY: Vail Ballou.

Heath, Shirley Brice. 1999 [1983]. *Ways with Words*. Cambridge: Cambridge University Press.

Henige, David. 1980. '"The Disease of Writing"': Ganda and Nyoro Kinglists in a Newly Literate World. In *The African Past Speaks*, ed. J. Miller. Hamden, CT: Archon/Shoe String Press.

Innes, Harold. 1999. *The Bias of Communication*. Toronto: University of Toronto Press.

Jennings, Claire. 1991. *Children as Story-tellers: Developing Language Skills in the Classroom*. Melbourne: Oxford University Press.

Kane, Sean. 1994. *Wisdom of the Mythtellers*. Peterborough, ON: Broadview.

Kendrick, Maureen E. 2003. *Play, Literacy and Culture: Converging Worlds*. Bern: Peter Lang.

Kermode, Frank. 1967. *The Sense of an Ending: Studies in the Theory of Fiction*. New York: Oxford University Press.

Kindl, Patrice. 1997. *The Woman in the Wall*. Boston: Houghton Mifflin.

Lee, Carol D., and Peter Smagorinsky, eds. 2000. *Vygotskian Perspectives on Literacy Research: Constructing Meaning through Collaborative Inquiry*. Cambridge: Cambridge University Press.

Linde, Charlotte. 1993. *Life Stories: The Creation of Coherence*. New York: Oxford University Press.

Lopez, Barry. 1988. *Crossing Open Ground*. New York: Vintage.

MacDonald, Margaret Read. 1986. *Twenty Tellable Tales: Audience Participation Folktales for the Beginning Storyteller*. New York: HW Wilson.

– 1993. *The Storyteller's Start-up Book: Finding, Learning, Performing and Using Folktales*. Little Rock, AK: August House.

MacDonald, Margaret Read, ed. 1999. *Traditional Storytelling Today: An International Sourcebook*. Chicago: Fitzroy Dearborn.

Mary-Kate and Ashley in ACTION. New York: Harper Entertainment.

Mooney, Bill, and David Holt. 1996. *The Storyteller's Guide: Storytellers Share Advice for the Classroom, Boardroom, Showroom, Podium, Pulpit and Center Stage*. Little Rock, AK: August House.

National Storytelling Association, ed. 1994. *Tales as Tools: The Power of Story in the Classroom*. Jonesborough, TN: National Storytelling Press.

Nelson, Katherine, ed. 1989. *Narratives from the Crib*. Cambridge, MA: Harvard University Press.

Nodelman, Perry. 1996. 'Some Presumptuous Generalizations about Fantasy.' In *Only Connect: Readings on Children's Literature*, ed. S. Egoff, G. Stubbs, R. Ashley, and W. Sutton. Toronto: Oxford University Press.

Ong, Walter. 1977. *Interfaces of the Word: Studies in the Evolution of Consciousness and Culture*. Ithaca, NY: Cornell University Press.

– 1982. *Orality and Literacy*. New York: Methuen.

Paley, Vivian Gussin. 1984. *Boys and Girls: Superheroes in the Doll Corner*. Chicago: University of Chicago Press.

– 1990. *The Boy Who Would Be a Helicopter*. Cambridge, MA: Harvard University Press.

– 2002. *The Girl with a Brown Crayon*. Cambridge, MA: Harvard University Press.

– 2004. *A Child's Work: The Importance of Fantasy Play*. Chicago: University of Chicago Press.

Pellegrini, Anthony D., and Peter Blatchford. 2000. *The Child at School: Interactions with Peers and Teachers*. New York: Oxford University Press.

Pellegrini, Anthony D., Kentaro Kato, Peter Blatchford, and Ed Baines. 2002. A Short-Term Longitudinal Study of Children's Playground Games across the First Year of School: Implications for Social Competence and Adjustment to School. *American Educational Research Journal* 39 (4): 991–1015.

Pollak, Richard. 1997. *The Creation of Dr. B: A Biography of Bruno Bettleheim*. New York: Simon and Schuster.

Pullman, Philip. 1999. *I Was a Rat*. Toronto: Random House.

Purcell-Gates, Victoria. 1995. *Other People's Words: The Cycle of Low Literacy*. Cambridge, MA: Harvard University Press.

Reutzel, Ray D., and Robert B. Cooter. 2008. *Essentials of Teaching Children to Read: The Teacher Makes the Difference*. Needham, MD: Allyn and Bacon.

Ricoeur, Paul. 1992. *Oneself as Another*. Trans. K. Blamey. Chicago: University of Chicago Press.

Roney, R. Craig. 2001. *The Story Performance Handbook*. Mahwah, NJ: Lawrence Erlbaum Associates.

Rosen, Betty. 1988. *And None of It Was Nonsense: The Power of Storytelling in School*. London: Mary Glasgow Publications.

Saris, Jamie A. 1995. Telling Stories: Life Histories, Illness Narratives, and Institutional Landscapes. *Culture, Medicine and Psychiatry* 19 (1): 39–72.

Sawyer, Ruth. 1962. *The Way of the Storyteller*. New York: Viking.

Scribner, Sylvia, and Michael Cole. 1981. *The Psychology of Literacy*. Cambridge, MA: Harvard University Press.

Seeger, Pete. 1994. *Abiyoyo*. New York: First Aladdin Books.

Shor, Ira, and Paolo Freire. 1987. *A Pedagogy for Liberation: Dialogues on Transforming Education*. Westport, CT: Bergin and Garvey.

Sideman, Belle Becker, ed. 1977. *The World's Best Fairy Tales: A Reader's Digest Anthology*. Montreal: Reader's Digest Association.

– 1981. 'Language and Literature from a Pueblo Indian Perspective.' In *Opening Up the Canon*, ed. L. Fiedler and H. Baker. Baltimore: Johns Hopkins University Press.

Silko, Leslie Marmon. 1986. *Ceremony*. Toronto: Penguin.

Snicket, Lemony. 1999–2007. *A Series of Unfortunate Events*. New York: Harper-Collins.

Stine, Robert Lawrence. 1992–2008. *Goosebump* (series). New York: Scholastic.

Tatar, Maria. 1987. *The Hard Facts of the Grimms' Fairy Tales*. Princeton: Princeton University Press.

– 2002. *The Annotated Classic Fairy Tales*. New York: Norton.

Taylor, Charles. 1987. *Human Agency and Language: Philosophical Papers*. Vol 1. Cambridge: Campbridge University Press.

Vygotsky, L.S. 1962. 'Thought and Word.' In *Thought and Language*, ed. E. Hanfmann and G. L'akar. Cambridge, MA: MIT.

Wertsch, James V., ed. 1985. *Culture, Communication, and Cognition: Vygotskian Perspectives*. New York: Cambridge University Press.

Wood, David, Jerome Bruner, and Gail Ross. 1976. 'The Role of Tutoring in Problem Solving.' *Journal of Child Psychology and Psychiatry* 17 (2): 89–100.

Yee, Paul. 1989. *Tales from Gold Mountain: Stories of the Chinese in the New World*. Toronto: Groundwood Books.

– 1991. *Roses Sing on New Snow*. Toronto: Groundwood.

– 1996. *Ghost Train*. Toronto: Groundwood Books.

Yolen, Jane. 1988. *Favorite Folktales From Around the World*. New York: Knopf.

Zeman, Ludmila. 1998. *The Last Quest of Gilgamesh*. Toronto: Tundra.

Further Resources: Books for Storytellers

The following list is intended to help readers who are interested in learning more about storytelling. Topics include family storytelling, classroom practices, guidance for new tellers, storytelling as performance art, storytelling issues, story resources for tellers, histories of storytelling, and storytelling's socio-cultural character.

Alison, Christine. 1987. *I'll Tell You a Story, I'll Sing You a Song*. New York: Dell.

Baker, Augusta, and Ellin Greene. 1977. *Storytelling: Art and Technique*. New York: R.R. Bowker.

Barton, Bob. 1986. *Tell Me Another: Storytelling and Reading at Home*. Markham, ON: Pembroke.

– 1992. *Stories to Tell*. Markham, ON: Pembroke.

– 2000. *Telling Stories Your Way: Storytelling and Reading Aloud in the Classroom*. Markham, ON: Pembroke.

Barton, Bob, and David Booth. 1990. *Stories in the Classroom: Storytelling, Reading Aloud and Role-playing with Children*. Portsmouth, NH: Heinemann.

Basso, Kieth H. 1996. *Wisdom Sits in Places: Landscape and Language among the Western Apache*. Albuquerque: University of New Mexico Press.

Bauer, Caroline Feller. 1993. *New Handbook for Storytellers with Stories, Poems, Magic and More*. Chicago: American Library Association.

Benjamin, Walter. 1968. Chapter entitled 'The Storyteller: Reflections on the Works of Nikolai Leskov.' In Benjamin, *Illuminations; Essays and Reflections*. New York: Schocken.

Birch, Carol, and Heckler, Melissa. 1996. *Who Says: Essays on Pivotal Issues in Contemporary Storytelling*. Little Rock, AK: August House.

Blatt, Gloria T., ed. 1993. *Once upon a Folktale: Capturing the Folklore Process with Children*. New York: Teachers College Press.

Bosma, Bette. 1992. *Fairy Tales, Fables, Legends, and Myths: Using Folk Literature in Your Classroom*. New York: Teacher's College Press.

Bruner, Jerome. 1987. *Actual Minds, Possible Words*. Cambridge, MA: Harvard University Press.

– 1990. *Acts of Meaning*. Cambridge, MA: Harvard University Press.

Cabral, Len. 1996. *Len Cabral's Storytelling Book*. New York: Neal-Schurman.

Cassady, Marsh. 1994. *The Art of Storytelling: Creative Ideas for Preparation and Performance*. Colorado Springs, CO: Meriwether.

Champlin, Connie. 1985. *Storytelling with Puppets*. Chicago: American Library Association.

Coles, Robert. 1989. *The Call of Stories: Teaching and the Moral Imagination*. Boston: Houghton Mifflin.

Cooper, Pamela J., and Rives Collins. 1992. *Look What Happened to Frog: Storytelling in Education*. Scottsdale, AZ: Gorsuch Scarisbrick.

Cox, Allison, and David H. Albert, eds. 2003. *The Healing Heart ~ Families: Storytelling to Encourage Caring and Healthy Families*. Gabriola Island, BC: New Society.

– 2003. *The Healing Heart ~ Communities: Storytelling to Build Strong and Healthy Communities*. Gabriola Island, BC: New Society.

Crosson, Vicky L., and Jay C. Stailey. 1988. *Spinning Stories: An Introduction to Storytelling Skills*. Austin: Texas State Library.

Cruikshank, Julie. 1990. *Life Lived Like a Story*. Lincoln: University of Nebraska Press.

Dailey, Sheila. 1985. *Storytelling: A Creative Teaching Strategy*. Mount Pleasant, MI: Storytime Productions.

De Vos, Gail, and Merle Harris. 1995. *Telling Tales: Storytelling in the Family*. Edmonton: Dragon Hill.

De Wit, Dorothy. 1979. *Children's Faces Looking Up: Program Building for the Storyteller*. Chicago: American Library Association.

Donaldson, Margaret. 1978. *Children's Minds*. New York: W.W. Norton.

Dyson, Anne Haas. 1997. *Writing Superheroes: Contemporary Childhood, Popular Culture and Classroom Literacy*. New York: Teachers College Press.

Egan, Kieran. 1990. *Teaching as Storytelling: An Alternative Approach to Teaching and Curriculum in the Elementary School*. London, ON: Althouse.

– 1997. *The Educated Mind: How Cognitive Tools Shape Our Understanding*. Chicago: University of Chicago Press.

Frye, Northrop. 1963. *The Educated Imagination: Massey Lectures*. Toronto: Canadian Broadcasting Corporation.

Fulford, Robert. 1999. *The Triumph of Narrative: Storytelling in an Age of Mass Culture: Massey Lectures Series*. Toronto: House of Anansi.

Geisler, Harlynne. 1997. *Storytelling Professionally: The Nuts and Bolts of a Working Performer*. Englewood, CO: Libraries Unlimited.

Gillard, Marni. 1995. *Storyteller, Storyteacher: Discovering the Power of Storytelling for Teaching and Living*. Markham, ON: Pembroke.

Glassie, Henry. 1997. *Irish Folktales*. Toronto: Random House.

Greene, Ellin. 1996. *Storytelling Art and Technique*. 3rd ed. New Providence, NJ: R.R. Bowker.

Greene, Maxine. 2000. *Releasing the Imagination: Essays on Education, the Arts, and Social Change*. San Francisco: Jossey-Bass.

Hamilton, Martha, and Mitch Weiss. 1990. *Children Tell Stories: A Teaching Guide*. Katonah, NY: Richard C. Owen Publishers.

Heath, Shirley Brice. 1999. *Ways with Words*. Cambridge: Cambridge University Press.

Hedberg, Natalie L., and Carol E. Westby. 1993. *Analyzing Storytelling Skills: Theory to Practice*. Tucson: Communication Skill Builders.

Heinig, Ruth Beall. 1992. *Improvisation with Favorite Tales*. Portsmouth, NH: Heinemann.

Hiroko, Fujita. 1999. *Stories to Play With: Kids' Tales Told with Puppets, Paper, Toys, and Imagination*. Little Rock, AK: August House.

hooks, bell. 1994. *Teaching to Transgress: Education as the Practice of Freedom*. New York: Routledge.

Jennings, Claire. 1991. *Children as Story-tellers: Developing Language Skills in the Classroom*. Melbourne: Oxford University Press.

Kane, Sean. 1994. *Wisdom of the Mythtellers*. Peterborough, ON: Broadview.

Kinghorn, Harriet R., and Mary Helen Pelton. 1991. *Every Child a Storyteller: A Handbook of Ideas*. Englewood, CO: Teacher Ideas Press.

Linde, Charlotte. 1993. *Life Stories: The Creation of Coherence*. New York: Oxford University Press.

– 1994. *Storytelling Games: Creative Activities for Language Communication and Composition across the Curriculum*. Phoenix: Oryx.

– 1995. *The Storytelling Coach*. Little Rock, AK: August House.

Lipman, Doug. 1999. *Improving Your Story: Beyond the Basics for All Who Tell Stories in Work or Play*. Little Rock, AK: August House.

Livo, Norma, and Sandra Reitz. 1986. *Storytelling: Process and Practice*. Littleton, CO: Libraries Unlimited.

– 1987. *Storytelling Activities*. Littleton, CO: Libraries Unlimited.

– 1991. *Storytelling Folklore Sourcebook*. Englewood, CO: Libraries Unlimited.

Lopez, Barry. 1988. *Crossing Open Ground*. New York: Vintage.

MacDonald, Margaret Read. 1982. *The Storyteller's Sourcebook: A Subject, Title, and Motif Index to Folklore Collections for Children*. Detroit: Neal-Schuman.

— 1986. *Twenty Tellable Tales: A Collection of Audience Participation Folktales for the Beginning Storyteller*. New York: H.W. Wilson.

— 1991. *Look Back and See: Twenty Lively Tales for Gentle Tellers*. New York: H.W. Wilson.

— 1993. *The Storyteller's Start-up Book: Finding, Learning, Performing and Using Folktales*. Little Rock, AK: August House.

MacDonald, Margaret Read, ed. 1999. *Traditional Storytelling Today: An International Sourcebook*. Chicago: Fitzroy Dearborn.

Maguire, Jack. 1985. *Creative Storytelling: Choosing, Inventing, and Sharing Tales for Children*. New York: Yellow Moon.

— 1998. *The Power of Personal Storytelling: Spinning Tales to Connect with Others*. New York: Penguin Putnam.

Mallan, Kerry. 1992. *Children as Storytellers*. Portsmouth, NH: Heinemann.

Matthews, Gareth. 2002. *Dialogues with Children*. Cambridge, MA: Harvard University Press.

— 1994. *The Philosophy of Childhood*. Cambridge, MA: Harvard University Press.

Mooney, Bill, and David Holt. 1996. *The Storyteller's Guide: Storytellers Share Advice for the Classroom, Boardroom, Showroom, Podium, Pulpit and Center Stage*. Little Rock, AK: August House.

Moore, Robin. 1991. *Awakening the Hidden Storyteller How to Build a Storytelling Tradition in Your Family*. Boston: Shambhala.

National Storytelling Association, ed. 1994. *Tales as Tools: The Power of Story in the Classroom*. Jonesborough, TN: National Storytelling Press.

Niemi, Loren, and Elizabeth Ellis. 2001. *Inviting the Wolf In: Thinking about the Difficult Story*. Little Rock, AK: August House.

Ong, Walter. 1982. *Orality and Literacy*. New York: Methuen.

Opie, Iona, and Peter Opie. 2001 [1960]. *The Lore and Language of School Children*. New York: New York Review of Books.

Paley, Vivian Gussin. 2004. *A Child's Work: The Importance of Fantasy Play*. Chicago: University of Chicago Press.

Pellegrini, Anthony D., and Peter Blatchford. 2000. *The Child at School: Interactions with Peers and Teachers*. New York: Oxford University Press.

Pellowski, Anne. 1995. 1991. *The World of Storytelling: A Practical Guide to the Origins, Development and Applications of Storytelling*. Bronx, NY: H.W. Wilson.

— *The Storytelling Handbook: A Young People's Collection of Unusual Tales and Helpful Hints on How to Tell Them*. New York: Simon and Schuster.

Pellowski, Anne, Theresa Miller, Laura Simms, and Norma Livo. 1988. *Joining In: An Anthology of Audience Participation Stories and How to Tell Them*. Somerville, MA: Yellow Moon.

Ricoeur, Paul. 1992. *Oneself as Another*. Trans. K. Blamey. Chicago: University of Chicago Press.

Robinson, Harry, and Wendy Wickwire. 1992. *Nature Power: In the Spirit of an Okanagan Storyteller*. Vancouver: Douglas and McIntyre.

Roney, R. Craig. 2001. *The Story Performance Handbook*. Mahwah, NJ: Lawrence Erlbaum Associates.

Rosen, Betty. 1988. *And None of It Was Nonsense: The Power of Storytelling in School*. London: Mary Glasgow Publications.

Ross, R.R. 1996. *Storyteller*. Little Rock, AK: August House.

Rubright, Lynn. 1996. *Beyond the Beanstalk: Interdisciplinary Learning through Storytelling*. Portsmouth, NH: Heinemann.

Sarris, Greg. 1993. *Keeping Slug Woman Alive: A Holistic Approach to American Indian Texts*. Berkeley and Los Angeles: University of California Press.

Sawyer, Ruth. 1962 [1942]. *The Way of the Storyteller*. New York: Viking.

Schimmel, Nancy. 1982. *Just Enough to Make a Story*. Berkeley: Sisters Choice.

Shedlock, Marie. 1951. *The Art of the Storyteller*. New York: Dover.

Sobol, Joseph Daniel. 1999. *The Storytellers' Journey: An American Revival*. Urbana: University of Illinois Press.

Stone, Kay. 1998. *Burning Brightly: New Light on Old Tales Told Today*. Peterborough, ON: Broadview.

Sutton-Smith, Brian. 1981. *The Folkstories of Children*. Philadelphia: University of Pennsylvania Press.

– 1997. *The Ambiguity of Play*. Cambridge, MA: Harvard University Press.

Thompson, Loraine. 1993. *Tell Me a Story! Narrative in the Classroom*. Instructional Strategies Series No. 15. Regina: Saskatchewan Instructional Development and Research Unit.

Tolkien, J.R.R. 1975. *Tree and Leaf*. London: Unwin.

Tooze, Ruth. 1959. *Storytelling*. Englewood Cliffs, NJ: Prentice-Hall.

Van Deusen, Kira. 1999. *Raven and the Rock: Storytelling in Chukotka*. Seattle: University of Washington Press.

– 2001. *The Flying Tiger: Women Shamans and Storytellers of the Amur*. 1st ed. Montreal: McGill-Queen's University Press.

– 2004. *Singing Story, Healing Drum: Shamans and Storytellers of Turkic Siberia*. Montreal: McGill-Queen's University Press.

Vansina, Jan. 1985. *Oral Tradition as History*. Madison: University of Wisconsin Press.

Yolen, Jane. 2000. *Touch Magic: Fantasy, Faerie and Folklore in the Literature of Childhood*. Little Rock, AK: August House.

Zipes, Jack. 1995. *Creative Storytelling: Building Community, Changing Lives*. New York: Routledge.

– 2002. *Breaking the Magic Spell: Radical Theories of Folk and Fairy Tales*. Lexington: University Press of Kentucky.

Index